GOOD HOUSEKEEPING

400 LOW-FAT
RECIPES & TIPS

GOOD HOUSEKEEPING

400 LOW-FAT
RECIPES & TIPS

HEARST
books

HEARST BOOKS

An Imprint of Sterling Publishing Co., Inc.
1166 Avenue of the Americas
New York, NY 10036

ISBN 978-1-61837-229-1

Distributed in Canada by Sterling Publishing Co., Inc.
c/o Canadian Manda Group, 664 Annette Street
Toronto, Ontario, Canada M6S 2C8
Distributed in Australia by NewSouth Books
45 Beach Street, Coogee, NSW 2034, Australia

For information about custom editions, special sales, and premium and corporate purchases, please contact Sterling Special Sales at 800-805-5489 or specialsales@sterlingpublishing.com.

Manufactured in China

2 4 6 8 10 9 7 5 3 1

www.sterlingpublishing.com

CONTENTS

FOREWORD 6

INTRODUCTION | 8

1 BREAKFASTS & BRUNCHES | 12

2 SUPER-HEALTHY SALADS | 52

3 SOUPS, STEWS & CHILIS | 102

4 SANDWICHES, WRAPS & PIZZAS | 158

5 FISH & SHELLFISH | 204

6 POULTRY | 246

7 LEAN RED MEAT | 294

8 VEGGIE & WHOLE-GRAIN MAINS | 338

9 ON THE SIDE | 384

10 DESSERTS | 420

METRIC EQUIVALENT CHARTS 466
PHOTOGRAPHY CREDITS 467
INDEX 468

Saucy Creole Shrimp (page 214)

FOREWORD

Welcome to Good Housekeeping's new collection of low-fat recipes! We hear regularly from readers who are looking for smart ways to cut back on fat and calories. Whether it's for weight loss, to keep type 2 diabetes in check, or to stay in synch with dietary guidelines, *Good Housekeeping 400 Low-Fat Recipes & Tips* will help.

I hope you'll be happily surprised at the range of recipes we can include. We've rounded up satisfying dishes that are big on flavor, easy to make, and contain 10% or less of their calories from saturated fat. You'll find everything from satisfying Huevos Rancheros and Whole-Grain Pancakes, to Lasagna Toss with Spinach and Ricotta and Classic Beef Stew. If you're already following a low-fat diet, you're probably familiar with the basic drill for meal-planning guidelines. But for newbies (and as a refresher course for everyone), we review the basic nutrients you need for optimum health, and offer tried-and-true tips for low-fat success that will make meal prep a breeze!

As always, every recipe is triple-tested and includes complete nutritional information. With *Good Housekeeping 400 Low-Fat Recipes & Tips* in your kitchen, you'll never have to sacrifice flavor—or satisfaction!

—SUSAN WESTMORELAND
Food Director, *Good Housekeeping*

Strawberry Granola Yogurt Parfait (page 32)

INTRODUCTION

THE NEW THINKING ABOUT FAT

Over the years, conflicting guidelines have left us confused about what to eat—particularly when it comes to dietary fat. While it's often assumed that fat is the "enemy" with regard to weight-loss, it's important to clarify the distinction between a *low fat* diet versus a moderate *total fat* diet low in saturated fats—one that is actually healthy and can help lower our risk of chronic disease. This book will help you sort out the difference in types of fats and show you how you can incorporate good-for-you foods into your diet while staying healthy, lean, and energized.

Why Now?

With the release of the 2015 Dietary Guidelines, a lot of the "fat talk" appears to have evolved for the better—and for the long term!

One of the biggest changes you'll notice in the 2015 United States Dietary Guidelines for Americans is that there's no mention of total fat or dietary cholesterol. Instead, the DGA addresses saturated fat consumption, limiting it to 10% of your total calories for the day to lower the risk of chronic disease and obesity. Abundant research suggests diets high in saturated fats raise blood cholesterol levels and increase your risk for heart disease.

What's the difference between unsaturated and saturated fats?

The most healthful fats include all those that contain *mostly* mono and polyunsaturated fatty acids, while the ones to limit are known as saturated fats.

All types of fats are actually in all types of foods, but some foods contain a higher content of unsaturated rather than saturated, which makes it a little easier to group or generalize certain foods. Simply put, the best types of fats are the ones that are extracted from *plants* instead of animals.

In oil form, that's: canola, olive, safflower, sunflower, walnut, peanut, hazelnut, algae, palm, hemp seed, chia seed, flaxseed, pecan, sesame, tiger nut, grape seed, corn, and avocado oils. The types of oils that are highest in saturated fat include lard, butter, margarine, palm oil, and coconut oil, as well as the animals/animal products themselves: red meat, poultry, and of course, all full-fat dairy products.

But I heard that some full-fat dairy is good for me.

True! But all foods are "good for you" in moderation! That's why the 10% of total calories from saturated fat is so important—because it allows you to be extra choosy about *where* you get that saturated fat from (my dietitian vote: lean cuts of 100% grass-fed beef; fatty fish, such as salmon, tuna, and mackerel; a daily 3- to 5-ounce serving of full-fat yogurt). The point is, some of the high-in-saturated-fat foods are some of the most satisfying to eat, which means they can help stave off weight gain because they keep you fuller, longer.

Where do problems arise? When you eat a diet high in processed foods, red and processed meats, fried foods, or baked goods, all of which are a common culprit of weight gain and increased risk of heart disease and type 2 diabetes in the United States.

Does that mean I need to become a vegetarian?

No way! But it *is* a good idea to adopt a more plant-based style of eating, one that focuses more on veggies, fruits, whole grains, and plant-based proteins (like those from nuts, legumes, and beans). The health benefits of a high-fiber diet combined with a low-saturated-fat diet are integral to lowering your chronic disease risk (heart disease, diabetes, certain types of cancers, and Alzheimer's disease).

So I can eat as much "healthy fat" like olive oil and avocados as I want, right?

Nope! (Sorry!) Ultimately, in order to maintain a healthy weight, the most important thing is keeping total calories in check. Carbs and protein are both macronutrients that provide 4kcal per gram, while fat provides 9kcal per gram, making it a higher calorie nutrient comparatively. The benefit to eating healthy fat in the form of nuts, seeds, oils, fruits, and veggies: It *can* be much more satisfying, which is why you've heard a lot lately about eating a moderate-fat diet (25–35% of total calories) for weight-control rather than a traditional "low-fat diet."

The recipes in this book all contain 10% or fewer calories from saturated fat. To make that calculation yourself, simply multiply the number of saturated fat grams by 9 (the number of calories per 1 gram of fat) and then divide by the total amount of calories per serving. If your result is 10% or less, you're home-free!

Is a "moderate fat" diet just another diet trend?

No. Essentially, this message has always been a part of nutritional research, but it's only now that we're seeing the need to explicitly clarify the difference between saturated and unsaturated fats. Oftentimes, when fat is eliminated (mostly the saturated kind found in processed foods, like cookies or dairy products labeled "fat-free"), the nutrient will be replaced with sugar to optimize taste. Not only does it not change the total calories of the food, but it's often even less satisfying. On top of that, your blood sugar spikes, and you're hungry again within a half hour!

What about trans-fats?

This man-made fat is a huge no-no. First, it's an entirely processed type of fat that was created as a possible cost-effective substitute for butter and oil. The good news: It's impossible to find if you're cooking food from scratch! This solid-at-room-temperature fat has the combined detrimental effect of lowering your HDL ("good" cholesterol) and raising your LDL ("bad" cholesterol). While the FDA is attempting to remove this fat from the food supply, it's important that we all triple-check labels for "partially hydrogenated oils," since a current loophole in the law allows manufacturers to label a product as "0g trans-fat" if there's 0.5g or less of the stuff per serving. And since so many foods will contain these partially hydrogenated oils until 2018, it's particularly crucial that we stay aware of the processed foods in our food supply that may be sneaky sources of a highly processed health hazard.

So what's the bottom line?

Eating a diet that contains a moderate amount of fats and keeps saturated fat to a minimum—10% or less of your daily calorie intake—will help you get and keep the lean, healthy body you want!

—JACLYN LONDON, MS, RD, CDN
Nutrition Director, *Good Housekeeping*

Spiced Banana-Chocolate Muffins (page 47)

1 | **BREAKFASTS** & BRUNCHES

You've heard it your whole life, and it's true: A good breakfast is the foundation of any healthy diet. But how do you eat a good-for-you meal in the morning when you're rushing to get the whole family out of the house?

Here's a tasty solution: Try one of our 5-minute smoothies. This small investment of time will get your day started with the right balance of satisfying healthy fats, fresh fruits, and—if you sprinkle a tablespoon of chia seeds, flaxseeds, nuts, or oat bran on top—fill-you-up fiber. For more on the benefits of fiber, see "Fiber: The Fabulous Fat Fighter" on page 27.

You can grab a smoothie and go, or bake up a batch of our healthy-fat muffins and take one along. Pair it with a piece of fruit and you have a nutritious breakfast you can pack in your purse.

On weekends or more leisurely mornings, try one of our delicious, savory egg dishes. Eggs are a high-quality source of protein, and contrary to what you may have heard, you can eat them without guilt. Served with vegetables or beans, as in our South-of-the-Border Vegetable Hash or Breakfast Tortilla Stack, these dishes deliver a hefty amount of fiber. And because everyone needs a little sweetness in their life, we've shared whole-grain healthier-fat takes on brunch favorites like French toast and pancakes, as well.

MANGO STRAWBERRY SMOOTHIE

A colorful, good-for-you morning lift-off! Either way you make it—with mango or with apricot nectar—creates a wonderful combination. If you use frozen strawberries, skip the ice cubes.

TOTAL TIME: 5 minutes

MAKES: 2½ cups

1	cup fresh or frozen unsweetened strawberries
1	cup mango or apricot nectar, chilled
½	cup plain or vanilla yogurt
4	ice cubes

In blender, combine strawberries, mango nectar, yogurt, and ice and blend until mixture is smooth and frothy. Pour into two tall glasses. Serve with straws, if you like.

Each serving: About 125 calories, 4g protein, 27g carbohydrate, 1g total fat (0g saturated), 0g fiber, 44mg sodium

Eat Your Strawberries

These days, strawberries are easy to find all year long, but they are at their sweetest, juiciest peak in spring. Delicious and nutritious, twelve medium berries weigh in at 45 calories, 3 grams of fiber, and about 135% of the daily recommended requirement for vitamin C.

Healthy Smoothie Additions

Different superfoods not only boost the nutrition of your smoothie, they can increase your taste and texture experience. Here are our faves:

CHIA SEEDS: These tiny wonders can hold up to 9 times their weight in liquid, which makes their ability to form a gel the perfect way to thicken a smoothie. Chia seeds expand in your stomach, keeping you fuller for longer; their high protein and fiber content also boost satiety. Prior to blending, soak the seeds in a little water to give your smoothie a nice smooth consistency. Add 1 tablespoon per serving.

GROUND FLAXSEEDS: This all-star seed contains both the insoluble and soluble fibers important for both gastrointestinal health and reducing cholesterol levels. Flax gives you a protein boost, and it's high in omega-3s, a good fat shown to have heart-healthy effects and the ability to reduce inflammation, thereby cutting the risk of diabetes. Add 1 tablespoon per serving.

ALMOND, CASHEW, AND PEANUT BUTTER: These nut butters are a good source of heart-healthy unsaturated fats, protein, and fiber. They can also help provide long-lasting energy. Add 1 tablespoon per serving.

OATS AND OAT BRAN: Rich in soluble fiber, which can help slash cholesterol levels and stabilize blood sugar, this grain is also mild in taste, so it blends well with other ingredients. Oats may also increase appetite control hormones, leaving you feeling fuller longer. Add 1 tablespoon per serving.

BERRY SATISFYING SMOOTHIE

Add fiber-rich oats to a morning smoothie? Absolutely! Oats make the drink extra filling.

TOTAL TIME: 5 minutes
MAKES: 4 servings

2	cups frozen mixed berries
1	cup vanilla low-fat yogurt
1	ripe banana, sliced
½	cup quick-cooking oats
½	cup orange juice
4	teaspoons honey

In blender, combine mixed berries, yogurt, banana, oats, orange juice, and honey and blend until mixture is smooth and frothy. Pour into four glasses.

Each serving: About 185 calories, 6g protein, 40g carbohydrate, 2g total fat (0g saturated), 4g fiber, 41mg sodium

STRAWBERRY CHIA SMOOTHIE

OJ isn't the only way to get your vitamin C in the morning. Kiwis and strawberries are also a good source, and this fruity blend with healthy chia seeds is custom-made to rev up your day.

TOTAL TIME: 10 minutes
MAKES: 1 serving

1	cup frozen strawberries
2	kiwifruit, peeled and chopped
³/₄	cup skim milk
1	tablespoon chia seeds
1	teaspoon ground ginger
4	ice cubes

In blender, combine strawberries, kiwifruit, milk, chia seeds, ginger, and ice and blend until mixture is smooth and frothy. Pour into one tall glass.

Each serving: About 256 calories, 10g protein, 49g carbohydrate, 4g total fat (1g saturated), 11g fiber, 86mg sodium

TIP

When purchasing chia seeds, take note of the use-by date on the package. If buying in bulk, store the seeds in an airtight container in a cool, dry place for up to several months.

BANANA BERRY BLAST SMOOTHIE

Get your morning off to a "berry" good start with this tasty blend of fresh blueberries and your pick of raspberries or blackberries.

TOTAL TIME: 5 minutes
MAKES: About 3 cups or 2 servings

1	small ripe banana, cut up
5	cups pineapple-orange juice
1	cup ice cubes
1	container (6 ounces) blueberries
1	container (6 ounces) raspberries or blackberries
2	teaspoons honey
1	teaspoon grated, peeled fresh ginger

In blender, combine banana, pineapple-orange juice, ice, blueberries, raspberries or blackberries, honey, and ginger and blend until mixture is smooth and frothy. Pour into two tall glasses.

Each serving: About 125 calories, 3g protein, 51g carbohydrate, 1g total fat (0g saturated), 9g fiber, 8mg sodium

TIP

The freshest blueberries should have a soft, hazy white coating, called "bloom." Bloom is a completely natural part of blueberries that helps protect the fruit from harsh sunlight.

JUMP-START SMOOTHIE

Spiked with two teaspoons of fresh ginger, this smoothie has just the right *oomph* to get your morning off to a delicious start.

TOTAL TIME: 5 minutes
MAKES: 2 servings

1	cup frozen strawberries
1	cup fresh blueberries
1	cup orange-tangerine juice blend, chilled
2	teaspoons chopped, peeled fresh ginger
2	cups plain low-fat yogurt
2	ice cubes

In blender, combine strawberries, blueberries, orange-tangerine juice, ginger, yogurt, and ice. Blend until mixture is smooth and frothy, scraping down sides of container occasionally. Pour into two tall glasses.

Each serving: About 96 calories, 3g protein, 21g carbohydrate, 1g total fat (0g saturated), 2g fiber, 24mg sodium

TIP

One serving of strawberries (about one cup) contains 144% of the daily value of vitamin C. That's 24% more than a typical 8-ounce glass of OJ from a carton. Plus, a cup of strawberries has about as much fiber (4 grams) as 2 slices of whole wheat bread.

CHOCOLATE-BANANA SMOOTHIE

Chocolate and bananas are a proven kid-favorite. Plus, it's super simple to whip up!

TOTAL TIME: 5 minutes
MAKES: 2 cups or 1 serving

1	frozen banana, peeled and sliced
3/4	cup milk
3	tablespoons chocolate syrup, or to taste
3	ice cubes

In blender, combine banana, milk, chocolate syrup, and ice cubes and blend until mixture is smooth and frothy. Pour into one tall glass.

Each serving: About 430 calories, 9g protein, 85g carbohydrate, 8g total fat (4g saturated), 4g fiber, 145mg sodium

TIP

A single serving of bananas is high in vitamin B_6, which is important for the health of our nervous system as well as key to the synthesis of most essential molecules in our bodies. Bananas are also a good source of vitamin C, bone-building manganese, potassium, and dietary fiber.

If you want to eat bananas right away, buy solid-yellow fruit with some brown spots. Bananas that are somewhat green in color will ripen within a few days at room temperature.

Frozen Assets

For a lusciously thick smoothie, use a creamy fruit like mango, banana, or avocado. However, frozen fruit will make your healthy smoothie even creamier. In fact, frozen fruit is a smoothie's BFF. This is especially true with summer fruit: Freezing is a great way to preserve color, flavor, and nutrient value. (Plus frozen fruit is a great sub for ice cubes.)

BERRY PICKING POINTERS

- Berries should be plump, fresh-looking, and uniformly colored.
- Avoid crushed or bruised fruit and cartons stained with juice.
- Beware of fuzzy fruit—mold spreads quickly from berry to berry.

PREFREEZING PREP

- STRAWBERRIES: Rinse, drain, then hull; halve or quarter, if you like.
- RASPBERRIES: Remove stems or leaves. Rinse carefully; drain.
- BLUEBERRIES: Remove stems and freeze un-rinsed. Quickly rinse under cold water just before using.
- BLACKBERRIES: Remove stems or leaves. Rinse carefully; drain.
- PEACHES, APRICOTS, NECTARINES, AND PLUMS: Remove pits; cut into halves or wedges and toss with a bit of lemon juice to prevent browning.
- BANANAS: Peel and break into small chunks.

HOW TO CHILL

- Arrange fruit in a single layer, without touching, on a jelly-roll pan lined with parchment paper.
- Freeze uncovered until hard, about 4 hours.
- Transfer fruit to freezer-weight bags (the quart size is great for single-serving portions), press out excess air, lay flat, and freeze for up to six months.

JAVA BANANA SMOOTHIE

Here's a frosty glass of Joe with a bonus: 1 banana per serving. Potassium-rich bananas not only stimulate your muscles, nerves, and brain cells, they can also help reduce blood pressure and risk of stroke.

TOTAL TIME: 5 minutes

MAKES: 2 servings

2	ripe bananas (preferably frozen), cut up
³/₄	cup cold-brewed coffee (See Perfect Cold-Brewed Coffee, opposite)
³/₄	cup low-fat (1%) milk
2	teaspoons brown sugar
1	cup ice cubes

In blender, combine bananas, coffee, milk, brown sugar, and ice and blend until mixture is smooth and frothy. Pour into two glasses.

Each serving: About 162 calories, 4g protein, 36g carbohydrate, 1g total fat (1g saturated), 3g fiber, 44mg sodium

Perfect Cold-Brewed Coffee

Making authentic cold-brewed coffee for smoothies couldn't be easier—or tastier. Cold brewing reduces the acidity of coffee, which in turn enhances its sweetness and other complex flavor notes. Here's how:

1. In a small pitcher or 1-quart measuring cup, whisk together ⅓ cup ground coffee and 1⅓ cups cold water until all the lumps are gone.

2. Cover tightly and refrigerate for at least 5 hours, but it's best left overnight (not much longer or it'll get bitter).

3. Strain the coffee through a coffee filter-lined strainer, pushing it through with a spatula. Makes ¾ cup.

COFFEE ICE CUBES

Double the above recipe. Pour cold-brewed coffee into an ice cube tray and freeze until solid. Place frozen cubes in a large freezer-weight bag, press out excess air, and freeze for up to two weeks.

CREAMY KALE SMOOTHIE

Frozen pineapple chunks, skim milk, and Greek yogurt give this super K smoothie its creamy taste and texture.

TOTAL TIME: 5 minutes
MAKES: 1 serving

1	cup coarsely chopped kale
1½	cups frozen pineapple chunks
⅓	cup plain fat-free Greek yogurt
½	cup skim milk
1	teaspoon honey
1	teaspoon brown sugar

In blender, combine kale, pineapple, yogurt, milk, honey, and brown sugar and blend until mixture is smooth and frothy. Pour into one tall glass.

Each serving: About 288 calories, 17g protein, 58g carbohydrate, 0g total fat, 5g fiber, 102mg sodium

TIP
Frozen pineapple chunks are available in convenient 1-pound bags at the supermarket. You can also substitute frozen mango chunks in this recipe.

FRUITY GREEN SMOOTHIE

Talk about fully loaded with goodness! Five varieties of fruit—plus spinach, celery, and cucumber—make this a truly super smoothie.

TOTAL TIME: 10 minutes
MAKES: 2 servings

2	cups water
½	cup baby spinach
2	stalks celery, chopped
1	Bartlett pear, cut up
1	green apple, cut up
1	ripe banana (preferably frozen), cut up
2	slices ripe mango
¼	cup diced pineapple
¼	English (seedless) cucumber, sliced
2	teaspoons honey

In blender, combine water, spinach, celery, pear, apple, banana, mango, pineapple, cucumber, and honey and blend until mixture is smooth and frothy. Pour into two tall glasses.

Each serving: About 217 calories, 3g protein, 53g carbohydrate, 1g total fat (Og saturated), 9g fiber, 46mg sodium

SEVEN-MINUTE MULTIGRAIN CEREAL

Get a great-grains start to your day with a hot and tasty serving of three kinds of grains.

TOTAL TIME: 5 minutes
MAKES: 1 serving

2	tablespoons quick-cooking barley
2	tablespoons bulgur
2	tablespoons old-fashioned oats, uncooked
²/₃	cup water
2	tablespoons raisins

Pinch ground cinnamon

1	tablespoon chopped walnuts or pecans

Low-fat (1%) milk or soy milk (optional)

In microwave-safe 1-quart bowl, combine barley, bulgur, oats, and water. Microwave on high for 2 minutes. Stir in raisins and cinnamon; microwave for 3 minutes longer. Stir, then top with walnuts and, if desired, milk.

Each serving: About 265 calories, 8g protein, 50g carbohydrate, 6g total fat (1g saturated), 7g fiber, 5mg sodium

Fiber: The Fabulous Fat Fighter

Switching to a high-fiber diet can be like taking a magic weight-loss pill. But how exactly does fiber work?

IT'S FILLING. It swells a little in the stomach, quelling hunger. So, a 100-calorie portion of bran cereal (18g fiber) will make you feel a lot fuller than a 100-calorie portion of corn flakes (1g fiber).

IT LOWERS BLOOD SUGAR. Many high-fiber foods (think oatmeal) help moderate your blood sugar and insulin levels. Lower insulin levels have been linked to lower body fat and a lower risk of diabetes.

IT FLUSHES OUT FAT. Some types of fiber, particularly those in fruits and vegetables, can sweep out fat before the body absorbs it.

IT'S LOW-CAL. Pure fiber itself has virtually no calories. Your body can't break it down, so it runs right through your digestive system, providing only bulk. That's why high-fiber foods are usually lower in calories than low-fiber foods. For example, 1 cup of apple juice has 0g fiber and 117 calories; 1 cup of sliced, unpeeled apple has 34g fiber and 74 calories.

GOOD SOURCES OF FIBER: Fruits, vegetables, legumes, brans, breads, cereals, pasta, and starchy foods made with whole grains.

PAPRIKA PARMESAN GRANOLA BARS

If you have extra bars crumble up a few, and transform them from hearty breakfast to delicious salad ingredient!

ACTIVE TIME: 10 minutes **TOTAL TIME**: 30 minutes plus cooling
MAKES: 8 bars

1	cup rolled oats, toasted
1/2	cup crisp rice cereal
1/2	cup grated Parmesan cheese
1/2	cup freeze-dried vegetable bits
1/3	cup smoked almonds, chopped
3	tablespoons chia seeds
1/2	teaspoon smoked paprika
1/2	teaspoon salt
1/2	teaspoon ground black pepper
2	large egg whites, beaten
1/2	cup unsweetened nut butter

1. Preheat oven to 350°F. Line 8" by 8" metal pan with foil; grease foil.

2. In large bowl, combine oats, cereal, Parmesan, vegetable bits, almonds, chia seeds, paprika, salt, and pepper. Stir in egg whites and nut butter.

3. Press mixture firmly into prepared pan. Bake for 30 minutes. Cool completely on wire rack.

4. Once cool, remove from pan; cut into 8 bars. Store in airtight container at room temperature for up to 1 week.

Each bar: About 235 calories, 10g protein, 18g carbohydrate, 16g total fat (2g saturated), 5g fiber, 305mg sodium

TIP
Feel free to sub in cumin, chili powder, or garlic powder for the paprika in this recipe.

LOWER-FAT GRANOLA

Oats, almonds, quinoa, wheat germ, and sesame seeds are baked with apple juice instead of oil.

ACTIVE TIME: 20 minutes   **TOTAL TIME**: 45 minutes plus cooling
MAKES: 6 cups or 12 servings

4	cups old-fashioned oats, uncooked
1/2	cup honey
1/2	cup apple juice
1 1/2	teaspoons vanilla extract
3/4	teaspoon ground cinnamon
1/2	cup natural almonds
1/4	cup quinoa, thoroughly rinsed
1/4	cup toasted wheat germ
2	tablespoons sesame seeds
1/2	cup dried apricots, cut into 1/4-inch dice
1/2	cup dark seedless raisins

1. Preheat oven to 350°F. Place oats in two 15 1/2″ by 10 1/2″ jelly-roll pans. Bake until lightly toasted, about 15 minutes, stirring twice.

2. In large bowl, with wire whisk, mix honey, apple juice, vanilla, and cinnamon until blended. Add toasted oats, almonds, quinoa, wheat germ, and sesame seeds; stir well to coat.

3. Spread oat mixture evenly onto same jelly-roll pans; bake until golden brown, 20 to 25 minutes, stirring frequently. Cool in pans on wire rack.

4. When cool, transfer granola to large bowl; stir in apricots and raisins. Store at room temperature in airtight container for up to 1 month.

Each 1/2-cup serving: About 350 calories, 12g protein, 64g carbohydrate, 8g total fat (2g saturated), 8g fiber, 10mg sodium

GRANOLA-YOGURT PARFAIT

A healthy low-fat breakfast doesn't get any easier than this.

TOTAL TIME: 5 minutes

MAKES: 1 serving

¹/₂	cup fresh or frozen (partially thawed) raspberries, or other favorite berry
³/₄	cup vanilla low-fat yogurt
2	tablespoons Lower-Fat Granola (opposite)

Into parfait glass or wineglass, spoon some of the raspberries, vanilla yogurt, and granola. Repeat layering until all ingredients are used.

Each serving: About 255 calories, 10g protein, 47g carbohydrate, 3g total fat (2g saturated), 5g fiber, 160mg sodium

Eat Your Yogurt

Need to fit more calcium and protein into your diet? This creamy, tangy snack is the way to go. Any low-fat or nonfat all-natural brand has health benefits (it contains bacteria that aids in digestion, for starters), but we really love Greek-style yogurt. This special, strained yogurt has a dense texture and rich flavor—even the nonfat versions. Perk up plain yogurt with add-ins like fresh fruit, honey, reduced-fat granola, and nuts. Or, use yogurt in place of mayo or sour cream to create low-fat dips and dressings. Greek yogurt is so creamy, it can even be used in some sauces to replace butter or cream.

STRAWBERRY GRANOLA YOGURT PARFAIT

The key ingredient in this yummy parfait is a pureed fruit sauce called a coulis (pronounced "ku-LEE"). Drizzle over ice cream, pancakes, or oatmeal, too. (See photograph on page 8.)

TOTAL TIME: 20 minutes
MAKES: 1 serving

½ cup granola
½ cup nonfat plain yogurt
¼ cup coulis (see recipe, below)
Strawberries, for garnish

In 8-ounce jar, distribute ½ cup granola, ½ cup nonfat plain yogurt, and ¼ cup coulis in layers. Can be refrigerated, sealed, overnight. Garnish with strawberry.

COULIS

In 3-quart saucepan, cook **1 pound strawberries**, hulled; **¾ cup sugar**; **½ teaspoon cinnamon**; and **½ teaspoon lemon peel** on medium until strawberries are soft but still red, stirring, 8 to 10 minutes. Transfer to blender; puree until smooth. Stir in **½ teaspoon vanilla** and **1 tablespoon lemon juice**. Makes 2 cups coulis. Refrigerate up to 2 weeks.

Each serving: About 295 calories, 11g protein, 53g carbohydrate, 5g total fat (0g saturated), 3g fiber, 120mg sodium

SPINACH SOUFFLÉ

Even though this recipe requires about 40 minutes total, only 20 minutes is active prep. During the remaining time, while the soufflé bakes, you can relax!

ACTIVE TIME: 20 minutes   **TOTAL TIME**: 40 minutes
MAKES: 4 main-dish servings

Nonstick cooking spray

3	tablespoons plain dried bread crumbs
1½	cups low-fat (1%) milk
⅓	cup cornstarch
2	large eggs, separated
1	package (10 ounces) frozen chopped spinach, thawed and squeezed dry
3	tablespoons grated Parmesan cheese
½	teaspoon salt
¼	teaspoon coarsely ground black pepper
½	teaspoon cream of tartar
4	large egg whites

1. Preheat oven to 425°F. Spray 10-inch quiche dish or shallow 2-quart casserole with cooking spray and sprinkle with bread crumbs to coat. Set aside.

2. In 2-quart saucepan, with wire whisk, beat milk with cornstarch until blended. Heat milk mixture over medium-high heat until mixture thickens and boils, stirring constantly. Boil for 1 minute. Remove saucepan from heat.

3. In large bowl, with rubber spatula, mix egg yolks, spinach, Parmesan, salt, and pepper until blended; stir in warm milk mixture. Cool slightly (if spinach mixture is too warm, it will deflate beaten egg whites when folded in).

4. In another large bowl, with mixer on high speed, beat cream of tartar and egg whites until stiff peaks form. Gently fold egg-white mixture, one-third at a time, into spinach mixture.

5. Spoon soufflé mixture into quiche dish. Bake for 20 minutes or until top is golden and puffed. Serve immediately.

Each serving: About 195 calories, 15g protein, 23g carbohydrate, 5g total fat (2g saturated), 2g fiber, 590mg sodium

BREAKFAST TORTILLA STACK

Looking for a breakfast that will keep you full all morning long? Top a whole wheat tortilla with fluffy eggs, fat-free refried beans, and salsa.

ACTIVE TIME: 25 minutes   **TOTAL TIME**: 30 minutes
MAKES: 4 main-dish servings

1/4	cup chopped red onion
1	cup ice water
2	ripe medium tomatoes, chopped
1/4	cup loosely packed fresh cilantro leaves, chopped
4	large eggs
4	large egg whites
1/8	teaspoon salt
1/8	teaspoon ground black pepper
Nonstick cooking spray	
1	cup fat-free refried beans
1/4	teaspoon chipotle chile powder
4	(7-inch) whole wheat tortillas

1. Prepare salsa: Soak onion in ice water for 10 minutes; drain well. In small bowl, combine onion, tomatoes, and cilantro; set aside.

2. In medium bowl, with wire whisk or fork, beat whole eggs, egg whites, salt, and pepper until blended.

3. Spray 10-inch nonstick skillet with cooking spray; heat over medium heat for 1 minute. Pour egg mixture into skillet; cook, stirring occasionally, for about 5 minutes or until egg mixture is set but still moist.

4. Meanwhile, in microwave-safe small bowl, mix beans and chile powder. Cover with vented plastic wrap; microwave on high for 1 minute or until hot.

5. Place stack of tortillas between damp paper towels on microwave-safe plate; microwave on high for 10 to 15 seconds to warm. To serve, layer each tortilla with eggs, beans, and salsa.

Each serving: About 200 calories, 13g protein, 29g carbohydrate, 4g total fat (1g saturated), 13g fiber, 635mg sodium

SOUTH-OF-THE-BORDER VEGETABLE HASH

To create a skinnier, lower-fat hash with a new flavor twist, we replaced the meat with kidney beans and added fresh lime and cilantro.

ACTIVE TIME: 20 minutes   **TOTAL TIME**: 50 minutes

MAKES: 4 main-dish servings

3	large Yukon Gold potatoes (1½ pounds), cut into ¾-inch chunks
1	tablespoon plus 1 teaspoon olive oil
1	large onion (12 ounces), cut into ¼-inch dice
1	red pepper, cut into ¼-inch-wide strips
3	garlic cloves, crushed with press
2	teaspoons ground cumin
¾	teaspoon salt
1	can (15 to 19 ounces) red kidney or black beans, rinsed and drained
2	tablespoons chopped fresh cilantro

Plain yogurt, lime wedges, salsa, and warmed corn tortillas, for serving (optional)

1. In 3-quart saucepan, place potato chunks and enough water to cover; heat to boiling over high heat. Reduce heat to low; cover and simmer until potatoes are almost tender, about 5 minutes; drain well.

2. Meanwhile, in 12-inch nonstick skillet, heat oil over medium heat until hot. Add onion, red pepper, garlic, cumin, and salt and cook for 10 minutes, stirring occasionally. Add drained potatoes and cook, turning occasionally, until vegetables are lightly browned, about 5 minutes longer. Stir in beans and cook until heated through, 2 minutes longer. Sprinkle with cilantro.

3. Serve vegetable hash with yogurt, lime wedges, salsa, and tortillas, if you like.

Each serving: About 340 calories, 12g protein, 63g carbohydrate, 6g total fat (1g saturated), 15g fiber, 618mg sodium

HUEVOS RANCHEROS

Fast and flavorful, these Mexican-inspired baked eggs are ideal for brunch. Baking rather than frying the tortilla cups keeps this dish low-fat.

ACTIVE TIME: 15 minutes   **TOTAL TIME**: 30 minutes
MAKES: 4 main-dish servings

4	(6-inch) corn tortillas
Nonstick cooking spray	
1	jar (16 ounces) mild low-sodium salsa
1	cup canned black beans, rinsed and drained
1	cup frozen corn kernels
3	green onions, sliced
1	teaspoon ground cumin
4	large eggs
$1/2$	cup loosely packed fresh cilantro leaves, thinly sliced
$1/2$	avocado, sliced into thin wedges
1	lime, sliced into wedges

1. Preheat oven to 350°F. In $15^1/2''$ by $10^1/2''$ jelly-roll pan, invert four 6-ounce custard cups. With kitchen shears, make four evenly spaced 1-inch cuts, from edge toward center, around each tortilla. Lightly spray both sides of tortillas with cooking spray and drape each over a custard cup. Bake tortilla cups for 8 minutes or until golden and crisp. Set aside to cool.

2. Meanwhile, in 12-inch nonstick skillet, combine salsa, beans, corn, green onions, and cumin; heat to boiling over medium heat. Cover and cook for 3 minutes to blend flavors. With large spoon, make four indentations for the eggs in salsa mixture, spacing them evenly around skillet. One at a time, break eggs into a cup and gently pour into an indentation in salsa mixture. Cover and simmer for 8 to 10 minutes or until eggs are set and cooked to desired doneness.

3. To serve, set each tortilla cup on a plate. Spoon an egg with some salsa mixture into each tortilla cup. Spoon any remaining salsa mixture around and on eggs in cups. Sprinkle with cilantro; serve with avocado and lime wedges.

Each serving: About 290 calories, 12g protein, 40g carbohydrate, 10g total fat (2g saturated), 11g fiber, 630mg sodium

CALIFORNIA FRITTATA

Mexican-style salsa, a medley of vegetables, and tortillas contribute California flavor to this substantial frittata. An egg substitute can be used instead of whole eggs, if you prefer.

ACTIVE TIME: 30 minutes   **TOTAL TIME**: 1 hour 5 minutes

MAKES: 4 main-dish servings

2 to 3	small potatoes (6½ ounces total)
1	tablespoon olive oil
1½	cups thinly sliced onions
1	zucchini (6 ounces), thinly sliced
1	cup thinly sliced cremini mushrooms
2	plum tomatoes (6½ ounces total), cored, halved, and thinly sliced
½	teaspoon kosher salt (optional)
½	teaspoon freshly ground black pepper
1	cup shredded spinach or Swiss chard
1	tablespoon slivered fresh basil leaves (optional)
2	large eggs
3	large egg whites
½	jicama (8 ounces), peeled and cut into 2" by ¼" matchstick strips
2	teaspoons lemon juice
2	tablespoons chopped fresh flat-leaf parsley
¾	cup bottled salsa
4	(6-inch) corn tortillas

1. Preheat oven to 350°F. In saucepan, heat potatoes and enough water to cover to a boil over high heat. Reduce heat to low; cover and simmer until fork-tender, 15 to 20 minutes. Drain and cool. Cut into ¼-inch slices.

2. In cast-iron or other heavy oven-safe skillet, heat oil over medium heat. Add onions and cook until softened, about 5 minutes. Add potatoes, zucchini, mushrooms, and tomatoes; cook, stirring gently, until zucchini begins to soften, 2 to 3 minutes. Add salt (if using), pepper, spinach, and basil (if using) and cook until spinach wilts, 1 to 2 minutes.

3. In medium bowl with wire whisk, mix eggs and egg whites. With spatula, stir vegetables while pouring eggs into skillet. Transfer skillet to oven and bake until eggs are set, 3 to 5 minutes.

4. While frittata bakes, sprinkle jicama sticks with lime juice; set aside.

5. When frittata is done, scatter parsley on top. Cut into 4 pieces and serve with salsa, tortillas, and jicama sticks.

Each serving: About 265 calories, 11g protein, 38g carbohydrate, 7g total fat (1g saturated), 8g fiber, 140mg sodium

Eat Your Tomatoes

Tomatoes are an excellent source of vitamin C, which enhances the body's ability to absorb iron. They also contain lycopene and other substances associated with lowering the risk of certain cancers. And, of course, they contain zero grams of fat. If you're not a fan of fresh tomatoes, you may just not have met the right one: Sample some firm and flavorful heirloom tomatoes from your local farmer's market. Come late summer, there's a tomato to suit every taste.

WHOLE-GRAIN PANCAKES

Have a stack of pancakes without a side of guilt. These flapjacks contain healthy oats and whole wheat flour. Plus, they're topped with delicious fresh fruit.

ACTIVE TIME: 15 minutes   **TOTAL TIME**: 30 minutes
MAKES: 12 pancakes or 4 main-dish servings

2	ripe peaches, pitted and chopped
1/2	pint raspberries (1 1/2 cups)
1	tablespoon granulated sugar
1/2	cup all-purpose flour
1/2	cup whole wheat flour
1/2	cup quick-cooking oats, uncooked
2	teaspoons baking powder
1/2	teaspoon salt
1 1/4	cups skim milk
1	large egg, lightly beaten
1	tablespoon vegetable oil
	Nonstick cooking spray

1. In medium bowl, combine peaches, raspberries, and sugar. Stir to coat; set aside.

2. Meanwhile, in large bowl, combine flours, oats, baking powder, and salt. Add milk, egg, and oil; stir just until flour mixture is moistened (batter will be lumpy).

3. Spray 12-inch nonstick skillet with cooking spray; heat over medium heat for 1 minute. Pour batter by scant 1/4-cups into skillet, making about 4 pancakes at a time. Cook until tops are bubbly, some bubbles burst, and edges look dry. With wide spatula, turn pancakes and cook until undersides are golden. Transfer pancakes to platter. Cover; keep warm.

4. Repeat with remaining batter, using more nonstick cooking spray if necessary.

5. To serve, top with fruit mixture.

Each serving: About 275 calories, 10g protein, 46g carbohydrate, 6g total fat (1g saturated), 6g fiber, 545mg sodium

HEALTHY MAKEOVER FRENCH TOAST

Our slimmed-down take on this Sunday-morning favorite is practically saintly. Subbing in low-fat milk and egg whites gives it half the fat and a third less cholesterol than traditional French toast. Plus, it's a cinch to whip up.

ACTIVE TIME: 15 minutes   **TOTAL TIME**: 25 minutes
MAKES: 4 main-dish servings

2	large egg whites
1	large egg
3/4	cup low-fat (1%) milk
1/4	teaspoon vanilla extract
1/8	teaspoon salt
2	teaspoons butter or margarine
8	slices firm whole wheat bread

Maple syrup and fresh blackberries, raspberries, and blueberries, for serving (optional)

1. Preheat oven to 200°F. In pie plate, with whisk, beat egg whites, egg, milk, vanilla, and salt until blended. In 12-inch nonstick skillet, melt 1 teaspoon butter over medium heat.

2. Dip bread slices, one at a time, in egg mixture, pressing bread lightly to coat both sides well. Place 3 or 4 slices in skillet and cook for 6 to 8 minutes or until lightly browned on both sides.

3. Transfer French toast to cookie sheet; keep warm in oven. Repeat with remaining butter, bread slices, and egg mixture. Serve French toast with maple syrup and berries, if you like.

Each serving: About 300 calories, 12g protein, 46g carbohydrate, 9g total fat (2g saturated), 6g fiber, 755mg sodium

PUMPKIN PANCAKES

Vitamin-rich pumpkin makes for a decadent breakfast treat.

TOTAL TIME: 20 minutes
MAKES: 4 servings

1	cup all-purpose flour
1	cup whole wheat flour
1	tablespoon baking powder
1	teaspoon pumpkin pie spice
½	teaspoon baking soda
½	teaspoon salt
1	cup whole milk
½	cup pumpkin puree
3	tablespoons brown sugar
2	large eggs
2	tablespoons vegetable oil

Maple syrup, for serving

1. In large bowl, whisk together all-purpose flour, whole wheat flour, baking powder, pumpkin pie spice, baking soda, and salt.

2. In small bowl, whisk together milk, pumpkin puree, brown sugar, eggs, and oil; stir into flour mixture until almost smooth.

3. Lightly grease 12-inch nonstick skillet; heat over medium heat until hot. In batches, scoop batter by ¼-cupfuls into skillet, spreading to 3½ inches each. Cook for 2 to 3 minutes or until bubbly and edges are dry. Turn; cook for 2 minutes or until golden.

4. Serve drizzled with syrup.

Each serving: About 415 calories, 13g protein, 63g carbohydrate, 13g total fat (3g saturated), 5g fiber, 930mg sodium

SPICED APPLE PANCAKE

This simple pancake makes delightful brunch fare. For the puffiest pancake, use a cast-iron skillet. If you don't have one, choose a heavy 12-inch skillet with an oven-safe handle and a bottom that is at least 10 inches in diameter.

ACTIVE TIME: 5 minutes   **TOTAL TIME**: 35 minutes
MAKES: 8 main-dish servings

1	tablespoon butter or margarine
2	tablespoons water
$1/2$	cup plus 2 tablespoons granulated sugar
$1^1/2$	pounds Granny Smith apples (3 to 4 medium), peeled, cored, and cut into 8 wedges
3	large eggs
$3/4$	cup milk
$3/4$	cup all-purpose flour
1	teaspoon pumpkin pie spice or $1/2$ teaspoon ground cinnamon
$1/4$	teaspoon salt

1. Preheat oven to 450°F. In 12-inch cast-iron skillet, heat butter, water, and $1/2$ cup sugar over medium-high heat to boiling. Add apple wedges; cook for 12 to 15 minutes or until apples are golden and sugar mixture begins to caramelize, stirring occasionally.

2. Meanwhile, in blender or food processor with knife blade attached, place eggs and milk. Add flour, pumpkin pie spice, salt, and remaining 2 tablespoons sugar. Blend until batter is smooth.

3. When apple mixture in skillet is deep golden, pour batter over apples. Place skillet in oven; bake for 15 to 17 minutes or until puffed and lightly browned. Serve immediately.

Each serving: About 190 calories, 5g protein, 34g carbohydrate, 4g total fat (2g saturated), 1g fiber, 110mg sodium

ULTIMATE CLASSIC WAFFLE

If you can resist devouring all of these mouthwatering waffles, freeze any leftovers. Then, just pop in the toaster for a quick weekday breakfast!

TOTAL TIME: 25 minutes
MAKES: 8 servings

1³⁄₄	cups all-purpose flour
1¹⁄₂	teaspoons baking powder
1	teaspoon baking soda
¹⁄₂	teaspoon salt
2	cups low-fat buttermilk
2	large eggs
3	tablespoons granulated sugar
3	tablespoons vegetable oil
1	tablespoon vanilla extract

Nonstick cooking spray

1. Preheat waffle maker.

2. In large bowl, whisk flour, baking powder, baking soda, and salt. In medium bowl, whisk buttermilk, eggs, sugar, oil, and vanilla. Add buttermilk mixture to flour mixture. Stir until just combined (small lumps are okay).

3. Spray waffle maker with nonstick cooking spray. Add ¹⁄₂ cup batter to waffle maker; close and cook for 2 to 5 minutes or until golden brown and crisp. Keep warm by placing directly on oven rack in 225°F oven. Repeat with remaining batter.

4. Cooked waffles may be cooled, wrapped tightly in plastic, and frozen for up to 1 month. Reheat in toaster oven or 350°F oven for 8 to 10 minutes (directly on oven rack) until hot and crisp.

Each serving: About 225 calories, 7g protein, 30g carbohydrate, 8g total fat (1g saturated), 1g fiber, 490mg sodium

SPICED BANANA-CHOCOLATE MUFFINS

These delicious chocolatey muffins feature good-for-you oats, whole wheat, and chia seeds. (See photograph on page 12.)

ACTIVE TIME: 15 minutes   **TOTAL TIME**: 35 minutes
MAKES: 18 muffins

2	cups old-fashioned oats, uncooked
1¼	cups white whole wheat flour
½	cup brown sugar
2	tablespoons chia seeds
2	teaspoons baking powder
¾	teaspoon baking soda
½	teaspoon salt
½	teaspoon ground cinnamon
¼	teaspoon ground ginger
1¼	cups mashed very ripe bananas (about 3 medium)
1	cup low-fat buttermilk
2	tablespoons vegetable oil
1	large egg, beaten
2	ounces bittersweet chocolate (60% to 70% cacao), melted

1. Preheat oven to 400°F. Line 18 muffin-pan cups with paper liners.

2. In large bowl, whisk oats, flour, sugar, chia seeds, baking powder, baking soda, salt, cinnamon, and ginger. In medium bowl, stir together bananas, buttermilk, oil, and egg. Fold banana mixture into flour mixture. Divide among 18 cups in muffin pan.

3. Bake for 20 to 25 minutes or until toothpick inserted into centers of muffins comes out clean. Cool on wire rack for 10 minutes. Remove muffins from pan and cool completely on wire rack.

4. Drizzle cooled muffin tops with melted chocolate.

Each 2-muffin serving: About 300 calories, 6g protein, 48g carbohydrate, 8g total fat (2g saturated), 6g fiber, 430mg sodium

APPLE-OAT MUFFINS

These muffins are wholesome and delicious.

ACTIVE TIME: 15 minutes   **TOTAL TIME**: 45 minutes

MAKES: 12 muffins

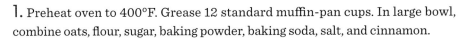

2	cups old-fashioned oats, uncooked
1¼	cups all-purpose flour
½	cup packed brown sugar
2	teaspoons baking powder
¾	teaspoon baking soda
¾	teaspoon salt
½	teaspoon ground cinnamon
1	cup buttermilk
2	tablespoons vegetable oil
1	large egg, lightly beaten
1	cup shredded Golden Delicious or Granny Smith apples (1 to 2 medium)
½	cup walnuts, chopped

1. Preheat oven to 400°F. Grease 12 standard muffin-pan cups. In large bowl, combine oats, flour, sugar, baking powder, baking soda, salt, and cinnamon.

2. In medium bowl, with fork, beat buttermilk, oil, and egg until well blended; stir in apples. Add apple mixture to flour mixture, and stir just until flour mixture is moistened; batter will be very thick and lumpy. Stir in chopped walnuts.

3. Spoon batter into prepared muffin-pan cups. Bake for 23 to 25 minutes or until muffins begin to brown and toothpick inserted in center comes out clean. Immediately remove muffins from pan. Serve warm, or cool on wire rack to serve later.

Each serving: About 210 calories, 5g protein, 33g carbohydrate, 7g total fat (1g saturated), 3g fiber, 320mg sodium

WHOLE-GRAIN BLUEBERRY MUFFINS

Deliciously dense, these muffins are made with a combination of all-purpose flour, whole wheat flour, and old-fashioned oats for the perfect blend of taste and health.

ACTIVE TIME: 20 minutes   **TOTAL TIME**: 40 minutes
MAKES: 12 muffins

1	cup old-fashioned oats, uncooked
1	cup whole wheat flour
1/2	cup all-purpose flour
2	teaspoons baking powder
1/2	teaspoon baking soda
1/2	teaspoon salt
1/4	cup plus 1 tablespoon packed brown sugar
1	cup low-fat buttermilk
1/4	cup fresh orange juice
2	tablespoons canola oil
1	large egg
1	teaspoon vanilla extract
2	cups fresh blueberries
1/4	cup natural almonds, chopped

1. Preheat oven to 400°F. Line 12-cup standard muffin pan with paper liners.

2. In blender, grind oats. In bowl, whisk together oats, all-purpose flour, whole wheat flour, baking powder, baking soda, salt, and 1/4 cup sugar. In small bowl, whisk together buttermilk, juice, oil, egg, and vanilla. Stir into flour mixture; fold in blueberries.

3. Combine almonds and remaining 1 tablespoon sugar. Spoon batter into prepared pan; sprinkle with almond sugar. Bake for 22 minutes or until toothpick inserted into center of muffin comes out clean. Cool in pan on wire rack for 5 minutes. Remove from pan; cool completely.

Each muffin: About 170 calories, 5g protein, 28g carbohydrate, 5g total fat (1g saturated), 3g fiber, 270mg sodium

LOW-FAT BANANA BREAD

We used egg whites and unsweetened applesauce to lighten up everyone's favorite quick bread without sacrificing moisture. For a whole-grain variation, substitute ½ cup whole wheat flour for the same amount of all-purpose flour.

ACTIVE TIME: 20 minutes   **TOTAL TIME**: 1 hour

MAKES: 1 loaf (16 slices)

1¾	cups all-purpose flour
½	cup granulated sugar
1	teaspoon baking powder
½	teaspoon baking soda
½	teaspoon salt
1	cup mashed very ripe bananas (2 medium)
⅓	cup unsweetened applesauce
2	large egg whites
1	large egg
¼	cup pecans, chopped

1. Preheat oven to 350°F. Grease 9" by 5" metal loaf pan. In large bowl, combine flour, sugar, baking powder, baking soda, and salt. In medium bowl, with fork, mix bananas, applesauce, egg whites, and egg until well blended. Stir banana mixture into flour mixture just until flour mixture is moistened.

2. Pour batter into prepared pan; sprinkle with chopped pecans. Bake until toothpick inserted in center comes out almost clean, 40 to 45 minutes. Cool in pan on wire rack for 10 minutes; remove from pan and cool completely on wire rack.

Each serving: About 120 calories, 3g protein, 23g carbohydrate, 2g total fat (0g saturated), 1g fiber, 155mg sodium

Go Nuts!

Dieters have long viewed nuts as the enemy. Sure, they're high in fat and calories, but when eaten in moderation (2 tablespoons daily), nuts can do wonders. By adding a bit of fat to a fat-free meal like cereal and skim milk, nuts can slow down the emptying of your stomach, making you feel fuller longer. In addition, nuts may suppress your appetite longer than other fatty foods do. Buy nuts roasted and unsalted for big flavor without the sodium. Or spread a little peanut butter—or almond or cashew butter—on your morning toast.

SKINNY CARROT MUFFINS

Moist muffins studded with raisins and carrots—perfect for breakfast on the go!

ACTIVE TIME: 15 minutes   **TOTAL TIME**: 45 minutes
MAKES: 12 muffins

Nonstick cooking spray

2¼   cups all-purpose flour
½   cup granulated sugar
1   teaspoon ground cinnamon
1   teaspoon salt
1   teaspoon baking soda
½   teaspoon baking powder
¼   teaspoon ground ginger
3   carrots, peeled and finely shredded (1½ cups)
1   cup vanilla nonfat yogurt
½   cup egg substitute
½   cup unsweetened applesauce
½   cup dark seedless raisins
⅓   cup packed light brown sugar
1   teaspoon vanilla extract
1   teaspoon confectioners' sugar

1. Preheat oven to 350°F. Spray 12 standard muffin-pan cups with nonstick cooking spray.

2. In medium bowl, combine flour, granulated sugar, cinnamon, salt, baking soda, baking powder, and ginger. In large bowl, with wire whisk or fork, mix carrots, yogurt, egg substitute, applesauce, raisins, brown sugar, and vanilla until well blended. Stir flour mixture into carrot mixture just until flour is moistened.

3. Spoon batter into muffin cups. Bake until toothpick inserted in center of muffins comes out clean, about 30 minutes. Let muffins sit in pan on wire rack for 10 minutes; remove to wire rack to cool completely. Sprinkle with confectioners' sugar while muffins are still warm.

Each serving: About 190 calories, 5g protein, 43g carbohydrate, 1g total fat (0g saturated), 1g fiber, 337mg sodium

Garden Greens and Pumpernickel Panzanella (page 97)

2 | SUPER-HEALTHY SALADS

Salad, in its most familiar guise, is composed of cool, crisp greens tossed with a piquant dressing. But, as the recipes in this chapter demonstrate, a winning salad can be created from a seemingly endless array of ingredients: beans, grains, or a combination; rice noodles or pasta; fresh veggies, fruits, and herbs—all bolstered with chicken, meat, or seafood to create a salad that's a meal in a bowl.

Since high-fat dressings are often the downfall of otherwise healthy salads, we offer several recipes for skinny salad dressings that contain 15 calories or less and zero grams of fat per serving. Citrus juice and zest, ginger, and fresh herbs keep the vinaigrettes flavorful, while a little reduced-fat buttermilk and low-fat mayo add tang and creaminess to the dressings. And since olive oil is rich in good-for-you monounsaturated fat—which may result in healthier levels of LDL and heart-boosting HDL—topping your salad with a moderate amount of this fragrant oil and vinegar is another appealing option.

Salads and healthy eating go hand-in-hand, so we offer an assortment of main-dish salads perfect for lunch or a light dinner. Our Tex-Mex-style Cobb salad brings new life to garden-variety classics. Grilled shrimp and pineapple dress up a simple mix of basil and baby greens, while stir-fried Korean steak in lettuce cups delivers salad you can eat out of hand.

From warm wheat berry and farro to six-bean salad and tabbouleh, our grain and bean salads can be served as nourishing main dishes, too. And don't miss our delicious Italian-inspired salads, such as Italian Tuna and White Bean Salad and Panzanella Salad with Grilled Chicken. Mediterranean meals like these follow the original heart-healthy diet!

PASTA SALAD WITH LEMON AND PEAS

Small shell or bow-tie pasta is dressed in a light, lemony mayonnaise made even more flavorful with the addition of green onions and basil.

ACTIVE TIME: 15 minutes   **TOTAL TIME**: 20 minutes
MAKES: 16 side-dish servings

1	pound bow-tie or small shell pasta
1	package (10 ounces) frozen baby peas
2	lemons
²/₃	cup low-fat (1%) milk
½	cup light mayonnaise
¼	teaspoon coarsely ground black pepper
1	cup loosely packed fresh basil leaves, chopped
4	green onions, thinly sliced
1	teaspoon salt

1. In large saucepot, cook pasta as label directs, adding frozen peas during last 2 minutes of cooking time. Drain pasta and peas; rinse under cold running water and drain well.

2. Meanwhile, from lemons, grate 1 tablespoon peel and squeeze 3 tablespoons juice. In large bowl, with wire whisk, mix lemon peel and juice with milk, mayonnaise, pepper, basil, green onions, and salt until blended.

3. Add pasta and peas to mayonnaise dressing; toss to coat well. Cover and refrigerate for up to 2 days if not serving right away.

Each serving: About 160 calories, 4g protein, 28g carbohydrate, 3g total fat (0g saturated), 2g fiber, 210mg sodium

Give It a Lift with Citrus

Grated peel or a splash of juice can perk up almost anything sweet or savory—without adding fat. Just a sprinkle or squeeze before serving can make the difference between a plain dish and a memorable one. Try these simple, flavor-boosting ideas.

GRATED PEEL

- Stir any citrus peel into rice pilaf to transform it from simple to sumptuous.
- Toss orange peel with lightly buttered carrots or roasted sweet potatoes.
- Sprinkle lime peel over coconut sorbet for a zesty fresh flavor.

JUICE

- Squirt some lemon, lime, or orange juice over steamed shellfish or grilled chicken just before eating.
- Add some lemon juice to bottled low-fat salad dressing to give it a sprightly homemade taste.
- Stir some lime juice into canned black beans or lentil soup to add zip before serving.

GRATED PEEL AND JUICE

- Stir grated lemon peel and juice into 1 tablespoon of low-fat mayonnaise for a tangy sandwich spread or dressing for steamed asparagus.
- Grate any citrus peel into a bowl with 1 tablespoon of butter or margarine, and add a squirt of juice plus a pinch of dried herb to make a citrus butter. Toss with cooked vegetables.
- Combine grated lime peel and juice with minced fresh ginger. Stir into a fruit salad (bananas, cantaloupe, and blueberries would be a nice match).

KALE CAESAR PASTA SALAD

Toss together this slimmer dinner in no time.

TOTAL TIME: 10 minutes
MAKES: 6 servings

1	pound bow-tie pasta
6	tablespoons light mayonnaise
1/3	cup grated Parmesan cheese
3	tablespoons lemon juice
1	tablespoon Dijon mustard
1	tablespoon extra-virgin olive oil
1	clove garlic, crushed with press
1/2	teaspoon salt
1/2	teaspoon pepper
1	large bunch kale, stemmed and chopped
8	medium radishes, cut into quarters

1. Cook pasta as label directs.

2. In a large bowl, whisk together mayonnaise, Parmesan, lemon juice, mustard, olive oil, garlic, salt, and pepper. Add kale, tossing to combine.

3. While cooked pasta is still hot, add to the kale mixture. Let cool slightly. Stir in the radishes and serve.

Each serving: About 390 calories, 14g protein, 62g carbohydrate, 10g total fat (2g saturated), 4g fiber, 435mg sodium

SKINNY SALAD DRESSINGS

These flavor-packed drizzles are so good, you'll forget they're no-fat.

HONEY-LIME VINAIGRETTE

MAKES: 1/2 cup or 8 servings

1/3	cup fresh lime juice (from 2 to 3 limes)	1	tablespoon rice vinegar
4	teaspoons honey	1/8	teaspoon salt

In small bowl, with wire whisk, mix lime juice, honey, vinegar, and salt until blended. Cover and refrigerate for up to 3 days.

Each 1-tablespoon serving: About 15 calories, 0g protein, 4g carbohydrate, 0g total fat, 0g fiber, 37mg sodium

TOMATO-ORANGE VINAIGRETTE

MAKES: 1/2 cup or 8 servings

1/2	cup tomato juice	1/4	teaspoon granulated sugar
1	tablespoon balsamic vinegar	1/4	teaspoon ground black pepper
1/4	teaspoon grated orange peel		

In small bowl, with wire whisk, mix tomato juice, vinegar, orange peel, sugar, and pepper until blended. Cover and refrigerate for up to 3 days.

Each 1-tablespoon serving: About 5 calories, 0g protein, 1g carbohydrate, 0g total fat, 0g fiber, 55mg sodium

ORANGE-GINGER VINAIGRETTE

MAKES: 1 cup or 16 servings

1/2	cup seasoned rice vinegar	1/2	cup orange juice
1/2	teaspoon grated, peeled fresh ginger	1/2	teaspoon soy sauce
		1/8	teaspoon Asian sesame oil

In small bowl, with wire whisk, mix vinegar, ginger, orange juice, soy sauce, and sesame oil until blended. Cover and refrigerate for up to 5 days.

Each 1-tablespoon serving: About 10 calories, 0g protein, 3g carbohydrate, 0g total fat, 0g fiber, 110mg sodium

BUTTERMILK-CHIVE DRESSING

MAKES: 3/4 cup or 12 servings

1/2	cup reduced-fat buttermilk	1	tablespoon low-fat mayonnaise
2	tablespoons distilled white vinegar	1/4	teaspoon salt
2	tablespoons chopped fresh chives	1/4	teaspoon ground black pepper

In small bowl, with wire whisk, mix buttermilk, vinegar, chives, mayonnaise, salt, and pepper until blended. Cover and refrigerate for up to 3 days.

Each 1-tablespoon serving: About 6 calories, 0g protein, 1g carbohydrate, 0g total fat, 0g fiber, 65mg sodium

CREAMY RANCH DRESSING

MAKES: 1 cup or 16 servings

3/4	cup plain nonfat yogurt	2	teaspoons Dijon mustard
1/4	cup low-fat mayonnaise	1/4	teaspoon dried thyme
1	green onion, minced	1/4	teaspoon coarsely ground black pepper
1	tablespoon cider vinegar		

In small bowl, with wire whisk, mix yogurt, mayonnaise, green onion, vinegar, mustard, thyme, and pepper until blended. Cover and refrigerate for up to 5 days.

Each 1-tablespoon serving: About 15 calories, 1g protein, 2g carbohydrate, 0g total fat, 0g fiber, 60mg sodium

BARLEY, CORN, AND TOMATO SALAD

The whole-grain goodness of pearl barley is combined with the fresh flavors of summer corn cut from the cob, tomatoes off the vine, and the heady perfume of basil.

ACTIVE TIME: 15 minutes **TOTAL TIME**: 40 minutes
MAKES: 12 side-dish servings

2½	cups water	1	teaspoon salt
1¼	cups pearl barley	¼	teaspoon ground black pepper
5	medium ears corn	2	large ripe tomatoes (about 8 ounces each), cut into ½-inch chunks
1	small bunch basil		
¼	cup rice vinegar	2	green onions, sliced
3	tablespoons olive oil		

1. In 2-quart saucepan, heat water to boiling over high heat. Stir in barley; return to boiling. Reduce heat to low; cover and simmer until barley is tender, 30 to 35 minutes.

2. Meanwhile, place corn on plate in microwave. Cook on high for 4 to 5 minutes, turning corn halfway through cooking. Cool slightly until easy to handle. Chop enough basil leaves to equal ⅓ cup; reserve remaining basil for garnish.

3. With sharp knife, cut corn kernels from cobs. In large bowl, with fork, mix vinegar, oil, salt, and pepper; stir in corn, warm barley, tomatoes, green onions, and chopped basil until combined. If not serving right away, cover and refrigerate for up to 4 hours. Garnish with basil leaves.

Each serving: About 145 calories, 4g protein, 26g carbohydrate, 4g total fat (1g saturated), 5g fiber, 205mg sodium

Get Your Grains: BARLEY

Barley is one of the oldest grains in cultivation. In most grains, the fiber is concentrated in the bran, which is removed when the kernel is refined. But even when all of barley's tough bran is removed (as with pearl barley, the most refined type), at least half of the original fiber remains. A half-cup of cooked barley contains 3 grams of fiber, compared to white rice's one-third gram.

SNAP PEA SALAD

This yummy double-pea salad is easy to prepare and pretty to serve. Use any leftover fresh dill in your next mayonnaise-based salad.

ACTIVE TIME: 10 minutes **TOTAL TIME**: 15 minutes
MAKES: 8 side-dish servings

1	pound sugar snap peas, strings removed
1	package (10 ounces) frozen peas
$\frac{1}{2}$	cup minced red onion
2	tablespoons white wine vinegar
2	tablespoons vegetable oil
2	tablespoons chopped fresh dill
1	tablespoon granulated sugar
$\frac{1}{2}$	teaspoon salt
$\frac{1}{4}$	teaspoon coarsely ground black pepper

1. In 5- to 6-quart saucepot, heat 2 inches water to boiling over high heat. Add snap peas and frozen peas and cook for 1 minute. Drain; rinse under cold running water to stop cooking. Drain again; pat dry between layers of paper towels.

2. In large bowl, stir onion, vinegar, oil, dill, sugar, salt, and pepper until mixed. Add peas and toss to coat. If not serving right away, cover and refrigerate for up to 4 hours.

Each serving: About 100 calories, 4g protein, 13g carbohydrate, 3g total fat (0g saturated), 4g fiber, 245mg sodium

PEACHES AND GREENS

Try this cool, refreshing alternative to a classic green salad.

ACTIVE TIME: 25 minutes
MAKES: 12 side-dish servings

1	large lime	2	bunches watercress (4 ounces each), tough stems discarded
2	tablespoons honey		
1	tablespoon olive oil	2	pounds ripe peaches (6 medium), peeled and cut into wedges
1	tablespoon chopped fresh mint leaves		
1/2	teaspoon Dijon mustard	1	large jicama (1¼ pounds), peeled and cut into 1½" by ¼" sticks
1/4	teaspoon salt		
1/4	teaspoon coarsely ground black pepper		

1. Prepare dressing: From lime, grate ¼ teaspoon peel and squeeze 2 tablespoons juice. In large bowl, with wire whisk, mix lime peel, lime juice, honey, oil, mint, mustard, salt, and pepper.

2. Just before serving, add watercress, peaches, and jicama to dressing in bowl; toss to coat.

Each serving: About 55 calories, 1g protein, 11g carbohydrate, 1g total fat (0g saturated), 3g fiber, 55mg sodium

Taste the Rainbow

The vibrant colors of fruits and vegetables do more than add visual appeal to a drab dinner. Natural pigments in produce, called phytochemicals, keep your body healthy, too. Scientists are still learning about the wide range of phytochemicals in nature, so don't expect to get these helpers from a pill. Instead, eat a colorful diet filled with reds, yellows, oranges, and greens. For instance, salad greens offer a wide variety of phytochemicals, so be sure to enjoy an assortment of types. Watercress or arugula add peppery notes to salad, mâche offers a delicious mild flavor and tender leaf, while baby spinach tastes as great on a sandwich as it does in a bowl.

BLACK BEAN AND AVOCADO SALAD

A satisfying combination of summer veggies, romaine lettuce, and black beans tossed with a creamy buttermilk dressing, this salad would also be good with our Creamy Ranch Dressing (page 59) or Honey-Lime Vinaigrette (page 58).

TOTAL TIME: 20 minutes

MAKES: 4 main-dish servings

Buttermilk-Chive Dressing (see recipe, page 59)

1	small head romaine lettuce (about 1 pound), cut into $^3/_4$-inch pieces (about 8 cups)
2	medium tomatoes, cut into $^1/_2$-inch pieces
2	Kirby cucumbers (about 4 ounces each), unpeeled, each cut lengthwise into quarters, then crosswise into $^1/_4$-inch-thick pieces
1	ripe avocado, cut into $^1/_2$-inch pieces
1	can (15 to 19 ounces) black beans, rinsed and drained

1. Prepare Buttermilk-Chive Dressing.

2. In large serving bowl, combine romaine, tomatoes, cucumbers, avocado, and beans. Add dressing and toss until evenly coated.

Each serving: About 235 calories, 11g protein, 36g carbohydrate, 6g fat (1g saturated), 15g fiber, 521mg sodium

TEX-MEX TURKEY COBB SALAD

Warm Southwestern accents give this classic a new attitude.

TOTAL TIME: 30 minutes

MAKES: 4 main-dish servings

1/4	cup fresh lime juice
2	tablespoons chopped fresh cilantro leaves
4	teaspoons olive oil
1	teaspoon granulated sugar
1/4	teaspoon ground cumin
1/4	teaspoon salt
1/4	teaspoon coarsely ground black pepper
1	medium head romaine lettuce (1 1/4 pounds), trimmed with leaves cut into 1/2-inch-wide strips
1	pint cherry tomatoes, cut into quarters
12	ounces cooked skinless roast turkey meat, cut into 1/2-inch pieces (2 cups)
1	can (15 to 19 ounces) pinto beans, rinsed and drained
2	small cucumbers (6 ounces each), peeled, seeded, and sliced 1/2-inch thick

1. Prepare dressing: In small bowl, with wire whisk, combine lime juice, cilantro, oil, sugar, cumin, salt, and pepper.

2. Place lettuce in large serving bowl. Arrange tomatoes, turkey, beans, and cucumbers in rows over lettuce and present the salad. Just before serving, toss salad with dressing.

Each serving: About 310 calories, 39g protein, 32g carbohydrate, 7g total fat (1g saturated), 13g fiber, 505mg sodium

PANZANELLA SALAD WITH GRILLED CHICKEN

This Florentine bread and tomato salad is popular in the summer, when tomatoes are at their peak. For a fresh and flavorful twist, we added chicken breasts to the mix and tossed the ingredients on the grill.

TOTAL TIME: 30 minutes

MAKES: 4 main-dish servings

2	tablespoons red wine vinegar	2	red peppers, cut lengthwise into quarters
1	garlic clove, crushed with press	1	red onion, cut into 1/2-inch-thick slices
3/4	teaspoon salt		
1/2	teaspoon coarsely ground black pepper	1	pound boneless skinless chicken breast halves
1/4	cup olive oil	2	pounds ripe plum tomatoes, cut into 1-inch chunks
4	ounces country-style bread (1/4 small loaf), cut into 3/4-inch-thick slices	1/4	cup loosely packed small fresh basil leaves, or 2 tablespoons chopped leaves

1. Prepare outdoor grill for direct grilling over medium heat.

2. Meanwhile, in large bowl, whisk together vinegar, garlic, 1/2 teaspoon salt, 1/4 teaspoon pepper, and 2 tablespoons oil until blended; set vinaigrette aside.

3. In jelly-roll pan, brush bread slices, peppers, and onion slices with remaining 2 tablespoons oil to lightly coat both sides; sprinkle with remaining 1/4 teaspoon each salt and pepper. With tongs, place bread slices, red peppers, onion slices, and chicken on hot grill grate. Cover grill and cook bread for about 3 minutes or until lightly toasted, turning over once. Cook peppers and onion for about 8 minutes or until lightly browned and tender, turning over once. Cook chicken for about 12 minutes or until meat thermometer inserted horizontally into breast registers 165°F, turning over once. As bread, vegetables, and chicken are done, transfer to cutting board. Cut bread slices, chicken, peppers, and onions into 1/2-inch pieces.

4. Stir tomatoes, basil, bread, peppers, onion, and chicken into vinaigrette in bowl; toss to combine. Scoop into bowls to serve.

Each serving: About 405 calories, 32g protein, 33g carbohydrate, 17g total fat (3g saturated), 6g fiber, 690mg sodium

CURRIED CHICKEN SALAD WITH CANTALOUPE SLAW

Curry, crystallized ginger, and crushed red pepper bring out the full sweet flavor of fresh fruit.

ACTIVE TIME: 25 minutes   **TOTAL TIME**: 35 minutes plus marinating
MAKES: 4 main-dish servings

1 to 2	limes
1	container (6 ounces) plain low-fat yogurt
3/4	teaspoon curry powder
1/4	cup chopped crystallized ginger
1	teaspoon salt
1/4	teaspoon crushed red pepper
4	medium boneless skinless chicken breast halves (about 1¼ pounds total)
1/2	small cantaloupe, rind removed and cut into julienne strips (2 cups)
1	large mango, peeled and cut into julienne strips (2 cups)
1/2	cup loosely packed fresh cilantro leaves, chopped
1	head Boston lettuce

Lime wedges, for serving (optional)

1. Prepare outdoor grill for covered direct grilling over medium heat.

2. From limes, grate ½ teaspoon peel and squeeze 2 tablespoons juice. In large bowl, with wire whisk, combine 1 tablespoon lime juice and ¼ teaspoon lime peel with yogurt, curry powder, 2 tablespoons ginger, ¾ teaspoon salt, and ⅛ teaspoon crushed red pepper. Add chicken, turning to coat with marinade. Cover and let stand for 15 minutes at room temperature or 30 minutes in refrigerator, turning occasionally.

3. Meanwhile, prepare slaw: In medium bowl, with rubber spatula, gently stir cantaloupe and mango with cilantro, remaining 2 tablespoons ginger, 1 tablespoon lime juice, ¼ teaspoon lime peel, ¼ teaspoon salt, and ⅛ teaspoon crushed red pepper; set aside. Makes about 4 cups.

4. Grease grill rack. Remove chicken from marinade; discard marinade. Place chicken on hot rack. Cover grill and cook chicken for 10 to 12 minutes or until juices run clear when thickest part of breast is pierced with tip of knife, turning chicken over once. Transfer chicken to cutting board; cool slightly until easy to handle, then cut into long thin slices.

5. To serve, arrange lettuce leaves on four dinner plates; top with chicken and slaw. Serve with lime wedges, if you like.

Each serving chicken with lettuce: About 205 calories, 34g protein, 5g carbohydrate, 4g total fat (1g saturated), 1g fiber, 330mg sodium

---

Each ½-cup slaw: About 50 calories, 1g protein, 13g carbohydrate, 0g total fat, 1g fiber, 150mg sodium

GRILLED CHICKEN TACO SALAD

A great way to prepare this Mexican favorite during the summer: Spicy chicken breasts are grilled and served over black-bean salsa, shredded lettuce, and crisp corn tortillas.

ACTIVE TIME: 25 minutes   **TOTAL TIME**: 35 minutes

MAKES: 4 main-dish servings

1	can (15 to 19 ounces) low-sodium black beans, rinsed and drained
3/4	cup medium-hot salsa
1	tablespoon fresh lime juice
1	cup loosely packed fresh cilantro leaves, chopped
2	tablespoons chili powder
1	teaspoon ground cumin
1	teaspoon ground coriander
1	teaspoon brown sugar
1/2	teaspoon salt
1/4	teaspoon cayenne (ground red) pepper
1	tablespoon olive oil
1	pound boneless skinless chicken breast halves
4	corn tortillas
4	cups thinly sliced lettuce
	Lime wedges, avocado slices, and reduced-fat sour cream, for serving (optional)

1. Prepare outdoor grill for direct grilling over medium-high heat.

2. In medium bowl, mix beans, salsa, lime juice, and half of cilantro; set aside.

3. In cup, stir chili powder, cumin, coriander, brown sugar, salt, cayenne, and oil until evenly mixed (mixture will be dry).

4. If necessary, place chicken breast halves between two sheets of plastic wrap and pound to uniform 1/4-inch thickness. With hands, rub chicken with chili-powder mixture.

5. Place chicken on hot grill and grill until juices run clear when thickest part of breast is pierced with tip of knife, 8 to 10 minutes, turning over once. Place tortillas on grill with chicken and cook until lightly browned, 3 to 5 minutes, turning over once.

6. Transfer chicken to cutting board. Place tortillas on four dinner plates. Cut chicken into long thin strips. Top tortillas with lettuce, bean mixture, and chicken. Sprinkle with remaining cilantro. If you like, serve with lime wedges, avocado slices, and sour cream.

Each serving: About 375 calories, 34g protein, 41g carbohydrate, 8g total fat (1g saturated), 11g fiber, 648mg sodium

ASIAN CHICKEN SALAD

This fast, easy chicken salad recipe is full of Far East–inspired flavors.

ACTIVE TIME: 20 minutes   **TOTAL TIME**: 30 minutes
MAKES: 6 main-dish servings

3	limes
4	medium boneless skinless chicken breast halves (1½ pounds total)
1	bag (16 ounces) frozen shelled edamame
⅓	cup low-sodium soy sauce
¼	cup loosely packed fresh cilantro leaves, chopped
1	tablespoon grated, peeled fresh ginger
2	teaspoons Asian sesame oil
1	pound napa (Chinese) cabbage (½ small head), sliced
1	bunch or 1 bag (6 ounces) radishes, trimmed and thinly sliced

1. Cut 2 limes into thin slices. From remaining lime, squeeze 2 tablespoons juice; set aside.

2. In covered 12-inch skillet, heat half of lime slices and 1 inch water to boiling over high heat. Add chicken; cover, reduce heat to medium-low, and cook for 13 to 14 minutes or until chicken loses its pink color throughout. With slotted spoon or tongs, remove chicken from skillet and place in large bowl of ice water; chill for 5 minutes. Drain chicken well; with hands, shred chicken into bite-size pieces.

3. Meanwhile, cook edamame as label directs; drain. Rinse with cold running water to stop cooking and drain again. In large bowl, whisk soy sauce, cilantro, ginger, sesame oil, and reserved lime juice. Add cabbage, edamame, radishes, and shredded chicken to bowl; toss to combine.

4. To serve, transfer to deep bowls and garnish with remaining lime slices.

Each serving: About 285 calories, 39g protein, 14g carbohydrate, 8g total fat (1g saturated), 6g fiber, 560mg sodium

KOREAN STEAK IN LETTUCE CUPS

Sliced round steak and shredded carrots are braised in a rich soy-ginger sauce and served in delicate Boston-lettuce leaves.

ACTIVE TIME: 15 minutes   **TOTAL TIME**: 20 minutes plus marinating
MAKES: 4 main-dish servings

3	tablespoons soy sauce
1	tablespoon granulated sugar
2	teaspoons Asian sesame oil
1	teaspoon minced, peeled fresh ginger
1/4	teaspoon cayenne (ground red) pepper
1	garlic clove, crushed with press
1	beef top round steak (about 1 pound), trimmed and cut into 1/2-inch cubes
4	celery stalks with leaves, thinly sliced
1/2	package (10 ounces) shredded carrots (1 3/4 cups)
1/2	cup water
3	green onions, thinly sliced
1	tablespoon sesame seeds, toasted (see Tip)
1	head Boston lettuce, separated into leaves
	Green-onion tops, for garnish

1. In medium bowl, stir soy sauce, sugar, oil, ginger, cayenne, and garlic until blended. Add beef, turning to coat with soy-sauce mixture, and marinate for 15 minutes at room temperature, stirring occasionally.

2. In 12-inch skillet, heat celery, carrots, and 1/2 cup water to boiling over medium-high heat. Cook for 2 to 3 minutes or until vegetables are tender-crisp, stirring occasionally. Add beef with its marinade and cook for 2 minutes or until meat just loses its pink color throughout, stirring quickly and constantly. Stir in green onions and sesame seeds; cook for 1 minute, stirring.

3. To serve, let each person place some beef mixture on a lettuce leaf. Garnish with green-onion tops. If you like, fold sides of lettuce leaf over filling to make a package to eat out of hand.

Each serving: About 300 calories, 28g protein, 12g carbohydrate, 10g total fat (3g saturated), 3g fiber, 855mg sodium

TIP

Toasting brings out the nutty flavor of sesame seeds. To toast, heat seeds in a small, dry skillet over medium heat, stirring constantly, until fragrant and a shade darker, 3 to 5 minutes.

GRILLED CAESAR SALAD

Grilling romaine or any other sturdy green that grows in a head (such as endive, radicchio, or chicory) transforms it into a totally different vegetable, with a rich "meaty" taste that adds instant flavor to any salad.

ACTIVE TIME: 10 minutes   **TOTAL TIME**: 15 minutes
MAKES: 4 side-dish servings

2	tablespoons olive oil
4	ounces Italian bread, cut into ½-inch-thick slices
¼	cup light mayonnaise
2	tablespoons freshly grated Parmesan cheese
3	tablespoons fresh lemon juice
1	teaspoon anchovy paste, or 2 anchovy fillets, mashed
¼	teaspoon coarsely ground black pepper
1	garlic clove, cut in half
1	package (18 to 22 ounces) hearts of romaine, each head cut lengthwise in half

1. Prepare outdoor grill for direct grilling over medium heat.

2. Use 1 tablespoon oil to lightly brush bread slices on both sides. Place bread on hot grill grate and cook for 2 to 3 minutes or until toasted, turning slices over once. Transfer to plate; cool until easy to handle.

3. Meanwhile, in small bowl, whisk together mayonnaise, Parmesan, lemon juice, anchovy paste, pepper, and remaining 1 tablespoon oil.

4. When bread is cool, lightly rub both sides of each slice with cut garlic clove. Cut bread into ½-inch cubes.

5. Place romaine halves on hot grill grate and cook for 4 to 5 minutes or until lightly browned and wilted, turning over once. Divide romaine among salad plates; drizzle with dressing and sprinkle with croutons to serve.

Each serving: About 229 calories, 5g protein, 22g carbohydrate, 14g total fat (2g saturated), 3g fiber, 394mg sodium

SUMMER TUNA SALAD WITH SWEET POTATO AND BASIL

Fodds of the Deep South combine with tuna for a hearty main-dish salad.

TOTAL TIME: 20 minutes

MAKES: 4 main-dish servings

3	sweet potatoes, thickly sliced
¼	cup water
2	tablespoons canola oil, plus more for brushing potatoes

Salt and freshly ground black pepper

2	cans (15 ounces each) black-eyed peas, rinsed and drained
2	cans (5 ounces each) oil-packed tuna, drained
1	cup shredded carrots
¼	cup cider vinegar
¼	cup chopped fresh basil

1. In large microwave-safe bowl, add sweet potato slices and water. Microwave on high for 8 minutes; drain. Meanwhile, prepare outdoor grill for direct grilling over medium-high heat.

2. Brush potatoes with canola oil and sprinkle with salt and pepper. Place on hot grill rack and grill for 10 to 15 minutes, turning once. Cut into chunks.

3. In large bowl, toss together black-eyed peas, tuna, shredded carrots, vinegar, basil, 2 tablespoons canola oil, and pinch salt. Fold in potatoes.

Each serving: About 445 calories, 27g protein, 49g carbohydrate, 17g total fat (2g saturated), 10g fiber, 750mg sodium

GRILLED PLUM AND PORK SALAD

This crunchy, savory salad gets an added sweetness from brown sugar and plums.

TOTAL TIME: 20 minutes
MAKES: 4 main-dish servings

1	pound pork tenderloin
2	teaspoons canola oil, plus more for brushing
Salt	
¼	cup hot sauce
2	tablespoons brown sugar
2	garlic cloves, crushed with press
3	plums, cut into wedges
8	cups thinly sliced cabbage

1. Prepare outdoor grill for covered direct grilling over medium-high heat.

2. Brush pork with oil and sprinkle with ¼ teaspoon salt. Place on hot grill rack and grill, covered, for 10 minutes, turning once.

3. In small bowl, whisk together hot sauce, brown sugar, and garlic. Set aside.

4. Brush plums with oil and place on grill, cut-sides down; cover and grill for 3 to 5 minutes, turning once. Toss plums with shredded cabbage, 2 teaspoons oil, and salt to taste; transfer to platter.

5. Brush pork generously with hot-sauce mixture; grill for 6 to 8 minutes more or until cooked through, brushing and turning. Slice pork and serve over plums and cabbage.

Each serving: About 265 calories, 24g protein, 22g carbohydrate, 10g total fat (2g saturated), 4g fiber, 875mg sodium

ITALIAN TUNA AND WHITE BEAN SALAD

Packed with protein, this tuna-topped salad is appropriate for lunch or dinner. Serve it with a warm, chewy baguette to round out the meal.

TOTAL TIME: 20 minutes
MAKES: 4 main-dish servings

1	lemon
1	can (6 ounces) solid white tuna in water, drained
1	can (15 to 19 ounces) white kidney beans (cannellini), rinsed and drained
1	ripe tomato, chopped
1/2	fennel bulb, cored and chopped (1¼ cups)
2	tablespoons chopped red onion
2	tablespoons chopped Kalamata olives
2	teaspoons finely chopped fresh rosemary leaves
1	tablespoon olive oil
1/2	teaspoon salt
1	bag (5 ounces) mixed greens

1. From lemon, grate 1 teaspoon peel and squeeze 2 tablespoons juice; place in medium bowl.

2. With fork, flake tuna into bowl with lemon. Add beans, tomato, fennel, onion, olives, rosemary, oil, and salt. Toss to mix well. (Tuna salad can be made up to 6 hours ahead; cover and refrigerate.)

3. To serve, divide greens among plates; top each with tuna salad.

Each serving: About 215 calories, 16g protein, 25g carbohydrate, 5g total fat (1g saturated), 8g fiber, 680mg sodium

RICE NOODLES WITH MANY HERBS

Whip up this light summery vegan dish with fast-cooking noodles, carrots, cucumber, herbs, and our delicious Asian dressing. Serve warm or at room temperature, and pass the Sriracha sauce to add some zest.

ACTIVE TIME: 20 minutes   **TOTAL TIME**: 30 minutes
MAKES: 4 main-dish servings

3	small carrots, peeled and cut into 2" by ¼" matchstick strips (1½ cups)
⅓	cup seasoned rice vinegar
5	quarts water
1	package (1 pound) ½-inch-wide flat rice noodles
⅓	English (seedless) cucumber, unpeeled and cut into 2" by ¼" matchstick strips (1 cup)
1	cup loosely packed fresh cilantro leaves
½	cup loosely packed fresh mint leaves
⅓	cup snipped fresh chives
2	teaspoons Asian sesame oil

1. In small bowl, stir carrots with rice vinegar. Let stand at room temperature while preparing noodles.

2. In 6-quart saucepot, heat 5 quarts water to boiling over high heat. Add noodles and cook just until cooked through, about 3 minutes. Drain noodles; rinse under cold running water and drain again.

3. Transfer noodles to large shallow serving bowl. Add carrots with their liquid, cucumber, cilantro, mint, basil, chives, and sesame oil; toss well.

Each serving: About 470 calories, 7g protein, 10g carbohydrate, 3g total fat (0g saturated), 2g fiber, 550mg sodium

TIP
These thin, translucent white noodles are made from rice flour and water; because of their neutral flavor they're a perfect foil for robust flavors.

GRILLED EGGPLANT CAPONATA SALAD

Eggplant simply inhales the smoky goodness from the grill. This delicious salad will be a recipe you go back to again and again.

ACTIVE TIME: 25 minutes   **TOTAL TIME**: 35 minutes
MAKES: 16 side-dish servings

2	small red onions, cut into $1/2$-inch slices
2	small eggplants (1 to $1^1/4$ pounds each), cut into $3/4$-inch-thick slices
	Nonstick cooking spray
4	medium stalks celery
$1/2$	teaspoon salt
2	tablespoons red wine vinegar
1	tablespoon extra-virgin olive oil
1	teaspoon granulated sugar
$1/4$	teaspoon coarsely ground black pepper
6	ripe medium plum tomatoes ($1^1/2$ pounds total), cut into $1/2$-inch chunks
1	cup Kalamata, Gaeta, or green Sicilian olives, pitted and chopped
$1/4$	cup golden raisins
3	tablespoons drained capers
$1/2$	cup loosely packed fresh flat-leaf parsley leaves

1. Prepare outdoor grill for covered direct grilling over medium heat.

2. Meanwhile, for easier handling, insert metal skewers through onion slices, if you like. Lightly spray both sides of eggplant slices with cooking spray. Sprinkle onions, eggplant, and celery with salt.

3. Place onions, eggplant, and celery on hot grill rack. Cover grill and cook vegetables until tender and lightly browned, 8 to 10 minutes, turning once and transferring to plate as they are done. Cool slightly until easy to handle.

4. Cut eggplant and celery into $3/4$-inch chunks; coarsely chop onions. In large bowl, mix vinegar, oil, sugar, and pepper until blended. Stir in tomatoes, olives, raisins, capers, and parsley. Add eggplant, onions, and celery, and gently toss to coat.

5. Serve salad at room temperature, or cover and refrigerate for up to 1 day.

Each serving: About 71 calories, 2g protein, 10g carbohydrate, 3g total fat (0g saturated), 3g fiber, 235mg sodium

BULGUR AND GRAPE SALAD WITH DRIED FIGS AND ALMONDS

Try this irresistible riff on the Middle Eastern bulgur salad, tabbouleh, dreamed up by Barbara Estabrook, finalist in the side-dish category of our second Cook Your Heart Out contest. It's tossed with sweet grapes, figs, and crunchy roasted almonds and dressed with a shallot-and-parsley vinaigrette.

ACTIVE TIME: 15 minutes **TOTAL TIME**: 1 hour
MAKES: 6 side-dish servings

1	cup uncooked bulgur
2	cups water
3	tablespoons extra-virgin olive oil
3	tablespoons champagne or white wine vinegar
¼	cup shallots, finely chopped
1	small garlic clove, grated
¼	teaspoon salt
¼	teaspoon cracked black pepper
1½	cups champagne or black grapes, halved
⅓	cup dry Calymyrna figs, sliced with tiny stems removed
3	tablespoons chopped fresh flat-leaf parsley
3	tablespoons coarsely chopped roasted almonds (skin on)
1	tablespoon chopped fresh mint

1. Place bulgur in large bowl. Bring water to a boil in microwave or small pan. Pour boiling water over bulgur, cover, and seal top of bowl with foil. Let bulgur stand for 30 minutes or until water is absorbed. Uncover and fluff with fork. Let stand for 15 to 20 minutes more.

2. Meanwhile, in small bowl, whisk together oil, vinegar, shallots, garlic, salt, and pepper. When bulgur is ready, add grapes, figs, and parsley to bowl; gently toss to combine. Gradually add vinaigrette to bulgur mixture while tossing to coat. Stir in almonds, then scatter mint over top of salad and serve.

Each serving: About 215 calories, 5g protein, 33g carbohydrate, 9g total fat (1g saturated), 6g fiber, 104mg sodium

MINTED CORN AND BROWN RICE SALAD

Here's a fresh-from-the-garden salad—sweet corn, tangy crispy radishes, and refreshing bright mint—combined with toothsome brown rice.

ACTIVE TIME: 35 minutes   **TOTAL TIME**: 55 minutes plus cooling
MAKES: 12 side-dish servings

1	cup long-grain rice
1¼	teaspoons salt
¼	cup fresh lemon juice
3	tablespoons olive oil
¼	teaspoon freshly ground black pepper
3	quarts water
8	medium ears corn, husks and silk removed
1	bunch radishes, chopped (1¼ cups)
¾	cup shelled fresh peas or thawed frozen peas
½	cup loosely packed fresh mint leaves, thinly sliced
2	tablespoons snipped fresh chives

1. Prepare rice as label directs, but do not add butter and use only ½ teaspoon salt.

2. While rice is cooking, prepare dressing: In large bowl, with wire whisk, mix lemon juice, oil, pepper, and remaining ¾ teaspoon salt until blended.

3. Add hot rice to dressing and toss to coat. Cool slightly, about 30 minutes, tossing occasionally.

4. Meanwhile, in 5-quart Dutch oven, bring 3 quarts water to a boil over high heat. Add corn and cook for 5 minutes; drain. When corn is cool enough to handle, cut kernels from cobs (you should have about 4 cups).

5. Add corn to rice with radishes, peas, mint, and chives. Toss until evenly mixed. If not serving right away, cover and refrigerate for up to 8 hours.

Each serving: About 140 calories, 3g protein, 25g carbohydrate, 4g total fat (1g saturated), 4g fiber, 255mg sodium

ROASTED SHRIMP AND POBLANO SALAD

Using just one baking sheet to roast the shallots, poblanos, and shrimp makes for speedy cleanup.

TOTAL TIME: 20 minutes
MAKES: 4 servings

2	medium shallots, sliced
3	poblano peppers, seeded and sliced
1	tablespoon canola oil
2	teaspoons chili powder
1	pound large shrimp, peeled and deveined
4	radishes, sliced
3	tablespoons lime juice
1/2	teaspoon salt
1/2	container (5 ounces) mixed greens
1	avocado, thinly sliced

1. Preheat oven to 450°F. Toss shallots and poblanos with oil and chili powder. Arrange on large baking sheet. Roast for 20 minutes.

2. Add shrimp to baking sheet and roast for 5 minutes more; cool slightly. Combine shrimp mixture, radishes, lime juice, salt, and mixed greens. Top with sliced avocado.

Each serving: About 215 calories, 17g protein, 9g carbohydrate, 12g total fat (2g saturated), 2g fiber, 940mg sodium

WARM FRENCH LENTIL SALAD

A classic French dish, warm lentil salad is at once healthful, hearty, and comforting. The bell peppers offer a good source of vitamin C and antioxidants.

ACTIVE TIME: 20 minutes   **TOTAL TIME**: 50 minutes
MAKES: 4 servings

7	ounces French green (de Puy) lentils (1 cup), picked over and rinsed
3	sprigs fresh oregano
3	cups water, plus 2 tablespoons
1	medium (8 ounces) onion
3	large stalks celery
2	large peppers (red, orange, or yellow)
2	tablespoons extra-virgin olive oil
$^{1}/_{2}$	teaspoon salt
$^{1}/_{2}$	teaspoon ground black pepper
3	tablespoons red wine vinegar
1	tablespoon fresh dill, chopped, plus more for garnish
$^{1}/_{4}$	teaspoon oregano leaves, chopped
6	ounces baby spinach
2	ounces feta cheese, crumbled ($^{1}/_{2}$ cup)

1. In 4-quart saucepan, combine lentils, oregano sprigs, and 3 cups water. Cover; heat to boiling. Reduce heat to maintain simmer; cook for 25 to 30 minutes or until tender.

2. Meanwhile, chop onion, celery, and peppers. In 12-inch skillet, heat 1 tablespoon oil over medium heat. Add onion and celery; cook for 7 to 8 minutes or until tender, stirring. Add peppers, 2 tablespoons water, and $^{1}/_{4}$ teaspoon each salt and pepper. Cook for 5 minutes or until peppers are tender-crisp, stirring.

3. Drain lentils (discard sprigs); transfer to bowl. Stir in vinegar, dill, oregano leaves, onion mixture, $^{1}/_{4}$ teaspoon each salt and pepper, and remaining oil.

4. Divide spinach among 4 serving plates; spoon lentil mixture over. Top with feta, and garnish with dill.

Each serving: About 340 calories, 16g protein, 47g carbohydrate, 12g total fat (3g saturated), 11g fiber, 565mg sodium

FATTOUSH

This Lebanese vegan salad is packed with juicy summer-ripe tomatoes and fresh herbs. Pieces of toasted pita absorb the tasty dressing.

TOTAL TIME: 25 minutes plus standing
MAKES: 4 main-dish servings

3	tablespoons fresh lemon juice
3	tablespoons olive oil
1	teaspoon salt
½	teaspoon ground black pepper
4	medium tomatoes (about 1¼ pounds total), cut into ½-inch pieces
3	green onions, trimmed and chopped
1	medium cucumber (8 ounces), peeled, seeded, and cut into ½-inch pieces
1	cup loosely packed fresh parsley leaves
½	cup loosely packed fresh mint leaves, chopped
4	(6-inch) pitas, split horizontally in half
1	small head romaine lettuce (about 1 pound), coarsely chopped

1. In large salad bowl, with wire whisk or fork, mix lemon juice, oil, salt, and pepper. Add tomatoes, green onions, cucumber, parsley, and mint; toss to coat. Let tomato mixture stand for 15 minutes to allow flavors to blend.

2. Meanwhile, toast pitas; cool. Break pitas into 1-inch pieces.

3. Just before serving, toss lettuce and pitas with tomato mixture.

Each serving: About 315 calories, 9g protein, 47g carbohydrate, 12g total fat (2g saturated), 2g fiber, 935mg sodium

WHEAT BERRY SALAD WITH DRIED CHERRIES

This salad is a wonderful mix of textures and flavors—the chewy nutty taste of wheat berries, combined with the pucker of tart dried cherries and lemon juice, the crunch of celery, and the hot-sweetness of Dijon and honey.

ACTIVE TIME: 15 minutes   **TOTAL TIME**: 1 hour 45 minutes
MAKES: 12 side-dish servings

2	cups wheat berries (whole wheat kernels)
8	cups water
1	large shallot, minced
3	tablespoons fresh lemon juice
1	tablespoon Dijon mustard
1	tablespoon olive oil
2	teaspoons honey
1½	teaspoons salt
½	teaspoon coarsely ground black pepper
3	medium stalks celery, each cut lengthwise in half, then cut crosswise into ¼-inch-thick slices
¾	cup dried tart cherries, chopped
½	cup chopped fresh flat-leaf parsley, plus sprigs for garnish

1. In 4-quart saucepan, heat wheat berries and water to boiling over high heat. Reduce heat to low; cover and simmer until wheat berries are just tender but still firm to the bite, about 1½ hours.

2. Meanwhile, in large bowl, with wire whisk or fork, mix shallot, lemon juice, mustard, oil, honey, salt, and pepper.

3. When wheat berries are cooked, drain well. Add warm wheat berries to dressing with celery, cherries, and chopped parsley; toss well. Serve salad at room temperature, or cover and refrigerate until ready to serve. Garnish with parsley sprigs.

Each serving: About 130 calories, 4g protein, 26g carbohydrate, 2g total fat (0g saturated), 6g fiber, 310mg sodium

CHICKPEA MANGO SALAD

This aromatic salad borrows flavors from Indian cuisine and is packed with vitamins and antioxidants, thanks to a combination of chickpeas, mango, baby spinach, and almonds.

TOTAL TIME: 20 minutes

MAKES: 4 main-dish servings

1/2	cup plain fat-free yogurt
1/2	cup loosely packed fresh cilantro leaves
2	tablespoons mango chutney
1	tablespoon extra-virgin olive oil
2	teaspoons fresh lime juice
1/2	teaspoon ground coriander
1/2	teaspoon salt
1/4	teaspoon pepper
2	cans (15 ounces each) no-salt-added garbanzo beans (chickpeas), drained
1	large ripe mango, chopped
1	package (5 to 6 ounces) baby spinach
1/2	cup sliced almonds, toasted

Naan (Indian-style flatbread) or pita bread, toasted, for serving

1. In food processor, puree yogurt, cilantro, chutney, oil, lime juice, coriander, salt, and pepper until smooth. Transfer to large bowl.

2. To same bowl, add beans and mango. Toss until well-coated. Chickpea mixture can be made ahead and refrigerated in airtight container up to overnight. To serve, add spinach and almonds; toss to combine. Serve with naan.

Each serving: About 435 calories, 18g protein, 69g carbohydrate, 11g total fat (1g saturated), 12g fiber, 560mg sodium

SHRIMP AND PINEAPPLE SALAD WITH BASIL

No grill basket? Thread shrimp onto skewers instead. If you use wooden skewers, presoak them in hot water for at least 30 minutes to prevent them from burning.

ACTIVE TIME: 10 minutes   **TOTAL TIME**: 25 minutes
MAKES: 6 main-dish servings

3 to 4 limes
3   tablespoons olive oil
1½   cups loosely packed fresh basil leaves
½   teaspoon salt
¼   teaspoon coarsely ground pepper
1½   pounds large shrimp, peeled and deveined
1   pineapple (3 pounds)
12   corn tortillas
Olive oil cooking spray
1   bag (5 to 6 ounces) baby greens
2   medium heads Belgian endive, sliced

1. Prepare outdoor grill for direct grilling over medium heat.

2. Prepare dressing: From limes, grate ½ teaspoon peel and squeeze ¼ cup juice. In blender, place lime peel and juice, oil, ½ cup basil leaves, salt, and pepper. Blend until pureed.

3. Spoon 2 tablespoons dressing from blender into medium bowl. Add shrimp to bowl and toss to coat with dressing.

4. Cut off crown and stem ends from pineapple. Stand pineapple upright and slice off rind and eyes. Cut pineapple lengthwise into 8 wedges, then cut off core from each wedge.

5. Place pineapple wedges on hot grill rack and cook until lightly charred and tender, about 10 minutes, turning over once. Place shrimp in grill basket on same grill rack with pineapple wedges and cook until opaque throughout, 5 to 8 minutes, turning over once. Transfer shrimp to large bowl. Transfer pineapple to cutting board and cut into ½-inch chunks.

6. Lightly spray both sides of tortillas with cooking spray and place on hot grill rack. Cook until toasted, 4 to 5 minutes, turning over once.

7. To bowl with shrimp, add greens, endive, pineapple, and remaining 1 cup basil and dressing; toss to coat. Place 2 tortillas on each of six plates; top with salad.

Each serving: About 350 calories, 23g protein, 43g carbohydrate, 11g total fat (2g saturated), 6g fiber, 420mg sodium

VIETNAMESE NOODLE SALAD

Use thin vermicelli noodles in this Asian-inspired salad—made from rice, they cook quickly and absorb sauce easily.

TOTAL TIME: 20 minutes
MAKES: 4 servings

8	ounces thin rice noodles
3	tablespoons fish sauce
2	tablespoons granulated sugar
2	tablespoons white vinegar
1	tablespoon vegetable oil
1	pound ground pork
3	garlic cloves, crushed with press
1	jalapeño chile, finely chopped
1	romaine heart, sliced
¼	cup chopped peanuts

Fresh herbs (mint, cilantro, and/or basil), for garnish

1. Prepare rice noodles as label directs. In cup, whisk together fish sauce, sugar, and vinegar; set aside.

2. In 12-inch skillet, heat oil over medium-high heat. Add pork, garlic, jalapeño, and 2 tablespoons fish-sauce dressing. Cook for 5 minutes or until pork is cooked through, breaking up meat with side of spoon.

3. Cut cooked noodles with kitchen shears. Add to large bowl along with pork, romaine, and remaining fish-sauce dressing; toss to combine. Garnish with peanuts and fresh herbs.

Each serving: About 465 calories, 28g protein, 60g carbohydrate, 13g total fat (2g saturated), 2g fiber, 980mg sodium

WARM FARRO SALAD WITH ROASTED VEGETABLES

If you've never eaten farro, this hearty main-dish salad is the perfect opportunity to enjoy its nutty goodness. Try it as a side-dish alongside grilled fish or chicken, or serve on a bed of lettuce for a main dish.

ACTIVE TIME: 25 minutes   **TOTAL TIME**: 1 hour 5 minutes
MAKES: 6 side-dish servings

2	large carrots, peeled and cut into ¹/₂-inch dice	1	bunch radishes, cut into ¹/₂-inch dice
2	small fennel bulbs, trimmed and cut into 1-inch pieces	1	tablespoon red wine vinegar
1	red onion, halved and sliced through root end	2¹/₂	cups water
		1	cup farro
3	tablespoons olive oil	3	tablespoons fresh lemon juice
1	teaspoon salt	2	teaspoons freshly grated lemon peel
¹/₄	teaspoon ground black pepper	1	cup lightly packed fresh basil leaves, chopped

1. Preheat oven to 400°F.

2. In large bowl, combine carrots, fennel, red onion, 1 tablespoon oil, ¹/₂ teaspoon salt, and ¹/₈ teaspoon pepper; toss. Turn onto 15¹/₂″ by 10¹/₂″ jelly-roll pan and spread evenly. Roast for 20 minutes, stirring once. Stir in radishes and roast until vegetables are tender, about 10 minutes. Stir in vinegar.

3. Meanwhile, in medium saucepan, bring water, farro, and ¹/₄ teaspoon salt to boiling over high heat. Reduce heat to medium-low; cover and simmer until farro is tender and water is absorbed, 25 to 30 minutes.

4. In large bowl, whisk lemon juice, lemon peel, remaining 2 tablespoons oil, ¹/₄ teaspoon salt, and ¹/₈ teaspoon pepper. Add farro, roasted vegetables, and basil; toss to combine. Serve warm.

Each serving: About 215 calories, 6g protein, 34g carbohydrate, 7g total fat (1g saturated), 6g fiber, 472mg sodium

 TIP

A good source of fiber and protein, farro has a nutty wheat flavor and chewy texture.

SIX-BEAN SALAD WITH TOMATO VINAIGRETTE

This salad is a tasty powerhouse of protein, iron, bone-building vitamin K, and a host of heart-healthy antioxidants.

ACTIVE TIME: 20 minutes   **TOTAL TIME**: 45 minutes plus chilling
MAKES: 18 side-dish servings

1½	teaspoons salt	1½	cups (half of 16-ounce bag) frozen shelled edamame, thawed
8	ounces green beans, trimmed and cut into 1-inch pieces		
8	ounces wax beans, trimmed and cut into 1-inch pieces	1	small ripe tomato (4 ounces), coarsely chopped
1	can (15 to 19 ounces) garbanzo beans	1	small shallot, coarsely chopped
		¼	cup olive oil
1	can (15 to 19 ounces) black beans or black soybeans	2	tablespoons red wine vinegar
		1	tablespoon Dijon mustard
1	can (15 to 19 ounces) red kidney beans	¼	teaspoon ground black pepper

1. In 12-inch skillet, heat 1 inch water with 1 teaspoon salt to boiling over high heat. Add green and wax beans; return water to a boil. Reduce heat to low; simmer until beans are tender-crisp, 6 to 8 minutes. Drain beans. Rinse with cold running water to stop cooking; drain again. Transfer beans to large serving bowl.

2. While green and wax beans are cooking, rinse and drain garbanzo, black, and kidney beans. Add canned beans and edamame to bowl with green and wax beans.

3. In blender, combine tomato, shallot, oil, vinegar, mustard, remaining ½ teaspoon salt, and pepper. Blend until smooth.

4. Add vinaigrette to beans in bowl. Toss until beans are evenly coated. Cover and refrigerate for at least 1 hour, or up to 8 hours, to blend flavors.

Each serving: About 130 calories, 7g protein, 18g carbohydrate, 4g total fat (0g saturated), 7g fiber, 360mg sodium

SHREDDED BEETS WITH CELERY AND DATES

This simple salad features raw grated beets, which lend crunchy appeal and a rich garnet color.

TOTAL TIME: 10 minutes

MAKES: 4 cups or 8 side-dish servings

1	pound beets, peeled
3	stalks celery, thinly sliced
½	cup pitted dried dates, chopped
3	tablespoons fresh lemon juice
¼	teaspoon salt
¼	teaspoon coarsely ground black pepper

1. Cut beets into quarters. In food processor with shredding blade attached, shred beets; transfer to large bowl.

2. Stir in celery, dates, lemon juice, salt, and pepper. If not serving right away, cover and refrigerate for up to 4 hours.

Each serving: About 50 calories, 1g protein, 13g carbohydrate, 0g total fat, 2g fiber, 110mg sodium

Eat Your Beets

Just one cooked cup of this super veggie packs 34% of your daily need for folate (which can help lower levels of heart-threatening homocysteine), 15% of potassium (which reduces blood pressure levels), and 27% of manganese (which helps maintain your bones). To bring out beets' natural juices, peel and grate them. Then subdue the earthy flavor with lemon juice and sweet dates; see Shredded Beets with Celery and Dates, above. The celery slices add crunch.

GARDEN GREENS AND PUMPERNICKEL PANZANELLA

This fresh, crunchy salad features the watermelon radish—a big, mild, and slightly sweet veggie. Look for bunches at your local farmers' market! (See photograph on page 52.)

ACTIVE TIME: 25 minutes   **TOTAL TIME**: 35 minutes
MAKES: 6 main-dish servings

1	pound asparagus, trimmed and cut into 1-inch lengths
1	bunch green onions, cut into 1-inch lengths
2	teaspoons plus 2 tablespoons extra-virgin olive oil
3/4	teaspoon salt
6	cups pumpernickel bread cubes (each about 3/4 inch)
2	tablespoons fresh lemon juice
1	tablespoon white wine vinegar
1	tablespoon spicy brown mustard
1	tablespoon prepared horseradish
1/4	cup chopped fresh dill
4	cups arugula
1/2	bunch watermelon radishes or regular radishes, trimmed and thinly sliced

1. Arrange two oven racks in upper and lower thirds of oven. Preheat oven to 450°F. On large rimmed baking sheet, toss asparagus, green onions, 2 teaspoons oil, and 1/4 teaspoon salt; spread in single layer. Bake on lower rack for 15 minutes or until vegetables are browned and tender. On another large rimmed baking sheet, arrange bread cubes in single layer. Bake on upper rack for 10 to 12 minutes or until crisp and dry, stirring once.

2. Meanwhile, in large bowl, whisk remaining 2 tablespoons oil, lemon juice, vinegar, mustard, horseradish, and remaining 1/2 teaspoon salt; stir in dill.

3. Toss bread cubes with vinaigrette in bowl; add roasted vegetables, arugula, and radishes. Toss until well combined.

Each serving: About 330 calories, 11g protein, 51g carbohydrate, 10g total fat (1g saturated), 9g fiber, 870mg sodium

TOMATO AND MINT TABBOULEH

Tabbouleh, the popular bulgur wheat and vegetable salad, is one of the best ways to enjoy tomatoes, cucumbers, and herbs.

TOTAL TIME: 20 minutes plus standing and chilling
MAKES: 12 side-dish servings

1½	cups boiling water
1½	cups bulgur
¼	cup fresh lemon juice
1	pound ripe tomatoes (3 medium), cut into ½-inch pieces
1	medium cucumber (8 ounces), peeled and cut into ½-inch pieces
3	green onions, chopped
¾	cup loosely packed fresh flat-leaf parsley leaves, chopped
½	cup loosely packed fresh mint leaves, chopped
1	tablespoon olive oil
¾	teaspoon salt
¼	teaspoon coarsely ground black pepper

1. In medium bowl, combine water, bulgur, and lemon juice, stirring to mix. Let stand until liquid has been absorbed, about 30 minutes.

2. To bulgur mixture, add tomatoes, cucumber, green onions, parsley, mint, oil, salt, and pepper, stirring to mix. Cover and refrigerate to blend flavors, at least 1 hour or up to 4 hours.

Each serving: About 85 calories, 3g protein, 17g carbohydrate, 2g total fat (0g saturated), 4g fiber, 157mg sodium

CRUNCHY CARROT COLESLAW

A mix of shredded cabbage and carrots gives this slaw its crunch; cider vinegar and a little cayenne give it a bite.

TOTAL TIME: 10 minutes

MAKES: 10 cups or 8 side-dish servings

⅓	cup fresh orange juice
¼	cup cider vinegar
2	tablespoons granulated sugar
2	tablespoons Dijon mustard
1	tablespoon vegetable oil
1	teaspoon salt
¼	teaspoon dried mint
⅛	teaspoon cayenne (ground red) pepper
1	bag (16 ounces) shredded cabbage for coleslaw
1	bag (10 ounces) shredded carrots

In large bowl, with wire whisk, mix orange juice, vinegar, sugar, mustard, oil, salt, mint, and cayenne until blended. Add cabbage and carrots; toss well. Serve slaw at room temperature, or cover and refrigerate until ready to serve.

Each serving: About 65 calories, 1g protein, 12g carbohydrate, 2g total fat (0g saturated), 2g fiber, 385mg sodium

MESCLUN WITH PEARS AND PUMPKIN SEEDS

Instead of the pecans we used to include in this recipe, we've swapped in toasted pumpkin seeds, or pepitas, which have become supermarket staples in recent years. They're also great on-the-go snacks.

TOTAL TIME: 10 minutes
MAKES: 12 side-dish servings

¼	cup pumpkin seeds (pepitas)
3	tablespoons cider vinegar
1	tablespoon Dijon mustard
2	teaspoons pure honey
¼	cup extra-virgin olive oil
3	ripe red pears, cored and thinly sliced
2	packages (5 ounces each) mixed baby greens
¼	teaspoon salt
¼	teaspoon freshly ground black pepper

1. In small skillet, heat pumpkin seeds over medium heat until all are toasted and some start to pop, 2 to 3 minutes. Cool completely. Toasted seeds can be stored in an airtight container for up to 1 week.

2. In small bowl, with wire whisk, stir vinegar, mustard, and honey until blended. Continue whisking and add oil in slow, steady stream; whisk until well blended and emulsified. Dressing can be made ahead. Cover tightly and refrigerate for up to 3 days.

3. In large bowl, combine sliced pears, greens, toasted pumpkin seeds, dressing, salt, and pepper. Toss until evenly coated.

Each serving: About 100 calories, 1g protein, 9g carbohydrate, 7g total fat (1g saturated), 2g fiber, 85mg sodium

TIP

To prevent the sliced pears from turning brown, combine them with the dressing up to 1 hour before serving. When ready to serve, toss with the greens, pumpkin seeds, and seasonings.

WARM QUINOA SALAD WITH TOASTED ALMONDS

Quinoa is often called a super-grain. Because it contains all eight essential amino acids, it is considered a complete protein. Toast it to reduce bitterness and bring out its tasty, nutty flavor.

ACTIVE TIME: 5 minutes   **TOTAL TIME**: 30 minutes
MAKES: 5 side-dish servings

1½	cups quinoa, thoroughly rinsed and drained
2½	cups plus 1 tablespoon water
¼	teaspoon salt
2	tablespoons reduced-sodium soy sauce
1	tablespoon rice vinegar
1	tablespoon Asian sesame oil
1	teaspoon grated, peeled fresh ginger
2	green onions, thinly sliced diagonally
¼	cup sliced natural almonds, toasted

1. In 12-inch skillet, toast quinoa over medium heat until fragrant and golden, about 5 minutes, stirring frequently.

2. Stir 2½ cups water and salt into toasted quinoa; heat to boiling over high heat. Reduce heat to low; cover and simmer until all water is absorbed, 15 to 17 minutes.

3. Meanwhile, in small bowl, stir together soy sauce, vinegar, oil, ginger, green onions, and remaining 1 tablespoon water.

4. Transfer quinoa to large serving bowl. Stir in soy sauce mixture until quinoa is evenly coated. Sprinkle with toasted almonds to serve.

Each serving: About 305 calories, 9g protein, 38g carbohydrate, 7g total fat (1g saturated), 4g fiber, 460mg sodium

TIP

To toast nuts, preheat the oven to 350°F. Spread the shelled nuts in a single layer on a cookie sheet. Bake, stirring occasionally, until lightly browned and fragrant, about 10 minutes.

Chilled Tuscan-Style Tomato Soup (page 104)

3 | **SOUPS, STEWS** & CHILIS

Whether your go-to soup-making tool is a stock pot or a slow cooker, one-pot meals like soups, stews, and chilis are a super simple way to cook up healthy food—and lots of it. You'll find good-for-you recipes that call for plenty of fiber-rich grains and beans, vitamin-packed veggies, and lean poultry and meat.

Check out our cool, refreshing soups that require little or no cooking, just right for hot summer days. Hit the farmer's market, and then make our chilled tomato soup, or buttermilk and corn soup. When the weather has a brisk snap, opt for warm, soothing vegetable soups like pureed carrot and dill or ginger-spiced carrot.

If you have a yen for heartier fare, look no further than our soups and chilis bursting with flavorful, filling, and totally low-fat beans. There's three-bean vegetable chili with a surprise ingredient—edamame—and a red chili made even redder with delicious beets. See "Eat Your Beans" on page 122 to learn about all the good things beans can do for you, including fighting cancer and diabetes.

Chicken soup lovers are in luck. We've gone global, with recipes for this world-class favorite from France, Italy, Mexico, even Thailand. For truly homemade fare, whip up a pot of chicken broth on your own stove to get started. You'll save on sodium. Make enough to freeze a batch so you can have a pot of soup bubbling on your stove whenever inspiration strikes.

CHILLED TUSCAN-STYLE TOMATO SOUP

The lush summer flavors of Tuscany shine in this refreshing, easy-to-make cold tomato soup. We blend cubes of country bread in with the tomatoes to achieve a thicker body and a velvety texture. (See photograph on page 102.)

TOTAL TIME: 15 minutes plus chilling

MAKES: 6 cups or 4 first-course servings

1	teaspoon olive oil
1	garlic clove, minced
2	cups country-style bread (3 ounces), cut into 1-inch cubes
3	pounds ripe tomatoes, cut into quarters
¼	cup loosely packed fresh basil leaves, chopped, plus more for garnish
1	teaspoon granulated sugar
½	teaspoon salt

1. In small skillet, heat oil over medium heat until hot. Add garlic and cook for 1 minute, stirring. Remove skillet from heat.

2. In food processor with knife blade attached, pulse bread until coarsely chopped. Add tomatoes and garlic; pulse until soup is almost pureed. Pour soup into bowl; stir in chopped basil, sugar, and salt. Cover and refrigerate until well chilled, at least 2 hours or overnight. Garnish each serving with basil leaves.

Each serving: About 145 calories, 5g protein, 28g carbohydrate, 3g total fat (1g saturated), 4g fiber, 445mg sodium

CHILLED BUTTERMILK AND CORN SOUP

This refreshing refrigerator soup—featuring corn, tomatoes, cucumber, and basil—is both low in fat and satisfying.

TOTAL TIME: 20 minutes plus chilling
MAKES: 4½ cups or 6 first-course servings

1	quart buttermilk
4	ripe medium tomatoes (1½ pounds total), seeded and chopped
1	small cucumber, peeled, seeded, and chopped
2	cups corn kernels, cut from cobs (about 4 ears)
½	teaspoon salt
¼	teaspoon coarsely ground black pepper
10	fresh basil sprigs

1. In large bowl, combine buttermilk, tomatoes, cucumber, corn, salt, and pepper. Cover and refrigerate until very cold, at least 2 hours.

2. To serve, set aside 6 small basil sprigs; pinch 12 large basil leaves from remaining sprigs and thinly slice. Spoon soup into bowls; garnish with sliced basil and small basil sprigs.

Each serving: About 135 calories, 8g protein, 24g carbohydrate, 2g total fat (1g saturated), 2g fiber, 365mg sodium

CARROT AND DILL SOUP

Combine sweet carrots with fresh orange, dill, and a touch of milk for a refreshing, creamy soup without the cream.

ACTIVE TIME: 25 minutes

TOTAL TIME: 1 hour 10 minutes

MAKES: 10½ cups or 10 first-course servings

1	tablespoon olive oil
1	large onion (12 ounces), chopped
1	stalk celery, chopped
2	large oranges
2	bags (16 ounces each) carrots, peeled and chopped
1	can (14½ ounces) vegetable broth, or 1¾ cups homemade (see recipe, page 136)
1	tablespoon granulated sugar
¾	teaspoon salt
¼	teaspoon coarsely ground black pepper
4	cups water
1	cup milk
¼	cup chopped fresh dill

Dill sprigs, for garnish

1. In 5-quart Dutch oven, heat oil over medium-high heat. Add onion and celery; cook until tender and golden, about 15 minutes, stirring occasionally.

2. Meanwhile, with vegetable peeler, remove 4 strips of peel (3" by 1" each) from oranges and squeeze 1 cup juice.

3. Add orange-peel strips to Dutch oven and cook for 2 minutes, stirring. Add orange juice, carrots, broth, sugar, salt, pepper, and water; heat to boiling over high heat. Reduce heat to low; cover and simmer until carrots are very tender, about 25 minutes.

4. Remove strips of orange peel from soup. In blender, with center part of lid removed to allow steam to escape, blend soup in small batches until smooth. Pour pureed soup into large bowl after each batch.

5. Return soup to Dutch oven; stir in milk and chopped dill. Heat just to simmering over medium heat. Spoon soup into bowls; garnish each serving with dill sprigs.

Each serving: About 95 calories, 3g protein, 16g carbohydrate, 3g total fat (1g saturated), 3g fiber, 3mg cholesterol, 335mg sodium

The Skinny on Soup

Looking to lose a few pounds? Embrace soup. Research shows that the best way to start a meal may be with a broth- or water-based soup. It fills you up—even more so than salad or other low-calorie foods—so you'll eat less at that meal. You can also make soup a meal in itself. Try our veggie- and grain-based recipes; they provide fiber to keep you feeling satisfied longer.

GINGER-SPICED CARROT SOUP

With one-and-a-half pounds of pureed carrots and two cups of peas, this creamy-smooth vegetable soup is supercharged with vitamin A, a vision-enhancing nutrient. Subbing ginger-steeped green tea for stock slashes the sodium, and may help protect against memory loss.

ACTIVE TIME: 25 minutes **TOTAL TIME**: 55 minutes
MAKES: 4 main-dish servings

4	green onions
1	(1-inch) piece fresh ginger
5	cups water
3	bags green tea
1	tablespoon olive oil
1	medium onion, finely chopped
1½	pounds carrots, peeled and cut into ³/₄-inch-thick pieces
1	medium all-purpose potato, peeled and chopped
½	teaspoon salt
¼	teaspoon ground black pepper
2	cups frozen peas

1. From green onions, cut off white and pale green parts and place in 5-quart saucepot. Thinly slice dark green onion parts; set aside. From ginger, cut 4 thin slices; set aside. Peel remaining piece of ginger and grate enough to make 1 teaspoon; set aside.

2. To saucepot, add sliced ginger and water. Heat to boiling over high heat. Add tea bags. Cover, remove from heat, and let stand for 10 minutes.

3. While tea steeps, in 12-inch skillet, heat oil over medium-high heat. Add onion, carrots, potato, and ¼ teaspoon each salt and pepper. Cook, stirring, for 6 minutes or until golden. Add grated ginger; cook for 1 minute, stirring.

4. With slotted spoon, remove ginger, tea bags, and green onion pieces from pot and discard after squeezing excess liquid back into pot. Heat ginger tea to boiling over high heat; stir in carrot mixture. Reduce heat to maintain simmer. Cook for 10 minutes or until vegetables are tender, stirring.

5. Transfer half of soup to blender; keep remaining soup simmering. Carefully puree until smooth; return to pot. Stir in peas and remaining $1/4$ teaspoon salt. Cook for 3 minutes or until peas are bright green and hot. Divide among soup bowls; garnish with sliced green onions.

Each serving: About 205 calories, 7g protein, 37g carbohydrate, 4g total fat (1g saturated), 6g fiber, 410mg sodium

SPRING PEA SOUP

Healthy, creamy, and full of flavor, this pea soup makes an excellent start to a spring dinner.

ACTIVE TIME: 12 minutes   **TOTAL TIME**: 35 minutes

MAKES: 10 first-course servings

2	tablespoons butter or margarine
2	large shallots, thinly sliced (³/₄ cup)
1	carton (32 ounces) reduced-sodium chicken broth (4 cups)
2	cups water
2	bags (16 ounces each) frozen peas, thawed
¹/₂	cup loosely packed fresh mint leaves, chopped
1	large all-purpose potato (8 ounces), peeled and cut into 1-inch chunks
³/₄	teaspoon salt
¹/₄	teaspoon freshly ground black pepper
3	tablespoons fresh lemon juice
10	nasturtium flowers, for garnish (see Tip)

1. In 4-quart saucepan, heat butter over medium-low heat until melted. Add shallots and cook for 10 to 12 minutes or until very tender.

2. Add broth, water, peas, half of mint, potato, salt, and pepper; heat to boiling over high heat. Reduce heat to medium; simmer for 10 minutes, stirring occasionally.

3. Spoon half of mixture into blender; cover, with center part of lid removed to let steam escape, and puree until smooth. Pour puree into medium bowl. Repeat with remaining mixture. Return soup to saucepan and reheat over medium heat if necessary. Stir in lemon juice and remaining ¹/₄ cup mint.

4. To serve, spoon soup into ten serving bowls; garnish with nasturtiums.

Each serving: About 120 calories, 6g protein, 19g carbohydrate, 3g total fat (1g saturated), 5g fiber, 475mg sodium

TIP
Nasturtiums and other edible flowers can be found in the produce section of supermarkets and at farmers' markets.

NOT YOUR GRANDMA'S BORSCHT

It's impossible to peel beets without getting red all over your hands—unless you wear rubber gloves. For easy cleanup, peel beets in the sink.

ACTIVE TIME: 15 minutes   **TOTAL TIME**: 1 hour 15 minutes

MAKES: 5 main-dish servings

1	tablespoon olive oil
1	onion, chopped
1	garlic clove, crushed with press
$1/2$	teaspoon ground allspice
1	can (14$1/2$ ounces) diced tomatoes
1	pound beets (not including tops)
6	cups sliced green cabbage (1 pound)
3	large carrots, peeled and cut into $1/2$-inch chunks

4	cups water
1	can (14$1/2$ ounces) vegetable broth, or 1$3/4$ cups homemade (see recipe, page 136)
1	bay leaf
$3/4$	teaspoon salt
2	tablespoons red wine vinegar
$1/4$	cup loosely packed fresh dill or parsley leaves, chopped
	Reduced-fat sour cream, for serving (optional)

1. In 5- to 6-quart saucepot, heat oil over medium heat until hot. Add onion and cook until tender, about 8 minutes. Stir in garlic and allspice; cook for 30 seconds. Add tomatoes with their juice and cook for 5 minutes.

2. Meanwhile, peel beets and shred in food processor (or on coarse side of box grater).

3. Add beets to onion mixture along with cabbage, carrots, water, broth, bay leaf, and salt; heat to boiling over high heat. Reduce heat to medium-low; cover and simmer until all vegetables are tender, about 30 minutes.

4. Remove bay leaf. Stir in vinegar and dill. Serve with sour cream, if desired.

Each serving: About 160 calories, 5g protein, 27g carbohydrate, 5g total fat (1g saturated), 6g fiber, 920mg sodium

CREAMY ITALIAN WHITE-BEAN SOUP

Canned beans make this Tuscan classic a snap to put together. But, if you have the time, substitute dried beans—they'll make this soup even more delicious. For this recipe, prepare two cups dried beans; they'll double in volume during soaking and cooking. See "Homemade Bean Basics" on page 117 for instructions.

ACTIVE TIME: 15 minutes **TOTAL TIME**: 55 minutes

MAKES: 6 cups or 4 main-dish servings

1	tablespoon vegetable oil
1	onion, finely chopped
1	celery stalk, finely chopped
1	garlic clove, minced
2	cans (15½ to 19 ounces each) white kidney beans (cannellini), rinsed and drained, or dried beans (see note, above)
1	can (13¾ to 14½ ounces) chicken broth

¼	teaspoon coarsely ground black pepper
⅛	teaspoon dried thyme leaves
2	cups water
1	bunch (10 to 12 ounces) spinach
1	tablespoon fresh lemon juice
	Freshly grated Parmesan cheese, for serving (optional)

1. In 3-quart saucepan, heat oil over medium heat until hot. Add onion and celery and cook for 5 to 8 minutes or until tender, stirring occasionally. Add garlic; cook for 30 seconds, stirring. Add beans, chicken broth, pepper, thyme, and water; heat to boiling over high heat. Reduce heat to low; simmer, uncovered, for 15 minutes.

2. Meanwhile, discard tough stems from spinach; thinly slice leaves.

3. With slotted spoon, remove 2 cups bean-and-vegetable mixture from soup; set aside. In blender at low speed, with center part of cover removed to allow steam to escape, blend remaining soup in small batches until smooth. Pour pureed soup into large bowl after each batch.

4. Return soup to saucepan; stir in reserved beans and vegetables. Heat to boiling over high heat, stirring occasionally. Stir in spinach and cook for 1 minute or until wilted. Stir in lemon juice and remove from heat. Serve with Parmesan, if you like.

Each serving: About 295 calories, 8g protein, 46g carbohydrate, 5g total fat (1g saturated), 22g fiber, 945mg sodium

MACARONI, CABBAGE, AND BEAN SOUP

A light yet chunky vegetable soup that's ready in less than half an hour.

ACTIVE TIME: 5 minutes **TOTAL TIME**: 20 minutes

MAKES: 12 cups or 6 main-dish servings

1½	cups elbow macaroni or mini penne (pennette) pasta
1	tablespoon olive oil
1	onion, cut in half and thinly sliced
½	small head savoy cabbage (about 1 pound), thinly sliced
2	garlic cloves, crushed with press
¼	teaspoon ground black pepper
3	cans (14½ ounces each) low-sodium vegetable broth, or 5½ cups homemade (see recipe, page 136)
2	cans (15 to 19 ounces each) white kidney beans (cannellini), rinsed and drained
1½	cups water

Freshly grated Parmesan or Pecorino-Romano cheese, for serving (optional)

1. Cook macaroni as label directs; drain.

2. Meanwhile, in 5- to 6-quart saucepot, heat oil over medium-high heat until hot. Add onion, cabbage, garlic, and pepper; cook, stirring often, until cabbage begins to wilt, 6 to 8 minutes. Stir in broth, beans, and water; heat to boiling.

3. Stir macaroni into cabbage mixture; heat through. Serve with Parmesan, if you like.

Each serving: About 305 calories, 15g protein, 53g carbohydrate, 4g total fat (1g saturated), 11g fiber, 397mg sodium

CHICKEN AND ESCAROLE SOUP

Here's a comforting Italian take on chicken noodle soup. It pairs leftover cooked chicken with tiny orzo pasta and escarole, a mild-flavored green beloved by Italians.

ACTIVE TIME: 15 minutes   **TOTAL TIME**: 35 minutes
MAKES: 10 cups or 5 main-dish servings

1	tablespoon olive oil
2	cups shredded or matchstick carrots
1	small onion, finely chopped
2	garlic cloves, minced
3	cans (14½ ounces each) chicken broth
2	cups water
2	heads escarole (1½ pounds total), cut into 1-inch pieces
½	cup orzo pasta
2	cups chopped leftover cooked chicken (10 ounces)
⅛	teaspoon coarsely ground black pepper
½	cup freshly grated Parmesan cheese

1. In 6-quart Dutch oven, heat oil over medium-high heat. Add carrots, onion, and garlic; cook for 4 minutes or until onion softens, stirring frequently. Stir in broth and water; heat to boiling. Stir in escarole and orzo; heat to boiling.

2. Reduce heat to medium-low; simmer, uncovered, for 6 minutes or until escarole and orzo are tender. Stir in chicken and pepper. Reduce heat to low and simmer for 3 minutes or until chicken is heated through. Serve with Parmesan.

Each serving: About 285 calories, 28g protein, 25g carbohydrate, 9g total fat (3g saturated), 6g fiber, 890mg sodium

BARLEY MINESTRONE WITH PESTO

Top this soup with a dollop of our homemade pesto, which you can make in a mini food processor or blender. In a hurry? Store-bought refrigerated pesto makes an excellent stand-in—although it's not as light as our version.

ACTIVE TIME: 50 minutes **TOTAL TIME**: 1 hour 15 minutes
MAKES: 10½ cups or 6 main-dish servings

MINESTRONE

1	cup pearl barley	3	cups water
1	tablespoon olive oil	2	cans (14½ ounces each) vegetable broth, or 3½ cups homemade (see recipe, page 136)
2	cups thinly sliced green cabbage (about ¼ small head)		
2	large carrots, peeled, cut lengthwise in half, then crosswise into ½-inch-thick slices	1	can (14½ ounces) diced tomatoes
		¼	teaspoon salt
2	large stalks celery, cut into ½-inch dice	1	medium zucchini (8 to 10 ounces), cut into ½-inch dice
1	onion, cut into ½-inch dice	4	ounces green beans, trimmed and cut into ½-inch pieces (1 cup)
1	garlic clove, finely chopped		

LIGHT PESTO

1	cup firmly packed fresh basil leaves	¼	teaspoon salt
2	tablespoons olive oil	¼	cup freshly grated Pecorino-Romano cheese
2	tablespoons water	1	garlic clove, finely chopped

1. Heat 5- to 6-quart Dutch oven over medium-high heat until hot. Add barley and cook until toasted and fragrant, 3 to 4 minutes, stirring constantly. Transfer barley to small bowl; set aside.

2. Add oil to same Dutch oven, still over medium-high heat. When oil is hot, add cabbage, carrots, celery, and onion; cook until vegetables are tender and lightly browned, 8 to 10 minutes, stirring occasionally. Add garlic and cook until fragrant, 30 seconds. Stir in barley, water, broth, tomatoes with their juice, and salt. Cover and heat to boiling over high heat. Reduce heat to low and simmer for 25 minutes.

3. Stir zucchini and green beans into barley mixture; increase heat to medium, cover, and cook until all vegetables are barely tender, 10 to 15 minutes longer.

4. Meanwhile, prepare pesto: In blender container with narrow base or in mini food processor, combine basil, oil, water, and salt; cover and blend until mixture is pureed. Transfer pesto to small bowl; stir in Romano and garlic. Makes about 1/2 cup pesto.

5. Ladle minestrone into six large soup bowls. Top each serving with some pesto.

Each serving soup with 1 teaspoon pesto: About 230 calories, 7g protein, 42g carbohydrate, 5g total fat (0g saturated), 9g fiber, 725mg sodium

MIXED VEGETABLE MINESTRONE

Hearty vegetables, cannellini beans, and tubetti pasta combine in this rustic Italian soup.

ACTIVE TIME: 20 minutes **TOTAL TIME**: 40 minutes
MAKES: 6 main-dish servings

2	tablespoons extra-virgin olive oil
1	onion, finely chopped
2	garlic cloves, crushed with garlic press
$3/4$	teaspoon salt
$3/4$	teaspoon ground black pepper
1	can (28 ounces) diced tomatoes
4	cups water
1	pound carrots, peeled and cut into $1/2$-inch pieces
1	small bunch Swiss chard (12 ounces), stems removed and discarded, leaves thinly sliced ($5^1/2$ cups)
8	ounces green beans, trimmed and cut into 1-inch pieces
$8^1/2$	cups frozen shelled edamame (soybeans)
1	can (15 to 19 ounces) white kidney beans (cannellini), rinsed and drained
1	cup tubetti or other short pasta
$1/2$	cup plus 6 tablespoons freshly grated Parmesan cheese

1. In 5- to 6-quart saucepot, heat 1 tablespoon oil over medium heat. Stir in onion, garlic, and $1/2$ teaspoon each salt and pepper. Cover and cook for 4 to 5 minutes or until tender. Add tomatoes and water. Bring to boiling over medium-high heat. Add carrots; cover and cook for 10 minutes, stirring occasionally. Add chard and green beans; cook for 6 minutes or until beans are just tender, stirring occasionally. Add edamame and white beans; cook for 5 minutes or until edamame are just cooked through. (Soup can be prepared to this point up to 2 days ahead; transfer to airtight container and refrigerate. Reheat before continuing with recipe.)

2. Meanwhile, cook pasta in boiling salted water as label directs. Drain well and stir into saucepot with soup. Stir in $1/2$ cup Parmesan and remaining $1/4$ teaspoon each salt and pepper. Ladle into soup bowls. Sprinkle each portion with 1 tablespoon Parmesan and drizzle with $1/2$ teaspoon olive oil.

Each serving: About 575 calories, 38g protein, 63g carbohydrate, 21g total fat (3g saturated), 17g fiber, 775mg sodium

☆ Good, easy, low carb

BLACK BEAN SOUP

This simple but hearty soup is sure to become a standby. The cilantro and fresh lime juice add some Latin flavor.

ACTIVE TIME: 15 minutes   **TOTAL TIME**: 45 minutes plus cooling

MAKES: ~~6½ cups or 6 main-dish servings~~

1	tablespoon olive oil
2	medium carrots, peeled and chopped
2	garlic cloves, finely chopped
1	large onion (10 to 12 ounces), chopped
1	medium red pepper (4 to 6 ounces), chopped
2	teaspoons ground cumin
¼	teaspoon crushed red pepper *← Smoked paprika*
½	teaspoon salt
2	cups water
2	cans black beans (15 to 19 ounces each), rinsed and drained
1	can (14½ ounces) reduced-sodium chicken broth
¼	cup fresh cilantro leaves, chopped, plus sprigs for garnish
1	tablespoon fresh lime juice

1. In 6-quart saucepot, heat oil over medium heat until hot. Add carrots, garlic, onion, and pepper; cook for 12 to 15 minutes or until vegetables are lightly browned and tender, stirring occasionally. Add cumin, crushed red pepper, and salt; cook for 1 minute.

2. Stir in water, beans, and broth; heat to boiling over medium-high heat. Reduce heat to low and simmer uncovered for 15 minutes to blend flavors.

Eat Your Beans

Whether you choose black, garbanzo, pinto, or cannellini, beans are packed with protein and insoluble and soluble fiber. Insoluble fiber helps promote regularity and may stave off such digestive disorders as diverticulosis. Soluble fiber can reduce LDL cholesterol levels and help control blood-sugar levels in people with diabetes. Beans are also high in saponin, a cancer-fighting plant compound.

3. Ladle 3 cups soup into blender; cover, with center part of lid removed to allow steam to escape, and blend until pureed. Stir puree into soup in saucepot; heat through over medium heat. Stir in cilantro and lime juice, and garnish with cilantro sprigs to serve.

Each serving: About 165 calories, 9g protein, 33g carbohydrate, 3g total fat (0g saturated), 11g fiber, 705mg sodium

HEARTY FISH CHOWDER

Cod, potatoes, and a sprinkling of crumbled bacon make every bite of this creamy chowder rich and satisfying.

ACTIVE TIME: 20 minutes   **TOTAL TIME:** 35 minutes

MAKES: 4 main-dish servings

4	slices center-cut bacon	2	tablespoons all-purpose flour
1	large carrot, peeled and chopped	1	cup bottled clam juice
1	medium celery root (13 ounces), peeled and chopped	1	pound skinless cod fillets, cut into 1-inch chunks
1	large all-purpose potato (12 ounces), peeled and chopped	½	cup reduced-fat (2%) milk
2	tablespoons plus ½ cup water	¼	teaspoon salt
2	small onions (4 to 6 ounces each), chopped	⅛	teaspoon freshly ground black pepper
			Fresh flat-leaf parsley leaves, chopped, for garnish

1. In 6- to 7-quart saucepot, cook bacon over medium heat for 5 to 7 minutes or until browned and crisp, turning occasionally. Drain on paper towels; set aside. Discard all but 1 tablespoon bacon fat. Keep saucepot with rendered bacon fat over medium heat.

2. While bacon cooks, in large microwave-safe bowl, combine carrot, celery root, potato, and 2 tablespoons water. Cover with vented plastic wrap and microwave on high for 5 minutes or until vegetables are just tender.

3. Add onion to saucepot and cook for 6 to 8 minutes or until tender, stirring occasionally. Add carrot mixture and cook for 2 minutes, stirring.

4. Add flour and cook for 2 minutes, stirring. Add clam juice and remaining ½ cup water and whisk until smooth. Heat to boiling, stirring occasionally. Add cod chunks, cover, and cook for 4 to 5 minutes or until fish just turns opaque throughout.

5. Stir in milk, salt, and pepper. Cook for 1 to 2 minutes or until hot but not boiling. Spoon chowder into shallow bowls; sprinkle with parsley and crumble 1 strip bacon over each serving.

Each serving: About 310 calories, 27g protein, 35g carbohydrate, 7g total fat (3g saturated), 5g fiber, 595mg sodium

TEX-MEX CHICKEN SOUP

This hearty soup combines the goodness of chicken with spicy jalapeños, smooth avocados, piquant cilantro, and bright lime.

ACTIVE TIME: 15 minutes **TOTAL TIME**: 4 hours 15 minutes
MAKES: 6 main-dish servings

2	medium russet potatoes, peeled and cut into ½-inch chunks
¼	cup water
1	pound boneless skinless chicken breast halves, cut into quarters
1	pound boneless skinless chicken thighs, cut into halves
4	cups chicken broth
3	large stalks celery, thinly sliced
1	jalapeño chile, finely chopped
2	teaspoons ground cumin
1	clove garlic, crushed with press
1	teaspoon salt
¼	teaspoon black pepper
2	cups frozen corn, thawed
½	cup lightly packed fresh cilantro leaves, finely chopped
1	tablespoon lime juice
1	ripe avocado, chopped

1. In large bowl, combine potatoes and water. Cover with vented plastic wrap and microwave on high for 5 minutes, or until almost tender. Drain and transfer potatoes to bowl of 7- to 8-quart slow cooker.

2. To same slow cooker bowl, add chicken, broth, celery, jalapeño, cumin, garlic, salt, and pepper. Replace lid and cook on low for 4 hours, or until chicken is cooked through (165°F) but not soft.

3. Transfer chicken to cutting board. Using two forks, pull chicken into bite-size pieces. Return chicken to slow cooker bowl.

4. Stir corn, cilantro, and lime juice into soup. Divide among serving bowls. Top with avocado.

Each serving: About 340 calories, 35g protein, 25g carbohydrate, 11g total fat (2g saturated), 5g fiber, 1,215mg sodium

CHICKEN SOUP, BOUILLABAISSE-STYLE

Instead of easy to overcook seafood, this slow-cooker bouillabaisse recipe boasts boneless, skinless chicken thighs simmered in a traditional saffron broth.

ACTIVE TIME: 30 minutes   **SLOW-COOK TIME**: 8 hours on Low or 4 hours on High

MAKES: 8 main-dish servings

1	tablespoon olive oil
3	pounds bone-in chicken thighs, skin and fat removed
1/2	teaspoon salt
1/4	teaspoon freshly ground black pepper
1	large bulb fennel (1 1/2 pounds)
1/2	cup dry white wine
1	onion, chopped
2	garlic cloves, finely chopped
1	can (14 1/2 ounces) chicken broth, or 1 3/4 cups homemade (see recipe, page 137)
1	can (14 1/2 ounces) diced tomatoes
1	bay leaf
1/2	teaspoon dried thyme
1/4	teaspoon saffron threads, crumbled

Crusty French bread, for serving (optional)

1. In 12-inch skillet, heat oil over medium-high heat until hot. Sprinkle chicken thighs with salt and pepper. Add chicken to skillet in two batches and cook, turning once and adding more oil if necessary, until lightly browned on both sides, 7 to 8 minutes per batch. With tongs, transfer chicken to bowl when browned.

2. Meanwhile, trim stems and tough outer layers from fennel bulb. Cut bulb into quarters, then thinly slice crosswise.

3. After chicken is browned, add wine to skillet and heat to boiling, stirring to loosen any browned bits. Boil for 1 minute.

4. In 4 1/4- to 6-quart slow-cooker bowl, combine fennel, onion, garlic, broth, tomatoes with their juice, bay leaf, thyme, and saffron. Top with chicken, any juices in bowl, and wine mixture from skillet; do not stir. Cover slow cooker and cook on low for 8 hours or on high for 4 hours.

5. With tongs, transfer chicken to serving bowls. Discard bay leaf. Skim and discard fat from sauce. Pour sauce over chicken. Serve with bread, if you like.

Each serving: About 175 calories, 22g protein, 9g carbohydrate, 6g total fat (1g saturated), 3g fiber, 580mg sodium

THAI CHICKEN-BASIL SOUP

Fresh basil and lime juice give this easy Thai noodle soup its perky personality.

ACTIVE TIME: 5 minutes   **TOTAL TIME**: 1 hour

MAKES: 15 cups or 8 main-dish servings

1	tablespoon vegetable oil
1	onion, chopped
1	medium poblano chile (3 ounces), seeded and chopped
4	teaspoons finely chopped, peeled fresh ginger
3	garlic cloves, thinly sliced
1/4	teaspoon crushed red pepper
3	tablespoons reduced-sodium Asian fish sauce (see Tip)
2	cartons (32 ounces each) reduced-sodium chicken broth
3	cups water
1/2	cup packed fresh basil leaves, thinly sliced, plus more for garnish
1 1/2	pounds boneless skinless chicken thighs, trimmed of fat and thinly sliced crosswise
1	package (14 ounces) linguine-style (1/4-inch-wide) rice noodles (see box, opposite)
	3 to 4 large limes

1. In 6-quart Dutch oven, heat oil over medium heat. Add onion and poblano, and cook for 10 minutes or until lightly browned and tender, stirring occasionally. Add ginger, garlic, crushed red pepper, and 1 tablespoon fish sauce; cook for 1 minute.

2. Add broth, water, and half of sliced basil; heat to boiling over high heat. Reduce heat to low; cover and simmer for 20 minutes. Uncover; increase heat to medium-high. Stir in chicken and uncooked noodles; heat to boiling. Boil for 1 minute.

3. Remove Dutch oven from heat. Skim off fat. Cut 1 lime into wedges and set aside for garnish. Squeeze enough juice from remaining limes to make 1/4 cup. To serve, stir in lime juice, remaining 2 tablespoons fish sauce, and remaining sliced basil. Garnish each serving with basil sprigs. Serve with additional fish sauce and lime wedges.

Each serving: About 315 calories, 19g protein, 47g carbohydrate, 6g total fat (1g saturated), 1g fiber, 925mg sodium

TIP

Highly pungent, Asian fish sauce is made from the liquid of salted fermented anchovies. That means a little goes a long way—happily, it has an extended shelf life. If you don't have any on hand, substitute half the amount of reduced-sodium soy sauce.

Asian Noodle Savvy

From rice vermicelli to udon, Asian noodles make stir-fries, soups, and salads feel new. The options below are available at supermarkets or Asian grocery stores, but if you can't locate them, we've provided pastas you can substitute for equally tasty results.

- **BEAN THREAD** (also known as cellophane, slippery, or mung bean noodles): Chewy, translucent, threadlike noodles made from the starch of mung beans. Bean threads become slippery when softened in hot water and cooked. Their understated flavor lets them absorb the other good tastes in the pan. Try them in brothy soups. Substitute: thin rice noodles, capellini, or vermicelli.
- **CHINESE WHEAT NOODLES:** Made with wheat flour and water, these round or flat noodles come in varying thicknesses and are available fresh or dried. The flat, wide noodles are called chow fun. The thinnest noodles are called Chinese somen. Use thinner ones in delicate soups; thicker ones hold their own in stir-fries. (Wheat noodles made with eggs are called mein; they resemble spaghetti.) Substitute: fresh or dried fettuccine.
- **RICE NOODLES:** Round or flat, these thin, translucent white noodles are made from rice flour and water; their neutral flavor makes them a perfect foil for robust, meaty flavors. Rice noodles may be called vermicelli (extra thin), thread (fine), or rice stick (flat). However, the labeling is not standardized, so look at the noodle rather than the name. Vermicelli is also known as mi fen (Chinese), bun (Vietnamese), and sen mee (Thai). Rice sticks are known as banh pho in Vietnam and jantaboon in Thailand. Substitute: vermicelli, linguine, or fettuccine (depending on size of rice noodle called for).
- **SOBA NOODLES:** Soba are thin, delicately textured Japanese noodles made from wheat flour and buckwheat, which lend them a brown color and nutty flavor. (See photo on page 134.) The more buckwheat these noodles contain, the more expensive they are. Soba noodles are often served cold with a dipping sauce or hot in soups, but they are versatile enough to be used in Chinese chicken salad or stir-fries, too. Substitute: whole wheat spaghetti.
- **UDON NOODLES:** These wheat-based Japanese noodles are available fresh or dried. Fat and bouncy in texture, delicate fresh udon noodles cook quickly, which makes them a great option for soups. Dried udon noodles are a good base for stir-fries. Substitute: linguine.

GOURMET RAMEN

Roasted chicken and mushrooms make this a hearty meal in a bowl.

TOTAL TIME: 20 minutes
MAKES: 4 servings

4	boneless skinless chicken thighs
2	tablespoons brown sugar
2	tablespoons soy sauce
2	quarts lower-sodium chicken broth
1	piece fresh ginger (1 inch), cut into matchsticks
12	ounces ramen noodles
6	ounces spinach
4	ounces shiitake mushrooms, sliced
1	tablespoon Asian sesame oil

Sliced green onions, for topping

1. Preheat broiler with oven rack 6 inches from heat source.

2. Toss chicken thighs with brown sugar and soy sauce; place on a foil-lined baking sheet. Broil for 8 to 10 minutes or until cooked through, turning once.

3. In saucepot, heat chicken broth and ginger; bring to a boil. Add ramen noodles and cook. During the last 2 minutes of cooking, stir in spinach, mushrooms, and sesame oil; cook for 3 minutes.

4. Divide among four serving bowls. Top with sliced broiled chicken and green onions.

Each serving: About 600 calories, 41g protein, 80g carbohydrate, 14g total fat (3g saturated), 5g fiber, 915mg sodium

SOBA NOODLES WITH SHRIMP, SNOW PEAS, AND CARROTS

Soba (Japanese noodles made from buckwheat flour) cook quickly, and the shrimp, peas, and carrots cook in the same water as the noodles. Just toss with an easy, delicious peanut sauce and dinner is served.

ACTIVE TIME: 15 minutes **TOTAL TIME:** 20 minutes
MAKES: 4 main-dish servings

1/4	cup creamy natural peanut butter	1	package (8 ounces) whole wheat soba noodles
2	teaspoons grated, peeled fresh ginger	1/2	bag (10 ounces) shredded or matchstick carrots (1 1/2 cups)
2	tablespoons reduced-sodium soy sauce	1	pound large shrimp, peeled and deveined, with tail left on, if preferred
1	tablespoon distilled white vinegar	4	ounces snow peas, strings removed
1	teaspoon Asian sesame oil		
1/2	teaspoon hot pepper sauce	1/2	cup loosely packed fresh cilantro leaves, chopped, plus more for garnish
1	teaspoon salt		

1. In small bowl, place peanut butter, ginger, soy sauce, vinegar, sesame oil, and hot pepper sauce. Set aside.

2. Heat covered 5- to 6-quart saucepot of water and salt to boiling over high heat. Add noodles and cook for 4 minutes. Add carrots and cook for 1 minute. Add shrimp and snow peas and cook for 2 minutes more. Reserve 1/2 cup noodle cooking water. Drain noodles, shrimp, and vegetables into large colander, then transfer to large bowl.

3. With wire whisk, beat peanut butter mixture until well blended. Add peanut sauce and chopped cilantro to noodle mixture in bowl and toss until evenly coated.

4. To serve, spoon into four large bowls; garnish each serving with a cilantro sprig.

Each serving: About 430 calories, 33g protein, 53g carbohydrate, 12g total fat (2g saturated), 6g fiber, 960mg sodium

HOMEMADE VEGETABLE BROTH

This broth is delicious, nutritious, and great in soups, risottos, and sauces. The optional fennel and parsnip lend natural sweetness and additional depth of flavor. For an Asian-flavored broth, add minced lemongrass, minced fresh ginger, or chopped fresh cilantro.

ACTIVE TIME: 25 minutes   **TOTAL TIME**: 2 hours 25 minutes
MAKES: 6 cups

4	large leeks	2	large carrots, peeled and thinly sliced
2 to 4	garlic cloves, not peeled		
13	cups water	3	stalks celery with leaves, thinly sliced
Salt			
1	large all-purpose potato, peeled, cut lengthwise in half, and thinly sliced	4	ounces mushrooms, trimmed and thinly sliced
		10	parsley sprigs
1	small fennel bulb, trimmed and chopped (optional)	4	thyme sprigs
		2	bay leaves
3	parsnips, peeled and thinly sliced (optional)	1	teaspoon whole black peppercorns, plus additional ground black pepper as needed

1. Cut off roots and trim dark green tops from leeks. Thinly slice leeks and rinse them in large bowl of cold water, swishing to remove sand. Transfer to colander to drain, leaving sand in bottom of bowl.

2. In 6-quart saucepot, combine leeks, garlic, 1 cup water, and pinch salt; heat to boiling. Reduce heat to medium; cover and cook until leeks are tender, about 15 minutes.

3. Add potato, fennel (if using), parsnips (if using), carrots, celery, mushrooms, parsley and thyme sprigs, bay leaves, peppercorns, and remaining 12 cups water. Heat to boiling; reduce heat and simmer, uncovered, for at least 1¹/₂ hours.

4. Taste and continue cooking if flavor is not concentrated enough. Season with salt and pepper, to taste. Strain broth through fine-mesh sieve into containers, pressing on solids with back of wooden spoon to extract liquid; cool. Cover and refrigerate to use within 3 days, or freeze for up to 4 months.

HOMEMADE CHICKEN BROTH

Nothing beats the rich flavor of homemade chicken broth. It serves as a base for many of our soups and stews. Make large batches and freeze it in sturdy containers for up to four months. Bonus: The cooked chicken can be used in casseroles and salads.

ACTIVE TIME: 30 minutes   **TOTAL TIME**: 4 hours 40 minutes plus cooling
MAKES: 5½ cups

1	chicken (3 to 3½ pounds), including neck (reserve giblets for another use)
2	carrots, peeled and cut into 2-inch pieces
1	stalk celery, cut into 2-inch pieces
1	onion, unpeeled, cut into quarters
5	parsley sprigs
1	garlic clove, unpeeled
½	teaspoon dried thyme
½	bay leaf
3	quarts water, plus more if needed

1. In 6-quart saucepot, combine chicken, chicken neck, carrots, celery, onion, parsley, garlic, thyme, bay leaf, and water. If necessary, add more water to cover broth ingredients; heat to boiling over high heat. With slotted spoon, skim foam from surface. Reduce heat to low; cover and simmer, turning chicken once and skimming foam occasionally, for 1 hour.

2. Remove from heat; transfer chicken to large bowl. When chicken is cool enough to handle, remove skin and bones and reserve meat for another use. Return skin and bones to pot and return to boiling over high heat. Skim foam; reduce heat to low and simmer, uncovered, for 3 hours.

3. Strain broth through colander into large bowl; discard solids. Strain again though fine-mesh sieve into containers; cool. Cover and refrigerate to use within 3 days, or freeze for up to 4 months.

4. Discard fat from surface of chilled broth before use.

MEDITERRANEAN SEAFOOD STEW

The fresh cod, shrimp, and mussels in this satisfying slow-cooker stew are added in the final 40 minutes to keep their scrumptious flavor.

ACTIVE TIME: 20 minutes   **SLOW-COOK TIME**: 3 hours 30 minutes on High
MAKES: 6 main-dish servings

2	large leeks, white and pale green parts only
1½	pounds fennel (2 large bulbs), trimmed and finely chopped
2¼	pounds tomatoes, chopped
2	garlic cloves, chopped
1	teaspoon salt
½	teaspoon freshly ground black pepper
4	sprigs fresh thyme
8	springs fresh flat-leaf parsley, stems and leaves separated
1	pound mussels, beards removed and scrubbed
1	pound shrimp (16 to 20 count), peeled and deveined
12	ounces skinless cod fillet, cut into 4-inch pieces
2	teaspoons extra-virgin olive oil
4	crusty dinner rolls

1. Cut off root ends from leeks and trim leaf ends. Cut each leek lengthwise in half, then into ¼-inch-thick slices. Place in large bowl of cold water. With hands, swish leeks to remove grit. Repeat process, changing water several times. Drain.

2. Transfer leeks to 6-quart slow-cooker bowl along with fennel, tomatoes, garlic, salt, and pepper. With kitchen twine, tie thyme and parsley stems together, reserving the parsley leaves. Bury in vegetable mixture.

3. Cover with lid and cook on high for 3 hours. Stir in mussels and shrimp, and lay fish on top. Immediately cover and cook for 30 to 40 minutes longer, or until mussels open and shrimp and fish turn opaque throughout.

4. Divide mussels among serving dishes. Discard herb bundle. Divide stew among serving dishes. Drizzle oil over stew. Chop reserved parsley leaves and sprinkle over stew. Serve with rolls.

Each serving: About 375 calories, 32g protein, 46g carbohydrate, 7g total fat (1g saturated), 6g fiber, 1,250mg sodium

TUSCAN VEGGIE STEW

This classic, vegetable-rich stew is a healthy way to warm up during the cold winter months.

ACTIVE TIME: 10 minutes **TOTAL TIME**: 40 minutes
MAKES: 6 servings

3	tablespoons extra-virgin olive oil, plus more for garnish
1	pound carrots, chopped
1	medium onion, finely chopped
2	quarts lower-sodium vegetable or chicken broth
1	bunch Tuscan or curly kale, chopped
4	ounces stale bread without crust, torn into small pieces (about 4 cups)
2	cans (14 ounces each) no-salt-added white (cannellini) beans, rinsed and drained
1	can (14 ounces) diced tomatoes
1/3	cup grated Parmesan cheese, plus more for garnish

1. In 6-quart saucepot, heat oil over medium heat. Add carrots and onion. Cook for 10 minutes, or until vegetables are beginning to soften, stirring occasionally.

2. Add broth, kale, bread, beans, and tomatoes. Heat to simmering over high heat. Reduce heat to maintain simmer. Cook for 20 minutes or until kale is tender, stirring occasionally. Stir in Parmesan. To serve, garnish with additional olive oil and Parmesan, if desired.

Each serving: About 355 calories, 15g protein, 53g carbohydrate, 11g total fat (2g saturated), 11g fiber, 830mg sodium

CLASSIC BEEF STEW

Lean beef, winter vegetables, and a richly flavored sauce make this a go-to for family suppers or casual entertaining.

ACTIVE TIME: 30 minutes **TOTAL TIME**: 1 hour 30 minutes

MAKES: 6 main-dish servings

1	tablespoon vegetable oil	3	medium carrots (8 ounces total), peeled and cut into 3/4-inch chunks
1	pound lean beef for stew, trimmed and cut into 1-inch cubes	3	medium turnips (12 ounces total), peeled and cut into 1-inch chunks
1/2	teaspoon salt		
2	stalks celery, chopped	1	tablespoon soy sauce
1	large onion (12 ounces), chopped	2	tablespoons all-purpose flour
1	can (14 1/2 ounces) stewed tomatoes	1	package (10 ounces) frozen peas
1	can (14 1/2 ounces) beef broth	2	tablespoons freshly grated lemon peel
1	cup plus 2 tablespoons water		
3	large potatoes (1 1/2 pounds total), peeled and cut into 1 1/2-inch chunks		

1. Pat beef dry with paper towels. In 5-quart Dutch oven, heat oil over medium-high heat until very hot. Add beef, sprinkle with salt, and cook, turning pieces occasionally, until beef is browned on all sides. Transfer beef to bowl.

2. Add celery and onion to drippings in Dutch oven and cook, stirring, until lightly browned. Return beef to Dutch oven; stir in stewed tomatoes, broth, and 1 cup water. Heat to boiling over high heat. Reduce heat to low; cover and simmer for 25 minutes.

3. Add potatoes, carrots, turnips, and soy sauce; heat to boiling over high heat. Reduce heat to low; cover and simmer until meat and vegetables in pot are fork-tender, about 20 minutes longer.

4. In cup, with fork, mix flour and remaining 2 tablespoons water until blended. Stir flour mixture into meat mixture; cook over medium-high heat until mixture boils and thickens slightly. Stir in frozen peas; heat through. Sprinkle with lemon peel.

Each serving: About 330 calories, 23g protein, 45g carbohydrate, 7g total fat (2g saturated), 7g fiber, 905mg sodium

Browning and Braising Basics

Mastering these techniques is essential to achieving rich, succulent meat stews.

- Make sure both the pan and the oil are very hot before adding the meat in small batches (a pound or less at a time). Overcrowding the pan will steam the meat instead of allowing it to brown.

- Let the meat brown on all sides, caramelizing the proteins and sugars. (Reduce the heat if the bits of meat clinging to the bottom of the pan begin to burn.)

- Add liquid to the meat in the pan only after browning is complete, and heat to boiling, scraping the bottom of the pan with a spoon to release the browned bits. (This process is known as deglazing.)

- Cover the pan and braise the mixture over lower heat on the stovetop or at a moderate temperature (325° to 350°F) in the oven, according to recipe instructions. Do not allow the stew to boil—the meat will toughen and dry out.

- When the meat is tender and fully braised, the tines of a fork will slip easily in and out of the pieces.

VALENTINE'S DAY RED CHILI

Beets and fire-roasted tomatoes color this vegetarian chili—and provide the inspiration for its name.

ACTIVE TIME: 35 minutes **TOTAL TIME**: 1 hour 30 minutes
MAKES: 9 cups or 6 main-dish servings

2	teaspoons ground cumin
1	teaspoon dried oregano
1/2	teaspoon chipotle chile powder
2	tablespoons vegetable oil
3	large beets (6 to 8 ounces each), trimmed, peeled, and chopped
1	jumbo red onion (1 pound), finely chopped
1	large red pepper (8 to 10 ounces), chopped
1/2	teaspoon ground black pepper
4	garlic cloves, crushed with press
1	can (28 ounces) fire-roasted diced tomatoes
1	can (15 ounces) low-sodium black beans, rinsed and drained
1	can (15 ounces) low-sodium red kidney beans, rinsed and drained
1	can (15 ounces) low-sodium pinto beans, rinsed and drained
1	cup water
1	cup reduced-fat sour cream
1/4	cup fresh cilantro leaves

1. In 7- to 8-quart Dutch oven or heavy saucepot, combine cumin, oregano, and chile powder. Cook over medium heat for 1 to 2 minutes or until toasted and fragrant. Transfer to sheet of waxed paper; set aside. In same Dutch oven, heat oil over medium heat until hot. Add beets, onion, red pepper, and 1/4 teaspoon pepper. Cook for 15 minutes or until vegetables are tender, stirring occasionally.

2. Add garlic and reserved spice mixture. Cook for 2 minutes, stirring constantly. Add tomatoes, all beans, and water. Heat to boiling over medium-high heat. Reduce heat to medium-low and simmer for 30 minutes, stirring and mashing some beans occasionally. Season with remaining 1/4 teaspoon pepper. (Can be prepared to this point up to 2 days ahead; transfer to airtight container and refrigerate. Reheat before serving.) Divide among serving bowls and top with sour cream and cilantro. Serve with corn bread, if desired.

Each serving: About 345 calories, 15g protein, 52g carbohydrate, 10g total fat (3g saturated), 15g fiber, 540mg sodium

THREE-BEAN VEGETABLE CHILI

This chili is so good we doubled the recipe. You can find edamame beans in the freezer case of most large supermarkets.

ACTIVE TIME: 35 minutes   **TOTAL TIME**: 1 hour 5 minutes

MAKES: 11½ cups or 8 main-dish servings

1	tablespoon vegetable oil
1	pound carrots, peeled and cut into ½-inch dice
2	large stalks celery, sliced
2	garlic cloves, crushed with press
1	jumbo onion (1 pound), chopped
4	teaspoons chili powder
1	tablespoon ground cumin
½	teaspoon ground cinnamon
¼	teaspoon cayenne (ground red) pepper
1	teaspoon salt
1	can (14½ ounces) diced tomatoes
1	can (14½ ounces) vegetable broth, or 1¾ cups homemade (see recipe, page 136)
1	cup water
2	cans (15 to 19 ounces) white kidney beans (cannellini), rinsed and drained
1	can (15 to 19 ounces) pink beans, rinsed and drained
2	cups frozen shelled edamame
¼	cup fresh cilantro leaves, chopped, plus more for garnish
	Reduced-fat sour cream and shredded reduced-fat Cheddar cheese, for serving (optional)

1. In 5- to 6-quart Dutch oven, heat oil over medium-high heat until hot. Add carrots, celery, garlic, and onion and cook for 10 to 12 minutes or until all vegetables are browned and tender, stirring occasionally.

2. Stir in chili powder, cumin, cinnamon, cayenne, and salt; cook for 30 seconds, stirring. Add tomatoes and their juice, broth, and water; heat to boiling. Reduce heat to low; cover and simmer for 15 minutes. Stir white kidney beans and pink beans into Dutch oven; cover and cook for 10 minutes longer. Stir in edamame and cook, uncovered, for 5 to 7 minutes or until edamame are just tender, stirring occasionally.

3. Stir chopped cilantro into chili. Spoon half of chili into serving bowls; garnish with cilantro leaves. Serve with sour cream and Cheddar, if you like. Spoon remaining chili into freezer-safe containers (see Tip).

Each serving: About 345 calories, 19g protein, 51g carbohydrate, 8g total fat (1g saturated), 15g fiber, 945mg sodium

Eat Edamame

These sweet, nutty soybeans have gone by many names over the years—beer beans, sweet beans, garden soys—but the Japanese edamame is the one that stuck. Cultivated in ancient China for medicinal purposes, edamame are a nutritional powerhouse. Rich in calcium, iron, vitamins A and C, and fiber, they don't contain saturated fat and are high in protein. Look for precooked edamame in your supermarket's freezer or produce section. Try whole beans as a snack or enjoy them in recipes.

- Toss shelled beans into stir-fries, soups, stews, and salads.

- Puree shelled, cooked beans, roasted garlic, olive oil, and spices to make a creamy dip for pita chips or crackers.

- Add edamame to a succotash in place of lima beans.

TIP

To reheat chili on the rangetop after thawing, in a covered saucepan, heat the chili to boiling and then simmer over medium heat for about 30 minutes, stirring occasionally. To use a microwave oven, place the chili in a microwave-safe bowl and heat, covered, on low for 10 minutes, stirring once or twice, then on high for 5 to 10 minutes, stirring once.

TURKEY AND WHITE BEAN CHILI

You can cut calories by a third and fat by half when you substitute ground turkey for beef chuck. The cannellini beans deliver an impressive 10 grams of fiber per serving—almost half your daily requirement.

ACTIVE TIME: 15 minutes   **TOTAL TIME**: 25 minutes
MAKES: 6 cups or 4 main-dish servings

1	tablespoon olive oil
1	pound lean (93%) ground turkey
½	teaspoon salt
1	onion, chopped
4	teaspoons chili powder
1	tablespoon ground cumin
1	can (28 ounces) whole tomatoes in juice, chopped
1	can (15 to 19 ounces) white kidney beans (cannellini)
½	cup water
½	cup plain nonfat yogurt

1. In 12-inch skillet, heat oil over medium-high heat until hot. Add turkey and salt, and cook for 6 to 8 minutes or until turkey loses its pink color throughout, stirring to break up meat with side of spoon. Add onion and cook for 4 minutes. Stir in chili powder and cumin; cook for 1 minute.

2. Add tomatoes with their juice, beans, and water; heat to boiling over high heat. Reduce heat to medium and cook, uncovered, for 10 minutes, stirring occasionally. Ladle chili into serving bowls and top with a dollop of yogurt.

Each serving: About 380 calories, 33g protein, 35g carbohydrate, 13g total fat (3g saturated), 10g fiber, 875mg sodium

SUPER BOWL CHILI

Our recipe for Texas-style chili contains small chunks of beef rather than ground. The classic version doesn't contain beans, but we replaced a portion of the meat with red kidney beans to cut some fat. Serve with corn bread or tortilla chips.

ACTIVE TIME: 30 minutes   **TOTAL TIME**: 2 hours 40 minutes

MAKES: 14 cups or 12 main-dish servings

2	tablespoons olive oil	2	cans (28 ounces each) whole tomatoes in puree
2	pounds boneless beef for stew, cut into ½-inch chunks	1	can (6 ounces) tomato paste
4	garlic cloves, crushed with press	¼	cup granulated sugar
2	red peppers cut into ½-inch pieces	2	teaspoons salt
2	jalapeño chiles, seeded and minced	2	teaspoons dried oregano
1	large onion, chopped	2	cups water
⅓	cup chili powder	2	cans (15 to 19 ounces each) red kidney beans, rinsed and drained

1. In 8-quart saucepot or Dutch oven, heat 1 teaspoon oil over high heat until hot. Add one-third of beef and cook until browned on all sides and liquid evaporates, 6 to 8 minutes, stirring often. With slotted spoon, transfer beef to bowl. Repeat with remaining beef, using 1 teaspoon oil per batch; set beef aside.

2. Add remaining 1 tablespoon oil to drippings in saucepot and heat over medium-high heat until hot. Stir in garlic, red peppers, jalapeños, and onion; cook until vegetables are tender, about 10 minutes, stirring occasionally. Stir in chili powder; cook for 1 minute.

3. Return beef to saucepot. Stir in tomatoes with their puree, tomato paste, sugar, salt, oregano, and water, breaking up tomatoes with side of spoon; heat to boiling over high heat. Reduce heat to low; cover and simmer for 1½ hours. Stir in beans and cook for 10 to 30 minutes longer or until meat is fork-tender, stirring occasionally.

Each serving: About 275 calories, 25g protein, 30g carbohydrate, 7g total fat (2g saturated), 7g fiber, 1,115mg sodium

SOUTHWESTERN CHICKEN STEW

Infuse your winter stew with the personality of the Southwest. This stew is brimming with bright, rich flavors and a subtle spice that will warm you up on the coldest winter nights.

ACTIVE TIME: 15 minutes   **TOTAL TIME**: 4 hours 15 minutes
MAKES: 8 servings

1	can (28 ounces) fire-roasted tomatoes
2	green onions, trimmed and cut into thirds
2	chipotle chiles in adobo sauce
2	tablespoons adobo sauce
2	garlic cloves, peeled
2	teaspoons chili powder
1	teaspoon ground cumin
1¼	teaspoons salt
1¼	pound boneless skinless chicken breast halves
2	cups chicken broth
½	cup water
1	pound thin spaghetti, broken into thirds
1½	cups finely shredded Monterey Jack cheese
2	green onions, thinly sliced
	Cilantro leaves, for garnish

1. In blender, purée tomatoes, onions, chipotles, adobo sauce, garlic, chili powder, cumin, and 1 teaspoon salt until smooth. Transfer to 6- to 7-quart slow-cooker bowl. Arrange chicken on top (do not submerge). Replace lid; cook on low for 3½ hours or until chicken is cooked through (165°F).

2. Transfer chicken to cutting board. In measuring cup, combine broth, water, and ¼ teaspoon salt. Microwave on high for 1 minute; add to slow cooker. Add spaghetti, pushing down to fully submerge. Replace lid; cook on low for 30 to 45 minutes, testing after 30 minutes, or until pasta is al dente and most of liquid has been absorbed, stirring once.

3. While pasta cooks, pull chicken into chunks. Once pasta is cooked, return chicken to bowl, tossing to combine. To serve, top with cheese, sliced green onions, and cilantro.

Each serving: About 410 calories, 29g protein, 50g carbohydrate, 10g total fat (4g saturated), 4g fiber, 1,120mg sodium

TIP
Use "thin spaghetti"—angel hair or spaghettini are too thin and will get overcooked and mushy.

CINCINNATI CHILI

Cincinnati has its own unique take on chili; there, they serve it over spaghetti. Try it at home by making an easy, tasty slow-cooker chili and then serving it over spaghetti.

ACTIVE TIME: 5 minutes **SLOW-COOK TIME**: 6 hours on Low
MAKES: 6 servings

1½	pounds lean (92%) ground beef
1	can (15 ounces) kidney beans, rinsed and drained
1	can (15 ounces) tomato sauce
1	medium onion, chopped
2	tablespoons brown sugar
2	tablespoons unsweetened cocoa
2	tablespoons ground chipotle chile
2	tablespoons ground cumin
1½	teaspoons ground cinnamon
1	pound spaghetti, cooked

Salt and black pepper

4	ounces sharp Cheddar cheese, shredded
4	green onions, thinly sliced

1. In 7- to 8-quart slow-cooker bowl, combine beef, beans, tomato sauce, onion, brown sugar, cocoa, chipotle, cumin, cinnamon, and ½ teaspoon each salt and black pepper; stir together, breaking up ground beef. Replace lid and cook on low for 6 hours.

2. When ready to serve, spoon over spaghetti. Top with shredded cheese and green onions.

Each serving (without spaghetti): About 565 calories, 47g protein, 81g carbohydrate, 7g total fat (5g saturated), 10g fiber, 885mg sodium

SOUTHWESTERN CHICKEN STEW

Infuse your winter stew with the personality of the Southwest. This stew is brimming with bright, rich flavors and a subtle spice that will warm you up on the coldest winter nights.

ACTIVE TIME: 15 minutes   **TOTAL TIME**: 4 hours 15 minutes
MAKES: 8 servings

1	can (28 ounces) fire-roasted tomatoes	1¼	pound boneless skinless chicken breast halves
2	green onions, trimmed and cut into thirds	2	cups chicken broth
		½	cup water
2	chipotle chiles in adobo sauce	1	pound thin spaghetti, broken into thirds
2	tablespoons adobo sauce	1½	cups finely shredded Monterey Jack cheese
2	garlic cloves, peeled		
2	teaspoons chili powder	2	green onions, thinly sliced
1	teaspoon ground cumin		Cilantro leaves, for garnish
1¼	teaspoons salt		

1. In blender, purée tomatoes, onions, chipotles, adobo sauce, garlic, chili powder, cumin, and 1 teaspoon salt until smooth. Transfer to 6- to 7-quart slow-cooker bowl. Arrange chicken on top (do not submerge). Replace lid; cook on low for 3½ hours or until chicken is cooked through (165°F).

2. Transfer chicken to cutting board. In measuring cup, combine broth, water, and ¼ teaspoon salt. Microwave on high for 1 minute; add to slow cooker. Add spaghetti, pushing down to fully submerge. Replace lid; cook on low for 30 to 45 minutes, testing after 30 minutes, or until pasta is al dente and most of liquid has been absorbed, stirring once.

3. While pasta cooks, pull chicken into chunks. Once pasta is cooked, return chicken to bowl, tossing to combine. To serve, top with cheese, sliced green onions, and cilantro.

Each serving: About 410 calories, 29g protein, 50g carbohydrate, 10g total fat (4g saturated), 4g fiber, 1,120mg sodium

TIP
Use "thin spaghetti"—angel hair or spaghettini are too thin and will get overcooked and mushy.

LAMB AND ROOT VEGETABLE TAGINE

Tagine, a traditional stew from North Africa, is known for its combination of sweet and salty ingredients. In this tender slow-cooker version, we include dried apricots, lamb, and lots of root vegetables.

ACTIVE TIME: 30 minutes   **SLOW-COOK TIME**: 8 hours on Low
MAKES: 10 main-dish servings

1	tablespoon vegetable oil	1	pound parsnips (6 medium), peeled and cut into 1-inch pieces
4	pounds well-trimmed leg of lamb, deboned and cut into 1-inch pieces	½	cup dried apricots, cut in half
½	teaspoon salt	2	teaspoons ground coriander
1¾	cups chicken broth	2	teaspoons ground cumin
1	medium onion, chopped	½	teaspoon ground cinnamon
2	garlic cloves, thinly sliced	2	cups plain couscous
1	pound sweet potatoes (2 medium), peeled and cut into 1-inch pieces	¾	cup pitted green olives, chopped
			Fresh cilantro leaves, for garnish

1. In 12-inch skillet, heat oil over medium-high heat until very hot. Sprinkle lamb with salt. Add lamb to skillet in three batches and cook, stirring occasionally and adding more oil if necessary, until lamb is browned on all sides, 5 to 6 minutes per batch. With slotted spoon, transfer lamb to medium bowl when browned.

2. After lamb is browned, add broth to skillet and heat to boiling over high heat, stirring to loosen browned bits. Boil for 1 minute.

3. Meanwhile, in 6- to 6 ½-quart slow-cooker bowl, combine onion, garlic, sweet potatoes, parsnips, apricots, coriander, cumin, and cinnamon. Top with lamb, any juices in bowl, and broth mixture; do not stir. Cover slow cooker and cook on low for 8 hours.

4. After lamb has cooked, prepare couscous as label directs.

5. Skim and discard fat from cooking liquid. Reserve ¼ cup chopped olives; stir remaining olives into lamb mixture. Spoon lamb mixture over couscous in bowls. Sprinkle with reserved chopped olives and garnish with cilantro.

Each serving: About 475 calories, 44g protein, 50g carbohydrate, 11g total fat (3g saturated), 6g fiber, 600mg sodium

VEAL AND MUSHROOM STEW

In this recipe, the veal is slowly simmered with mushrooms and a touch of sweet Marsala wine. Peas contribute subtle sweetness and color.

ACTIVE TIME: 30 minutes   **TOTAL TIME**: 1 hour 30 minutes
MAKES: 6 main-dish servings

1½	pounds boneless veal shoulder, cut into 1½-inch chunks	¼	pound shiitake mushrooms, stems removed
¾	teaspoon salt	½	cup water
¼	teaspoon ground black pepper	⅓	cup sweet Marsala wine (see box, below)
3	tablespoons vegetable oil		
1	pound white mushrooms, trimmed and cut in half	1	package (10 ounces) frozen peas, thawed

1. Preheat oven to 350°F. Pat veal dry with paper towels and sprinkle with salt and pepper. In nonreactive 5-quart Dutch oven, heat 2 tablespoons oil over medium-high heat until very hot. Add half of veal and cook until browned, using slotted spoon to transfer meat to bowl as it is browned. Repeat with remaining veal.

2. In Dutch oven, heat remaining 1 tablespoon oil over medium-high heat. Add both types of mushrooms and cook, stirring occasionally, until lightly browned.

3. Return veal to Dutch oven; stir in water and Marsala, stirring until browned bits are loosened from bottom of pan. Heat to boiling. Cover Dutch oven and bake, stirring occasionally, until veal is tender, 1 hour to 1 hour 15 minutes. Stir in peas and heat through.

Each serving: About 250 calories, 26g protein, 12g carbohydrate, 11g total fat (2g saturated), 3g fiber, 448mg sodium

Let's Talk Marsala

Marsala, Italy's most famous fortified wine, is produced by a process similar to the one used in Spain to make sherry. Marsala is made in several different styles: secco (dry), semisecco (semisweet), and dolce (sweet). It is also classified based on its flavor characteristics and aging: Fino is usually aged less than one year, Marsalas designated Superiore between two and four years, and Vergine between four and ten years.

Deep-Dish Veggie Supreme Pizza (page 199)

4 | SANDWICHES, WRAPS & PIZZAS

Surprise! Sandwiches, wraps, pizzas, and even burgers can be part of a low-fat diet. You just have to choose your fillings and toppings with care. And it certainly doesn't hurt to eat them on whole-grain pitas, tortillas, burger buns, or multigrain pizza dough!

About those fillings: In this chapter, you'll find healthier burgers made from beans, chicken, and turkey, which sidestep the unhealthy fats in the usual beef versions. Turkey fajitas offer an alternative take on Mexican fare. Our pizzas are topped with a cornucopia of veggies, and say no thanks to fatty meat toppings.

Pack a wholesome lunch for your kids (or yourself) with our Garden Turkey Sandwiches, Greek Salad Pitas, or our Healthy Club Sandwiches, and no one will be tempted by fast-food fare. Come dinnertime, warm sandwiches like our BBQ Ranch Chicken Wraps, Falafel Sandwiches, or PLTs (fire-seared portobello burgers) make quick and nutritious meals.

FALAFEL SANDWICHES

Serve these small, flat bean patties in pita pockets with lettuce, tomatoes, cucumbers, and tangy plain low-fat yogurt.

ACTIVE TIME: 10 minutes   **TOTAL TIME:** 20 minutes

MAKES: 4 sandwiches

4	green onions, cut into ½-inch pieces
2	garlic cloves, cut in half
½	cup packed fresh flat-leaf parsley leaves
2	teaspoons dried mint
1	can (15 to 19 ounces) no-salt-added garbanzo beans, rinsed and drained
½	cup plain dried bread crumbs
1	teaspoon ground coriander
1	teaspoon ground cumin
1	teaspoon baking powder
½	teaspoon salt
¼	teaspoon cayenne (ground red) pepper
¼	teaspoon ground allspice
	Olive oil nonstick cooking spray
4	(6- to 7-inch) whole wheat pita breads
	Sliced romaine lettuce, sliced ripe tomatoes, sliced cucumber, sliced red onion, and plain low-fat yogurt, for serving (optional)

1. In food processor with knife blade attached, finely chop green onions, garlic, parsley, and mint. Add beans, bread crumbs, coriander, cumin, baking powder, salt, cayenne, and allspice and blend until a coarse puree forms.

2. Shape bean mixture, by scant ½ cups, into eight 3-inch round patties and place on sheet of waxed paper. Coat both sides of patties with cooking spray.

3. Heat 10-inch nonstick skillet over medium heat until hot. Add half of patties and cook until dark golden brown, about 10 minutes, turning once. Transfer patties to paper towels to drain. Repeat with remaining patties.

4. Cut off top third of each pita to form a pocket. Reserve cut-off pieces for another use. Place 2 warm patties in each pita. Serve with choice of accompaniments.

Each sandwich (without accompaniments): About 305 calories, 13g protein, 58g carbohydrate, 3g total fat (0g saturated), 10g fiber, 755mg sodium

HEALTHY CLUB SANDWICHES

This carrot, sprout, and bean spread combo will satisfy your palate and ease your conscience.

TOTAL TIME: 25 minutes
MAKES: 4 sandwiches

2	tablespoons olive oil		Pinch cayenne (ground red) pepper
2	teaspoons plus 1 tablespoon fresh lemon juice	1	can (15 to 19 ounces) garbanzo beans, rinsed and drained
1	teaspoon honey	1	tablespoon water
1/8	teaspoon ground black pepper	12	slices multigrain bread, lightly toasted
3	carrots, peeled and shredded (1 cup)	1	large ripe tomato (12 ounces), thinly sliced
2	cups alfalfa sprouts		
1	garlic clove, finely chopped	1	bunch watercress (4 ounces), tough stems trimmed
1/2	teaspoon ground cumin		

1. In medium bowl, stir 1 tablespoon oil, 2 teaspoons lemon juice, honey, and pepper until mixed. Add carrots and alfalfa sprouts; toss until mixed and evenly coated with dressing.

2. In 2-quart saucepan, heat remaining 1 tablespoon oil over medium heat. Add garlic, cumin, and cayenne and cook until very fragrant, about 1 minute. Stir in beans and remove from heat. Add remaining 1 tablespoon lemon juice and water; mash to a coarse puree.

3. Spread garbanzo-bean mixture on 8 toast slices. Place tomato slices and watercress over 4 garbanzo-topped toast slices. Top remaining 4 garbanzo-topped slices with alfalfa-sprout mixture and place on watercress-topped bread. Cover with 4 remaining toast slices. Cut sandwiches in half.

Each sandwich: About 380 calories, 14g protein, 57g carbohydrate, 12g total fat (2g saturated), 17g fiber, 545mg sodium

BULGUR BEAN BURGERS

Why buy expensive veggie burgers when they're so easy to make at home? This version gets its "meaty" texture from a combination of bulgur and black beans. Add an extra helping of grains by serving these burgers on whole wheat buns.

ACTIVE TIME: 20 minutes   **TOTAL TIME**: 30 minutes

MAKES: 4 burgers

1	cup water
3/4	teaspoon salt
1/2	cup bulgur
1	can (15 to 19 ounces) reduced-sodium black beans, rinsed and drained
1	container (6 ounces) plain low-fat yogurt
1/4	teaspoon ground allspice
1/4	teaspoon ground cinnamon
1/4	teaspoon ground cumin
1/4	cup packed fresh mint leaves, chopped
	Nonstick cooking spray
1/8	teaspoon ground black pepper
1/2	cup grated Kirby (pickling) cucumber (1 small)
4	lettuce leaves
1	ripe tomato, sliced
4	whole wheat hamburger buns

1. In 1-quart saucepan, heat water and 1/2 teaspoon salt to boiling over high heat. Stir in bulgur. Reduce heat to low; cover and simmer until water is absorbed, 10 to 12 minutes.

2. Meanwhile, in large bowl, with potato masher or fork, mash beans with 2 tablespoons yogurt until almost smooth. Stir in bulgur, allspice, cinnamon, cumin, and half of mint until combined. With lightly floured hands, shape bean mixture into four 3-inch round patties. Coat both sides of each patty lightly with cooking spray.

3. Heat 12-inch nonstick skillet over medium heat until hot. Add burgers and cook until lightly browned and heated through, about 8 minutes, turning once.

4. While burgers are cooking, prepare yogurt sauce: In small bowl, combine remaining yogurt, remaining mint, remaining $1/4$ teaspoon salt, and pepper. Makes about $1^{1}/4$ cups.

5. To serve, divide lettuce, tomato slices, and burgers among buns; top with some yogurt sauce. Serve with remaining yogurt sauce.

Each burger: About 295 calories, 16g protein, 58g carbohydrate, 3g total fat (1g saturated), 13g fiber, 960mg sodium

Get Your Grains:
BULGUR

This nutritious staple of the Middle East is a form of whole wheat kernel that has been parboiled and dried. Bulgur differs from cracked wheat in that it's precooked, so it is quick to prepare and can be served hot or cold. Not only does bulgur contain soluble fiber, it is also a low-fat source of protein, vitamins, and minerals.

PLT SANDWICHES

This substantial fire-seared portobello burger, slathered with basil mayo and sandwiched in a ciabatta bun, is brawny enough for beef lovers. Before grilling, brush the mushrooms with rosemary-garlic oil for a robust flavor.

ACTIVE TIME: 20 minutes   **TOTAL TIME**: 30 minutes
MAKES: 4 sandwiches

1	teaspoon finely chopped fresh rosemary leaves	1/4	teaspoon salt
1	garlic clove, crushed with press	1/4	teaspoon ground black pepper
3	tablespoons olive oil	4	ciabatta or other crusty rolls, split
3	tablespoons light mayonnaise	4	iceberg lettuce leaves
2	tablespoons packed, finely chopped fresh basil leaves	1/2	cup arugula (optional)
4	large portobello mushroom caps	1	ounce shaved Parmesan cheese
		4	large tomato slices

1. Prepare outdoor grill for direct grilling over medium-high heat.

2. In small bowl, combine rosemary, garlic, and oil. In another bowl, combine mayonnaise and basil.

3. Brush oil mixture all over mushrooms, then sprinkle them with salt and pepper. Place ciabatta halves and mushrooms on hot grill grate. Cook ciabatta for 3 minutes or until toasted, turning over once. Cook mushrooms for 6 to 8 minutes or until browned and tender, turning over once. Transfer to cutting board. Cut mushrooms at an angle into $1/2$-inch slices, keeping mushroom shape intact.

4. Spread basil mayonnaise on cut sides of ciabatta. Divide lettuce, then arugula (if using), among bottom halves. Place 1 mushroom on top, fanning slices apart slightly. Top with Parmesan, tomato, and ciabatta tops.

Each sandwich: About 463 calories, 17g protein, 55g carbohydrate, 18g total fat (3g saturated), 4g fiber, 880mg sodium

TIP

To turn this recipe vegan, just use vegan mayonnaise and omit the cheese.

VEGGIE WRAPS WITH GOAT CHEESE

An array of roasted veggies mix with tangy goat cheese for a filling, flavor-rich, and fiber-fabulous meal.

TOTAL TIME: 20 minutes

MAKES: 4 wraps

2	Portobello mushroom caps, sliced
1	large red pepper, sliced
8	ounces green beans
2	tablespoons olive oil
1/4	teaspoon salt
2	cans (15 ounces each) chickpeas, drained
3	tablespoons lemon juice
1/4	teaspoon ground black pepper
4	soft-taco-size whole-grain tortillas
1	ounce fresh goat cheese, crumbled

Lemon wedges, for serving

1. Preheat oven to 450°F. On two rimmed baking sheets, toss mushroom caps, red pepper, and green beans with olive oil and salt. Roast for 30 minutes.

2. In small bowl, mash chickpeas with lemon juice and pepper; spread mixture evenly on tortillas. Top with roasted veggies and goat cheese. Fold to wrap. Serve with lemon wedges.

Each wrap: About 465 calories, 19g protein, 66g carbohydrate, 16g total fat (3g saturated), 17g fiber, 910mg sodium

BBQ RANCH CHICKEN WRAPS

Sneaky cheat: Use store-bought ranch dressing instead of the buttermilk, green onions, and salt.

ACTIVE TIME: 20 minutes
TOTAL TIME: 30 minutes
MAKES: 4 wraps

1¼	pounds thin chicken breast cutlets
½	cup barbecue sauce
⅓	cup low-fat buttermilk
2	green onions, finely chopped
1	tablespoon cider vinegar
¼	teaspoon salt
1	large head romaine lettuce, chopped
1	medium red pepper, seeded and chopped
1	cup fresh or frozen (thawed) corn
4	plain or spinach soft wraps

1. Preheat oven to 425°F. In a large baking dish, toss chicken with ¼ cup barbecue sauce. Bake for 20 minutes or until cooked through.

2. Meanwhile, in a large bowl, whisk ¼ cup barbecue sauce, buttermilk, green onions, cider vinegar, and salt. Transfer cooked chicken to cutting board; chop into bite-size pieces.

3. To the bowl with the dressing, add romaine, red pepper, corn, and chopped chicken and toss until well coated.

4. To serve, divide among wraps and fold to enclose.

Each wrap: About 500 calories, 39g protein, 64g carbohydrate, 10g total fat (3g saturated), 9g fiber, 1,185mg sodium

VEGETARIAN SOUVLAKI

No one will miss the meat in these yummy sandwiches. Make the filling by cutting up your favorite veggie burgers.

ACTIVE TIME: 15 minutes **TOTAL TIME**: 35 minutes
MAKES: 4 sandwiches

1	tablespoon olive oil
1	large onion (12 ounces), cut in half and thinly sliced
4	frozen vegetarian soy burgers (10- to 12-ounce package), cut into 1-inch pieces
$1/2$	teaspoon salt
$1/4$	teaspoon ground black pepper
8	ounces plain nonfat yogurt
8	ounces English (seedless) cucumber, cut into $1/4$-inch pieces
1	teaspoon dried mint
1	small garlic clove, crushed with press
4	(6- to 7-inch) pitas, warmed
1	medium tomato, cut into $1/2$-inch pieces
1	ounce feta cheese, crumbled

1. In 12-inch nonstick skillet, heat oil over medium heat until hot. Add onion and cook, stirring occasionally, until tender and golden, 12 to 15 minutes. Add burgers, $1/4$ teaspoon salt, and pepper and cook until heated through, about 5 minutes.

2. Meanwhile, in medium bowl, stir yogurt, cucumber, mint, garlic, and remaining $1/4$ teaspoon salt until blended. Add burger mixture and toss gently to combine.

3. Cut 1-inch slice from each pita to form pocket. Spoon one-fourth burger mixture into each pita. Sprinkle with tomato and feta.

Each sandwich: About 390 calories, 24g protein, 45g carbohydrate, 13g total fat (3g saturated), 6g fiber, 945mg sodium

TUSCAN TUNA SALAD SANDWICHES

Tuna and cannellini beans are a popular combination in Italy. Tossed with a piquant dressing, it makes a great sandwich filling.

TOTAL TIME: 15 minutes

MAKES: 4 sandwiches

1	can (15 to 19 ounces) low-sodium white kidney beans (cannellini), rinsed and drained
½	cup chopped fresh basil
2	tablespoons capers, drained and chopped
2	tablespoons fresh lemon juice
2	tablespoons olive oil
½	teaspoon salt
¼	teaspoon coarsely ground black pepper
1	can (6 ounces) unsalted tuna packed in water, drained and flaked
1	bunch watercress (4 ounces), tough stems trimmed and sprigs cut in half
4	whole wheat pita breads
2	ripe medium tomatoes (6 ounces each), thinly sliced

1. In large bowl, mash 1 cup beans. Stir in basil, capers, lemon juice, oil, salt, and pepper until well blended. Add tuna, watercress, and remaining beans; toss to mix.

2. Cut pita breads in half. Spoon tuna mixture onto pita halves; top with tomato slices.

Each sandwich: About 330 calories, 20g protein, 44g carbohydrate, 10g total fat (1g saturated), 9g fiber, 724mg sodium

GREEK SALAD PITAS

Garbanzo beans ensure that this healthy sandwich is both low in fat and full of fiber.

TOTAL TIME: 20 minutes
MAKES: 4 sandwiches

1	can (15 ounces) low-sodium garbanzo beans, rinsed and drained
¼	cup plain low-fat yogurt
2	tablespoons olive oil
2	tablespoons fresh lemon juice
½	teaspoon salt
¼	teaspoon coarsely ground black pepper
¼	teaspoon ground cumin
1	garlic clove, peeled
4	(6- to 7-inch) whole wheat pita breads
3	cups sliced romaine lettuce
2	medium tomatoes, cut into ¼-inch pieces
1	medium cucumber, peeled and chopped (½ cup)
2	ounces feta, crumbled (½ cup)
2	tablespoons chopped fresh mint leaves

1. In food processor with knife blade attached or in blender, combine beans, yogurt, oil, lemon juice, salt, pepper, cumin, and garlic; puree until smooth.

2. Cut off top third of each pita to form pocket. Use half of bean mixture to divide evenly inside pockets.

3. Combine lettuce, tomatoes, cucumber, feta, and mint; use to fill pockets. Top with remaining bean mixture.

Each sandwich: About 392 calories, 17g protein, 54g carbohydrate, 13g total fat (4g saturated), 10g fiber, 542mg sodium

ASIAN TUNA BURGERS

For a light texture, finely chop the fish by hand; using a food processor will make the patties dense and dry. Serve with pickled ginger, with or without a bun.

ACTIVE TIME: 15 minutes **TOTAL TIME**: 20 minutes
MAKES: 4 burgers

1	tuna steak (about 1 pound)
1	green onion, thinly sliced
2	tablespoons reduced-sodium soy sauce
1	teaspoon grated, peeled fresh ginger
¼	teaspoon coarsely ground black pepper
¼	cup plain dried bread crumbs
2	tablespoons sesame seeds

Nonstick cooking spray

1. Prepare outdoor grill for direct grilling over medium heat.

2. With chef's knife, finely chop tuna and place in medium bowl. Add green onion, soy sauce, ginger, and pepper; mix until combined (mixture will be very soft and moist). Shape tuna mixture into four 3-inch patties.

3. On waxed paper, combine bread crumbs and sesame seeds. Carefully press patties into mixture, turning to coat both sides. Spray both sides of tuna patties with cooking spray.

4. Place patties on hot grill rack and cook for 6 to 7 minutes, until browned on the outside and still slightly pink in the center, or to desired doneness, turning over once.

Each burger: About 210 calories, 26g protein, 7g carbohydrate, 8g total fat (2g saturated), 1g fiber, 400mg sodium

CHICKEN CAKES WITH "ROASTED" TOMATO SALSA

Mexican flavors combine with chicken to create an enticing, healthy burger alternative.

TOTAL TIME: 25 minutes
MAKES: 8 cakes or 4 servings

1	cup loosely packed fresh cilantro leaves
3	medium plum tomatoes (12 ounces total)
1	teaspoon hot pepper sauce with chipotle, or 1 teaspoon adobo puree
1/4	teaspoon salt
1	small zucchini (6 ounces), cut into 1-inch chunks
2	cups skinless rotisserie chicken, light or dark meat (10 ounces), cut into 1-inch chunks
1/3	cup plain dried bread crumbs
1/4	cup light mayonnaise
1	tablespoon olive oil
2	large whole wheat hamburger buns or Kaiser rolls, split in half

1. Prepare salsa: In food processor with knife blade attached, pulse cilantro until coarsely chopped. Remove ¼ cup chopped cilantro; reserve. Place tomatoes directly on clean gas or electric burner over high heat. With tongs, turn tomatoes frequently as skins burst and blacken, 2 to 3 minutes. Transfer tomatoes as they are done to food processor bowl with cilantro. Add hot pepper sauce and salt. Pulse 4 to 6 times or just until chunky. With rubber spatula, scrape salsa from food processor bowl into small serving bowl. It's okay if some salsa remains in processor bowl. Makes about 1½ cups.

2. To same food processor bowl, add zucchini. Pulse 5 to 6 times or until coarsely chopped. Add chicken, bread crumbs, mayonnaise, and reserved ¼ cup cilantro. Pulse 5 to 6 times or just until well combined (chicken should be chunky). Shape mixture by scant ½ cups into eight 4-inch round patties.

3. In 12-inch nonstick skillet, heat oil over medium heat until very hot. Add chicken cakes; cook, turning once, until golden on both sides, 8 to 10 minutes. Serve 2 chicken cakes on top of each bun half with a heaping ⅓ cup tomato salsa to make a total of 4 open-face sandwiches.

Each serving (2 cakes with salsa and half bun): About 307 calories, 22g protein, 23g carbohydrate, 15g total fat (3g saturated), 3g fiber, 499mg sodium

CHICKEN CAESAR PITAS

Chicken Caesar salad served in whole wheat pitas makes for a terrific sandwich. Healthy and easy, this recipe takes only 20 minutes!

ACTIVE TIME: 10 minutes   **TOTAL TIME**: 20 minutes

MAKES: 4 sandwiches

3	tablespoons olive oil, plus more for pan
3/4	pound chicken breast tenders
1/4	teaspoon salt
1/4	teaspoon ground black pepper
2	tablespoons fresh lemon juice
1	tablespoon red wine vinegar
1	teaspoon Dijon mustard
1	teaspoon anchovy paste (optional)
1	garlic clove, cut in half
4	whole wheat pitas, cut in half
1	heart romaine lettuce, chopped
1/4	cup fresh basil, leaves sliced
1/4	cup freshly grated Parmesan cheese
1	cup grape tomatoes, cut in half

1. Heat ridged grill pan over medium-high heat until hot. Lightly brush with olive oil. Sprinkle chicken tenders with 1/8 teaspoon each salt and pepper. Cook for 6 to 7 minutes, or until chicken is browned and instant-read thermometer inserted into thickest part registers 165°F, turning over once.

2. Transfer chicken to cutting board and let cool completely. While chicken cools, in large bowl, with wire whisk, stir lemon juice, vinegar, mustard, remaining 1/8 teaspoon each salt and pepper, and anchovy paste (if using) until well mixed. Continuing to whisk, add oil in slow, steady stream until incorporated.

3. Rub cut sides of garlic all over insides of pitas; discard garlic. Microwave pitas on high for 15 seconds to soften.

4. Cut chicken into 1-inch pieces. In bowl with dressing, combine lettuce, basil, Parmesan, tomatoes, and chicken, tossing to coat. Divide mixture among pitas.

Each sandwich: About 340 calories, 25g protein, 29g carbohydrate, 15g total fat (3g saturated), 4g fiber, 540mg sodium

MANGO CHICKEN LETTUCE WRAPS

Mango, mint, and jicama add a Latin American zing to these speedy, no-cook chicken wraps.

TOTAL TIME: 20 minutes

MAKES: 4 main-dish servings

1	large ripe mango, peeled and chopped
1	cup finely chopped jicama
½	cup packed fresh mint leaves, finely chopped
¼	cup fresh lime juice
2	tablespoons extra-virgin olive oil
½	teaspoon Asian chili sauce (Sriracha), plus more to taste
¼	teaspoon salt
3	cups coarsely shredded chicken meat (from ½ rotisserie chicken)
12	Boston lettuce leaves

1. In large bowl, combine mango, jicama, mint, lime juice, oil, chili sauce, and salt. Toss well. If making ahead, cover bowl and refrigerate mixture up to overnight.

2. To serve, add chicken to mango mixture; toss to combine. Place 3 lettuce leaves on each serving plate; divide chicken mixture equally among lettuce leaves.

Each serving: About 325 calories, 32g protein, 17g carbohydrate, 15g total fat (3g saturated), 4g fiber, 400mg sodium

GINGERY CHICKEN IN LETTUCE CUPS

An Asian-inspired meal with lean chicken and edamame serves up healthy doses of protein, fiber, and heart-boosting phytochemicals—and few calories.

TOTAL TIME: 30 minutes
MAKES: 4 main-dish servings

3	tablespoons reduced-sodium soy sauce
2	teaspoons grated, peeled fresh ginger
1	teaspoon honey
2	teaspoons Asian sesame oil
1¼	pounds chicken tenders, cut into ¼-inch chunks
1	cup frozen shelled edamame
2	medium stalks celery, chopped
12	large Boston lettuce leaves

1. In cup, combine soy sauce, ginger, and honey. Set aside.

2. In 12-inch nonstick skillet, heat sesame oil over medium heat for 1 minute. Add chicken chunks and cook for 3 minutes, stirring occasionally.

3. Add edamame to chicken in skillet; cook for 2 minutes, stirring occasionally. Stir in celery; cook for 2 minutes longer. Add soy sauce mixture; cook for 1 to 2 minutes or until chicken is cooked through, stirring occasionally to coat chicken with sauce. Makes about 3½ cups.

4. Arrange lettuce leaves on 4 dinner plates. Divide chicken mixture among lettuce leaves, using a generous ¼ cup per leaf. Fold leaves over chicken mixture and eat out of hand.

Each serving: About 260 calories, 40g protein, 9g carbohydrate, 7g total fat (1g saturated), 3g fiber, 565mg sodium

CHICKEN QUESADILLAS WITH AVOCADO SALSA

This tasty Tex-Mex meal calls for lower-fat tortillas and cheese. The splurge: avocado. Though avocados are high in fat, it's mostly the heart-healthy kind; plus, they contain a natural cholesterol reducer.

ACTIVE TIME: 20 minutes   **TOTAL TIME**: 40 minutes
MAKES: 4 quesadillas

2	teaspoons canola oil
1	green onion, thinly sliced
1	large lime
1/4	teaspoon salt
1/8	teaspoon ground black pepper
1	pound boneless skinless thin-sliced chicken breasts, cut into 1-inch-wide strips
4	burrito-size low-fat flour tortillas
3/4	cup reduced-fat shredded Mexican cheese blend (3 ounces)
1/2	avocado, peeled and cut into 1/2-inch pieces
3/4	cup salsa

1. In 12-inch nonstick skillet, heat oil over medium heat for 1 minute. Add green onion and cook for about 6 minutes or until tender, stirring occasionally.

2. Meanwhile, from lime, grate 1 teaspoon peel and squeeze 2 tablespoons juice. Evenly season chicken strips on both sides with lime peel, salt, and pepper.

3. Add chicken to green onion in skillet; cook for 10 minutes or until chicken is no longer pink inside. Transfer to bowl; stir in lime juice.

4. Evenly divide chicken mixture and cheese on half of each tortilla; fold tortillas over to make 4 quesadillas.

5. In same skillet, cook quesadillas over medium heat, in two batches, for 8 minutes per batch or until browned on both sides and heated through. Cut each quesadilla into thirds. Stir avocado into salsa; serve alongside quesadillas.

Each quesadilla: About 400 calories, 36g protein, 30g carbohydrate, 14g total fat (3g saturated), 10g fiber, 884mg sodium

GRILLED ASPARAGUS AND SHIITAKE TACOS

These super-quick vegetarian tacos are the perfect spring dinner.

ACTIVE TIME: 15 minutes   **TOTAL TIME**: 20 minutes
MAKES: 4 servings

3	tablespoons canola oil
4	garlic cloves, crushed with press
1	teaspoon ground chipotle chile
½	teaspoon salt
1	pound asparagus, trimmed
8	ounces shiitake mushrooms, stems discarded
1	bunch green onions, trimmed
8	corn tortillas, warmed
1	cup homemade or prepared guacamole

Lime wedges, cilantro sprigs, and hot sauce, for serving

1. Prepare outdoor grill for direct grilling over medium heat.

2. In large baking dish, combine oil, garlic, ground chipotle, and salt. Add asparagus, shiitakes, and green onions; toss to coat. Grill asparagus for 5 to 6 minutes or until tender and lightly charred, turning occasionally. Grill shiitakes and green onions for 4 to 5 minutes or until lightly charred, turning occasionally. Transfer vegetables to cutting board.

3. Cut asparagus and green onions into 2-inch lengths. Slice shiitakes. Serve with corn tortillas, guacamole, lime wedges, cilantro, and hot sauce.

Each serving: About 350 calories, 7g protein, 36g carbohydrate, 21g total fat (2g saturated), 11g fiber, 445mg sodium

TURKEY BURGERS WITH MINTED YOGURT SAUCE

Pita patties, yogurt, feta, and mint add a taste of Greece to this flavorful but slimmed-down (and heart-healthy) summer favorite.

ACTIVE TIME: 20 minutes   **TOTAL TIME**: 35 minutes
MAKES: 4 burgers

$\frac{1}{2}$	cup plus 2 tablespoons plain fat-free yogurt
2	green onions, green and white parts separated and thinly sliced
$\frac{1}{2}$	cup packed fresh mint leaves, finely chopped
1	pound ground turkey breast meat
$1\frac{1}{2}$	ounces feta cheese, finely crumbled
$1\frac{1}{2}$	teaspoons ground coriander
$\frac{1}{8}$	teaspoon salt
$\frac{1}{8}$	teaspoon ground black pepper
2	whole wheat pitas, cut in half
2	tomatoes, thinly sliced

1. Prepare outdoor grill for covered direct grilling over medium heat.

2. In small bowl, combine $\frac{1}{2}$ cup yogurt, white parts of green onions, and half of chopped mint.

3. In large bowl, with hands, combine turkey, feta, coriander, salt, pepper, green parts of green onions, remaining mint, and remaining yogurt. Mix well, then form into $3\frac{1}{2}$-inch round patties, each $\frac{3}{4}$-inch thick.

4. Place turkey patties on hot grill grate; cover and cook for 12 to 13 minutes or just until meat loses its pink color throughout, turning once. (Burgers should reach an internal temperature of 165°F.) During last 2 minutes of cooking, add pitas to grill. Cook for 2 minutes or until warmed, turning once.

5. Open pitas. Divide burgers, tomato slices, and yogurt sauce among pitas.

Each burger: About 250 calories, 35g protein, 20g carbohydrate, 5g total fat (2g saturated), 4g fiber, 412mg sodium

BBQ BRISKET TACOS

These zesty tacos are definitely worth the wait. Pair them with a chunky salsa or creamy avocado for the perfect finish.

ACTIVE TIME: 15 minutes **TOTAL TIME**: 8 hours 30 minutes

MAKES: 10 servings

1	cup ketchup
3	tablespoons spicy brown mustard
3	tablespoons balsamic vinegar
1	tablespoon Worcestershire sauce
3	garlic cloves, crushed with press
¼	cup Ultimate Rub (see recipe, below)
1	beef brisket (about 3 to 4 pounds), trimmed of excess fat and cut in half
20	corn tortillas, warmed

Cilantro leaves, sliced radishes, lime wedges, and crumbled cotija cheese, for serving

1. Spray bowl of 6- to 8-quart slow cooker with nonstick cooking spray. Add ketchup, mustard, vinegar, Worcestershire sauce, and garlic; whisk to combine.

2. Coat brisket on all sides with Ultimate Rub; add to slow-cooker bowl. Cover and cook on low for 8 hours or until tender but not falling apart.

3. Transfer brisket to cutting board. With two forks, shred meat. Return meat to slow-cooker bowl; stir to coat with sauce.

4. Serve pulled brisket with tortillas and cilantro leaves, radishes, limes, and cheese.

Each serving: About 335 calories, 33g protein, 32g carbohydrate, 9g total fat (3g saturated), 4g fiber, 810mg sodium

ULTIMATE RUB

In medium bowl, stir together **¼ cup brown sugar, 2 tablespoons kosher salt, 2 tablespoons ground coriander, 2 tablespoons ground cumin, 2 tablespoons garlic powder, 1 tablespoon ground ginger, 1 tablespoon smoked paprika, 1 tablespoon black pepper,** and **1 teaspoon ground cinnamon.** Store rub in an airtight container or resealable plastic bag for up to 6 months. Makes scant 1 cup.

TURKEY MEATBALL PITAS

No one need ever know these meatballs are made with turkey instead of beef.

ACTIVE TIME: 20 minutes   **TOTAL TIME**: 30 minutes

MAKES: 5 sandwiches

1	pound ground turkey
2	slices whole-grain bread, chopped
2	tablespoons grated onion
1	large egg white
1½	teaspoons ground cumin
1	teaspoon salt
3	tablespoons water
5	whole wheat pita breads (6-inch)
½	large cucumber, peeled and cut into ¾-inch pieces
1	container (8 ounces) plain nonfat yogurt
2	tablespoons chopped fresh cilantro, or 1 teaspoon dried mint
4	cups thinly sliced romaine lettuce

1. Preheat oven to 425°F. Coat 15½" by 10½" jelly-roll pan with nonstick cooking spray.

2. In large bowl, with hands, mix turkey, bread, onion, egg white, cumin, ¾ teaspoon salt, and water. Wetting hands for easier shaping, form turkey mixture into 25 meatballs. Place meatballs in prepared jelly-roll pan and bake until cooked through (meatballs will not brown), 12 to 15 minutes.

3. Cut about 1 inch from top of each pita; reserve cut-off pieces for another use. Wrap pitas in foil. After meatballs have baked for about 10 minutes, warm pitas in oven until meatballs are done.

4. Meanwhile, in small bowl, mix cucumber, yogurt, cilantro, and remaining ¼ teaspoon salt. To serve, fill pitas with lettuce and meatballs; top with cucumber sauce.

Each sandwich: About 380 calories, 28g protein, 44g carbohydrate, 11g total fat (3g saturated), 5g fiber, 909mg sodium

Eat Your Onions

They may make you weep, but onions (and their brethren leeks, shallots, and garlic, known as alliums) contain sulfur compounds that account for their distinctive flavor and aroma—and their nutritional benefits. They can inhibit the formation of blood clots and reduce the body's production of cholesterol. Studies suggest they may also defend against bacteria, fungi, viruses, and parasites.

ROAST BEEF WALDORF SANDWICHES

Horseradish dressing and a crunchy celery-and-apple mixture make rare roast beef taste even better. Soaking the onions in ice water crisps them and tames their bite.

TOTAL TIME: 20 minutes plus standing

MAKES: 4 sandwiches

4	very thin slices red onion
1/2	Golden Delicious apple, peeled and finely chopped (1/2 cup)
2	stalks celery, finely chopped
4	tablespoons low-fat mayonnaise
2	tablespoons sour cream
1/2	teaspoon fresh lemon juice
1	tablespoon bottled white horseradish
8	slices pumpernickel bread, lightly toasted, if desired
8	ounces thinly sliced rare roast beef
1	bunch watercress (4 ounces), tough stems trimmed

1. In small bowl, combine onion with enough ice water to cover; let stand for 15 minutes. Drain.

2. In separate small bowl, combine apple, celery, 2 tablespoons mayonnaise, 1 tablespoon sour cream, and lemon juice until well blended. In cup, combine remaining 2 tablespoons mayonnaise, remaining 1 tablespoon sour cream, and horseradish until blended.

3. Spread horseradish mixture evenly on 4 bread slices. Layer roast beef, onion, and watercress on top. Spread celery mixture evenly on remaining 4 bread slices and invert onto sandwiches. To serve, cut sandwiches in half.

Each sandwich: About 295 calories, 22g protein, 40g carbohydrate, 7g total fat (3g saturated), 5g fiber, 726mg sodium

MEATLOAF BURGERS WITH SAUTÉED CARROTS

Here's a kid-pleasing meal: Meatloaf patties on hamburger buns with sautéed baby carrots on the side.

ACTIVE TIME: 15 minutes   **TOTAL TIME**: 25 minutes
MAKES: 4 burgers

1/2	cup water	1	tablespoon spicy brown mustard
1	tablespoon butter or margarine	1 1/4	pounds lean (90%) ground beef
1	bag (16 ounces) baby carrots	1	stalk celery, finely chopped
1/2	teaspoon salt	1/2	small onion, finely chopped
1/4	teaspoon freshly ground black pepper	1/4	cup plain dried bread crumbs
1	tablespoon brown sugar	1	garlic clove, crushed with press
Nonstick cooking spray		2	teaspoons Worcestershire sauce
1/4	cup ketchup	4	potato rolls, split and toasted
		4	lettuce leaves

1. In 12-inch skillet, heat water and butter over medium heat until simmering. Add carrots, 1/4 teaspoon salt, and 1/4 teaspoon pepper; cook, covered, for 10 minutes or until carrots are tender. Uncover; stir in sugar and cook for 3 minutes or until carrots are coated and liquid evaporates. Remove from heat; cover and keep warm.

2. Meanwhile, lightly spray ridged grill pan with nonstick cooking spray, then heat over medium heat until hot.

3. In cup, combine ketchup and mustard. In large bowl, mix 1 tablespoon ketchup mixture with beef, celery, onion, bread crumbs, garlic, Worcestershire, and remaining 1/4 teaspoon salt until blended, but do not overmix. Shape beef mixture into four 3/4-inch-thick patties, handling meat as little as possible for best texture.

4. Place burgers in hot grill pan; cook for 10 to 12 minutes for medium or until desired doneness, turning over once halfway through cooking. (Instant-read thermometer inserted horizontally into center of patties should register 160°F.)

5. Serve burgers on rolls with lettuce and remaining ketchup mixture. Serve carrots on the side.

Each burger: About 505 calories, 36g protein, 52g carbohydrate, 18g total fat (5g saturated), 6g fiber, 975mg sodium

STEAK SANDWICHES WITH GRILLED ONIONS

Marinating the steak with a delicious blend of Asian flavors and then grilling it takes this classic sandwich to a new level.

ACTIVE TIME: 15 minutes   **TOTAL TIME**: 30 minutes plus marinating

MAKES: 4 sandwiches

¼	cup reduced-sodium soy sauce	1	medium red onion (about 8 ounces), cut into 4 thick slices
¼	cup balsamic vinegar		
1	tablespoon brown sugar	8	slices multigrain bread, toasted on grill, if desired
1	teaspoon fresh thyme leaves		
¼	teaspoon ground black pepper	2	ripe medium tomatoes (6 to 8 ounces each), sliced
1	beef flank steak (about 1¼ pounds)	1	bunch (5 ounces) arugula, trimmed
1	(12-inch) metal skewer		

1. In large zip-tight plastic bag, mix soy sauce, vinegar, brown sugar, thyme, and pepper. Add steak, turning to coat. Seal bag, pressing out excess air. Place bag on plate; let marinate for 15 minutes at room temperature or for 1 hour in the refrigerator, turning several times.

2. Prepare outdoor grill for covered direct grilling over medium heat.

3. Meanwhile, for easier handling, insert skewer horizontally through onion slices; set aside.

4. Remove steak from marinade; pour marinade into 1-quart saucepan. Heat over high heat until boiling; boil for 2 minutes.

5. Place steak and onion slices on hot grill rack. Cover grill and cook steak and onions, brushing both with marinade occasionally and turning over once, until onions are browned and tender and meat is medium-rare, 12 to 15 minutes. Transfer steak to cutting board; let stand for 10 minutes to allow juices to set for easier slicing. Separate onions into rings.

6. Thinly slice steak diagonally across grain. Arrange onion rings and steak on 4 slices of bread; spoon any meat juices from board over onion and steak. Top with tomatoes, arugula, and remaining slices of bread.

Each sandwich: About 450 calories, 40g protein, 51g carbohydrate, 10g total fat (4g saturated), 4g fiber, 802mg sodium

SPIN

This classic

ACTIVE TIM
MAKES: 8 m

1	recip
1	teas
1	sma
1	teas
1	pac (see
¼	teas
1	cup
2	ou
12	Ka

1. Prepa

2. In sm
5 minute

3. Sprea
with cru
browne

Each serv
4g fiber,

TIP

To
spir
ju
a
plo
si
Pr
o

QUI
PIZ

Use this
whole v
your ne
will sell

TOTAL
MAKES

1¼
1¼
1
1
1
2

1. Sif
2 cup
come

2. T
8 mi
doug

3. G
pan,

BROCCOLI-MUSHROOM PIZZA

Veggies make this pizza healthy—and melted cheese makes it delicious!

ACTIVE TIME: 20 minutes plus time to make dough   **TOTAL TIME**: 40 minutes
MAKES: 8 main-dish servings

1	recipe Quick Homemade Pizza Dough (see recipe, page 196)
1	tablespoon light corn-oil spread (56% to 60% fat)
1	package (16 ounces) mushrooms, sliced
1	large garlic clove, crushed with press
1	package (16 ounces) broccoli florets
¼	teaspoon salt
½	cup tomato sauce
½	cup packed basil leaves, chopped
1	cup shredded part-skim mozzarella or Monterey Jack cheese

1. Prepare Quick Homemade Pizza Dough.

2. Preheat oven to 450°F.

3. In 12-inch nonstick skillet, melt corn-oil spread over medium-high heat. Add mushrooms and garlic; cook until mushrooms are golden. Meanwhile, in 10-inch skillet, heat 1 inch water to boiling over high heat. Place steamer basket in skillet; add broccoli. Reduce heat to medium; cover and steam until tender.

4. Remove broccoli; add to mushrooms with salt and toss well to mix.

5. Spread dough with tomato sauce and spoon broccoli mixture on top. Sprinkle with basil and cheese. Bake for 20 to 25 minutes.

Each serving: About 220 calories, 12g protein, 36g carbohydrate, 4g total fat (2g saturated), 4g fiber, 542mg sodium

Eat Your Broccoli

A super source of vitamins C and K (one cup cooked has more than a day's worth of each), broccoli also can help ward off cancer. Sulforaphane, one of its compounds, disarms cancer-causing substances.

APPLE-BRIE PIZZA WITH CARAMELIZED ONIONS

With these grandma-style slices baked on a sheet pan, everyone gets his or her favorite—from extra-crusty corners to topping-loaded middles.

ACTIVE TIME: 20 minutes   **TOTAL TIME:** 1 hour
MAKES: 8 main-dish servings

1	tablespoon olive oil
2	large sweet onions, thinly sliced
1	pound fresh or frozen (thawed) pizza dough
1	small Gala or Empire apple, thinly sliced
4	ounces Brie, thinly sliced
1	tablespoon balsamic vinegar

Fresh basil leaves, for garnish

1. In 12-inch skillet, heat oil on medium. Add onions and ¼ teaspoon salt. Cover and cook 15 minutes or until golden brown and almost tender, stirring occasionally.

2. Preheat oven to 475°F. Spread onions on dough and bake for 15 minutes. Top with apple and Brie and bake an additional 20 minutes or until crust is golden brown. Sprinkle with ½ teaspoon pepper and drizzle with vinegar. Garnish with basil.

Each serving: About 405 calories, 10g protein, 52g carbohydrate, 18g total fat (4g saturated), 3g fiber, 530mg sodium

GRILLED WHOLE WHEAT VEGGIE PIZZA

Everyone's favorite takeout gets a low-cal, high-fiber makeover with a heap of veggies—sweetened by a turn on the grill—a whole wheat crust, and a sprinkle of cheese.

ACTIVE TIME: 25 minutes   **TOTAL TIME**: 30 minutes
MAKES: 4 main-dish servings

2	medium portobello mushroom caps, sliced	1/4	teaspoon pepper
1	small red onion (4 to 6 ounces), sliced into rounds	1	pound whole wheat pizza dough (see Tip)
1	small yellow summer squash, sliced	2	plum tomatoes, thinly sliced
1	tablespoon olive oil	1/2	cup shredded smoked mozzarella cheese (2 ounces)
1/4	teaspoon salt	1/4	cup packed fresh basil leaves, sliced

1. Prepare outdoor grill for covered direct grilling over medium heat. Brush mushrooms, onion, and squash with oil; sprinkle with salt and pepper.

2. Grill vegetables, covered, for 6 minutes or until tender and browned, turning once. Remove from grill and separate onion rings; set aside. Reduce heat on grill to medium-low.

3. Cover large cookie sheet with foil; spray with cooking spray. Stretch dough into 10″ by 14″ rectangle. Place on cookie sheet.

4. Lift dough and foil; place dough-side down on grill, gently peeling off foil. Cover grill; cook for 3 minutes or until bottom is crisp. Turn crust over. Quickly top with tomatoes, vegetables, and cheese. Cover again; cook for 2 minutes longer or until bottom is crisp. Slide onto cutting board; garnish with basil.

Each serving: About 375 calories, 13g protein, 58g carbohydrate, 10g total fat (2g saturated), 9g fiber, 695mg sodium

TIP
You can purchase whole wheat dough, ready to roll out and bake, at a neighborhood pizza shop and some supermarkets.

Swordfish with Summer Salad (page 244)

5 | FISH & SHELLFISH

If your goal is to eat lighter and healthier, seafood should make regular appearances on your dinner menu. It's naturally low in fat and is a rich source of protein, vitamins, and minerals. And oily fish, such as salmon and tuna, are high in omega-3 fatty acids, which can lower blood cholesterol levels. So consider giving the chicken breasts and red meat a rest a couple of nights a week and replacing them with salmon, cod, or shrimp. You and your family will be enjoying a healthier, more varied diet.

If you're someone who orders fish in restaurants but rarely prepares it at home, this chapter brimming with simple, flavorful recipes will inspire you to make fish yourself. Keep frozen shrimp in the freezer and you can cook up our Shrimp and Zucchini Scampi, a shrimp and veggie risotto, or a handful of tasty stir-fries in a jiffy. If your kids like fish sticks, then they'll love our island-spiced version rolled in panko crumbs and baked in the oven until crisp and ready for dipping in a low-fat lime mayo.

Dinners like our Snapper Livornese can be quickly prepared in a pan, while Asian-style flounder is wrapped in parchment paper and baked in the oven. Pan-roasted cod sits on a bed of red cabbage and apples, while pan-seared scallops top a pile of lemony couscous.

These recipes use readily available options, but if you can't locate the fish or shellfish called for in a recipe, just ask your fishmonger for the best substitution. Many fish can be easily swapped for other varieties with equally good results.

MUSSELS WITH TOMATOES AND WHITE WINE

To enjoy every last drop, serve this saucy dish with crusty bread—or a spoon.

ACTIVE TIME: 20 minutes   **TOTAL TIME**: 45 minutes

MAKES: 8 first-course or 4 main-dish servings

1	tablespoon olive or vegetable oil	¾	cup dry white wine
1	small onion, chopped	4	pounds large mussels, scrubbed and debearded (see Tip)
2	garlic cloves, finely chopped		
¼	teaspoon crushed red pepper	2	tablespoons chopped fresh parsley
1	can (14 to 16 ounces) whole tomatoes		

1. In nonreactive 5-quart Dutch oven, heat oil over medium heat. Add onion and cook until tender and golden, 6 to 8 minutes. Add garlic and crushed red pepper and cook for 30 seconds longer. Stir in tomatoes with their juice and wine, breaking up tomatoes with side of spoon. Heat to boiling; boil for 3 minutes.

2. Add mussels; heat to boiling. Reduce heat; cover and simmer until mussels open, about 5 minutes, transferring mussels to large bowl as they open. Discard any mussels that have not opened after 5 minutes. Pour tomato sauce over mussels and sprinkle with parsley.

Each first-course serving: About 105 calories, 9g protein, 6g carbohydrate, 3g total fat (1g saturated), 1g fiber, 277mg sodium

MOULES À LA MARINIÈRE

Prepare Mussels with Tomatoes and White Wine as directed, but substitute **butter** for olive oil and ⅓ **cup chopped shallots** for onion. Omit crushed red pepper and tomatoes; use 1½ **cups dry white wine**.

TIP
Scrub mussels well under cold running water. To debeard, grasp the hairlike beard firmly with your thumb and forefinger and pull it away, or scrape it off with a knife. (Cultivated mussels usually do not have beards.)

SHRIMP AND ZUCCHINI SCAMPI

Looking for a super-quick dinner? This one, ready in just 20 minutes, is tough to beat.

TOTAL TIME: 20 minutes
MAKES: 6 servings

1	pound linguine
1½	tablespoons olive oil
1½	pounds shrimp, peeled and deveined
2	medium zucchini, sliced
4	garlic cloves, chopped
3	tablespoons butter
¾	cup white wine
⅛	teaspoon salt
2	teaspoons grated lemon peel

Chopped parsley, for garnish

1. Cook pasta as label directs; reserve ¼ cup cooking water before draining.

2. In 12-inch skillet, heat oil over medium-high heat; add shrimp and cook for 3 minutes or until cooked through, turning once. Transfer shrimp to plate.

3. To same skillet, add zucchini, garlic, and butter; cook for 3 minutes. Add wine and salt; cook for 2 minutes, stirring and scraping bits from bottom of pan. Remove from heat.

4. Return shrimp to skillet along with cooked pasta, cooking water, and lemon peel; garnish with parsley.

Each serving: About 460 calories, 31g protein, 60g carbohydrate, 11g total fat (5g saturated), 3g fiber, 216mg sodium

SHRIMP AND ASPARAGUS STIR-FRY

Flavored with ginger, soy, and sesame, this entreé is rich in vitamins and minerals (thanks to brown rice and asparagus).

ACTIVE TIME: 15 minutes **TOTAL TIME**: 30 minutes

MAKES: 4 main-dish servings

1	cup quick-cooking (10-minute) brown rice	1	tablespoon grated, peeled fresh ginger
3	teaspoons Asian sesame oil	2	tablespoons reduced-sodium soy sauce
1½	pounds asparagus, trimmed and cut into 1-inch pieces	2	tablespoons fresh lime juice
1	pound medium shrimp, peeled and deveined	¼	cup loosely packed fresh basil leaves, thinly sliced

1. Cook rice as label directs.

2. Meanwhile, in 12-inch nonstick skillet, heat 2 teaspoons sesame oil over medium heat for 1 minute. Add asparagus and cook for 7 to 8 minutes or until asparagus is tender-crisp, stirring occasionally. Add shrimp and ginger; cook for 5 to 6 minutes or until shrimp are opaque throughout, stirring occasionally.

3. Stir in soy sauce, lime juice, basil, and remaining 1 teaspoon sesame oil; remove from heat. Serve over rice.

Each serving: About 265 calories, 29g protein, 22g carbohydrate, 7g total fat (1g saturated), 2g fiber, 455mg sodium

Frozen Shrimp to the Rescue

With just fewer than 2 grams of fat in a 4-ounce serving, shrimp should be a health-conscious eater's go-to seafood. Although fresh shrimp can be expensive, frozen shrimp, available at wholesale food clubs and larger supermarkets, is a bargain. Because it is flash-frozen for easy transport, the flavor and texture are preserved. Keep some on hand in the freezer and it will be a snap to whip up low-fat stir-fries, pastas, and main-dish salads.

SPRING VEGETABLE RISOTTO WITH SHRIMP

Made in the microwave, this creamy dish—full of fiber, protein, and rich Parmesan flavor—is as healthy as it is easy.

ACTIVE TIME: 10 minutes **TOTAL TIME**: 35 minutes

MAKES: 10 cups or 6 main-dish servings

1	carton (32 ounces) chicken broth (4 cups)	2	cups Arborio or Carnaroli rice (short-grain Italian rice)
1¼	cups water	1	pound large shrimp, peeled and deveined
½	cup dry white wine		
8	ounces asparagus, cut into 1-inch pieces	1	cup frozen peas
		2	tablespoons fresh lemon juice
1	tablespoon olive oil	1	tablespoon chopped fresh parsley or basil leaves
1	small onion (4 to 6 ounces), finely chopped		
		¼	teaspoon salt
1	carrot, peeled and finely chopped	¼	teaspoon ground black pepper

1. In 2-quart saucepan, heat broth, water, and wine to boiling over high heat. When boiling, add asparagus and cook for 2 minutes. With slotted spoon, remove asparagus to small bowl; set aside.

2. Meanwhile, in microwave-safe 4-quart bowl or casserole, combine oil, onion, and carrot. Cook, uncovered, in microwave on high for 3 minutes or until vegetables begin to soften. Add rice and stir to coat with oil; cook, uncovered, on high for 1 minute.

3. Stir hot broth mixture into rice mixture. Cover bowl with vented plastic wrap, and cook in microwave on medium for 15 minutes or until most of liquid is absorbed and rice is tender but still firm, stirring halfway through cooking.

4. Add shrimp, frozen peas, and cooked asparagus; cover and cook in microwave on high for 3 to 4 minutes longer or just until shrimp lose their pink color throughout. Do not overcook; mixture will look loose and soupy but will soon thicken to the proper creamy consistency.

5. Stir in lemon juice, parsley, salt, and pepper.

Each serving: About 425 calories, 24g protein, 67g carbohydrate, 4g total fat (1g saturated), 3g fiber, 545mg sodium

CARAMELIZED CHILE SHRIMP

Thanks to a trio of insta-ingredients—peeled shrimp, thin vermicelli, and bagged broccoli—this streamlined seafood stir-fry is an ideal low-fat meal on time-is-tight nights.

ACTIVE TIME: 15 minutes **TOTAL TIME**: 25 minutes
MAKES: 4 main-dish servings

6	ounces rice stick noodles	3	garlic cloves, very thinly sliced
1	pound broccoli florets	1/4	teaspoon crushed red pepper
1	green onion, finely chopped	1	tablespoon reduced-sodium Asian fish sauce
1/4	teaspoon salt		
3	tablespoons granulated sugar	1	pound jumbo shrimp, peeled and deveined
1	tablespoon water		
1	tablespoon vegetable oil	1/4	cup packed fresh cilantro leaves
		1/4	teaspoon ground black pepper

1. In heavy 12-inch skillet, heat at least 1 inch water to boiling over high heat. Add noodles and cook for 1 to 2 minutes or until just tender. With tongs, transfer noodles to fine-mesh sieve. Rinse under cold water and drain.

2. When water in skillet returns to boiling, add broccoli. Cook for 3 minutes or until tender-crisp; drain and transfer to large bowl. Toss with green onion and salt. Wipe skillet dry.

3. In same skillet, cook sugar and water over medium-high (stirring just until sugar dissolves) for 3 to 4 minutes or until mixture turns dark amber. Stir in oil, garlic, and red pepper. Cook for 10 seconds, then stir in fish sauce and shrimp.

4. Cook for 2 to 3 minutes or until shrimp just turn opaque throughout, stirring frequently. Remove from heat, and stir in cilantro and black pepper.

5. Evenly divide noodles and broccoli among four dinner plates. Spoon shrimp with chile sauce on top of noodles.

Each serving: About 340 calories, 22g protein, 53g carbohydrate, 5g total fat (1g saturated), 4g fiber, 600mg sodium

"BBQ" SALMON AND BRUSSELS BAKE

This smoky-and-sweet seafood dinner can be roasted in (and served on!) a single sheet pan—making for the quickest, easiest cleanup ever.

ACTIVE TIME: 20 minutes   **TOTAL TIME**: 40 minutes

MAKES: 6 servings

2	tablespoons brown sugar
1	teaspoon garlic powder
1	teaspoon onion powder
1	teaspoon smoked paprika
3	tablespoons olive oil
1¼	pounds Brussels sprouts, trimmed and halved
1¼	teaspoons salt
¼	teaspoon ground black pepper
1	side of salmon (about 3½ pounds)

Snipped chives, for garnish

1. Preheat oven to 450°F. Line large rimmed baking sheet with foil. In small bowl, stir together brown sugar, garlic powder, onion powder, smoked paprika, and 2 tablespoons oil.

2. On another large rimmed baking sheet, toss Brussels sprouts with remaining 1 tablespoon oil, ¼ teaspoon salt, and pepper. Roast sprouts for 5 minutes.

3. Meanwhile, cut salmon into 10 fillets; arrange skin-side down on prepared baking sheet. Brush rub all over salmon; sprinkle with 1 teaspoon salt. Roast salmon with Brussels sprouts for 15 minutes or until sprouts are tender and salmon is just cooked through, stirring sprouts once halfway through roasting. Reserve 4 smaller salmon fillets for another use. Serve remaining salmon with Brussels sprouts; garnish with chives.

Each serving: About 280 calories, 35g protein, 11g carbohydrate, 11g total fat (2g saturated), 3g fiber, 380mg sodium

GREEK-STYLE TILAPIA

This healthy Mediterranean fish dish is ready in just 30 minutes.

ACTIVE TIME: 20 minutes   **TOTAL TIME**: 30 minutes
MAKES: 4 main-dish servings

2	lemons
1½	pounds tilapia fillets
1	tablespoon fresh oregano leaves, chopped, plus sprigs for garnish
¼	teaspoon salt
¼	teaspoon ground black pepper
1	pint grape tomatoes, cut lengthwise in half
8	ounces orzo

1. Preheat oven to 400°F. From lemons, grate ½ teaspoon peel and squeeze ¼ cup juice.

2. In 13" by 9" glass or ceramic baking dish, arrange tilapia fillets. Evenly sprinkle fillets with lemon juice and peel, chopped oregano, salt, and pepper. Add tomatoes to baking dish around tilapia; cover with foil and roast for 16 to 18 minutes or until tilapia is opaque throughout and tomatoes are tender.

3. Meanwhile, heat covered 4-quart saucepan of salted water to boiling over high heat. Add orzo and cook as label directs. Drain well.

4. Serve tilapia, tomatoes, and orzo with juices from baking dish.

Each serving: About 395 calories, 36g protein, 50g carbohydrate, 6g total fat (0g saturated), 2g fiber, 310mg sodium

ALMOND-CRUSTED CREOLE SALMON

This dish is just as tasty with finely chopped pistachios or pecans instead of sliced almonds.

TOTAL TIME: 20 minutes
MAKES: 4 servings

1	pound green beans, trimmed
1	tablespoon olive oil
¼	teaspoon salt
¼	teaspoon ground black pepper
⅓	cup plain nonfat Greek yogurt
2	teaspoons Creole seasoning
1	teaspoon grated lemon peel
4	skinless salmon fillets (6 ounces each)
¼	cup sliced almonds, coarsely chopped

1. Preheat oven to 450°F. Line large rimmed baking sheet with foil. In large bowl, toss green beans with oil, salt, and pepper. Arrange on prepared baking sheet and bake for 10 minutes.

2. In small bowl, stir together Greek yogurt, Creole seasoning, and lemon peel. Spread onto each salmon fillet and sprinkle chopped almonds on top. Push beans to one side of baking sheet; place salmon on other side. Spray salmon with cooking spray. Bake for 12 minutes or until salmon is cooked through and beans are tender.

Each serving: About 310 calories, 39g protein, 9g carbohydrate, 13g total fat (2g saturated), 4g fiber, 540mg sodium

Get Your Omega-3s

One type of polyunsaturated fat, omega-3, is thought to combat heart disease. Omega-3s help inhibit the formation of blood clots and reduce the incidence of heartbeat abnormalities. You'll find omega-3s in fish—and the oilier the fish, the more omega-3 it contains. So, be sure to include oily fish like salmon, bluefin tuna, mackerel, and sardines in your diet once a week.

SNAPPER LIVORNESE

Vibrant with olives, capers, and basil, this preparation works beautifully with any lean white fish.

ACTIVE TIME: 10 minutes   **TOTAL TIME**: 30 minutes
MAKES: 4 main-dish servings

1 tablespoon olive oil	1/8 teaspoon salt
1 garlic clove, finely chopped	1/2 cup fresh basil leaves, thinly sliced
1 can (14½ ounces) diced tomatoes	1/4 cup Kalamata or Gaeta olives, pitted and coarsely chopped
1/8 teaspoon crushed red pepper	
4 red snapper or flounder fillets (6 ounces each)	2 teaspoons capers, drained

1. In 12-inch nonstick skillet, heat oil over medium heat until hot. Add garlic and cook for 1 minute, stirring. Stir in tomatoes with their juice and crushed red pepper; heat to boiling over medium-high heat. Reduce heat to low and simmer, uncovered, for 8 to 10 minutes or until mixture thickens slightly.

2. Meanwhile, with tweezers, remove any bones from snapper fillets.

3. Place fillets, skin-side down, in tomato mixture in skillet; sprinkle with salt. Cover and cook for 8 to 10 minutes or just until fish turns opaque throughout.

4. With wide slotted spatula, transfer snapper to warm platter. Stir basil, olives, and capers into tomato mixture; spoon over snapper.

Each serving: About 250 calories, 36g protein, 6g carbohydrate, 8g total fat (1g saturated), 1g fiber, 571mg sodium

The Drill on Oil

Wondering which oil to use tonight? Olive oil is still a winner. It has big flavor, which means you can use less for more taste with fewer calories. And since olive oil is a predominantly monounsaturated fat, it's heart-healthy as well. When you're looking for more neutral-tasting oil at a reasonable price, canola oil is a standout. Not only is it rich in monounsaturated fat, it contains the plant version of an omega-3 fatty acid. Specialty oils—like grape seed, sesame, and walnut—are healthful but expensive, so use them in small quantities for an epicurean touch.

ISLAND-SPICED FISH STICKS

Turn cod fillets into spicy fish sticks, using thyme, allspice, a jalapeño chile pepper, and a coating of panko bread crumbs. Bake them in the oven for a low-fat finish.

ACTIVE TIME: 20 minutes   **TOTAL TIME:** 30 minutes plus chilling
MAKES: 4 main-dish servings

Nonstick olive oil cooking spray

2	limes
2	green onions, light and dark green parts only
1/4	cup packed fresh parsley leaves
1/2	jalapeño chile, seeds removed
1	teaspoon fresh thyme leaves
1/4	teaspoon ground allspice
1/2	teaspoon plus 1/8 teaspoon salt
1	large egg white
1	pound skinless cod fillet
3/4	cup panko (Japanese-style bread crumbs)
2	tablespoons light mayonnaise
2	tablespoons reduced-fat sour cream
1	bag (5 to 6 ounces) baby spinach

1. Lightly coat baking sheet with nonstick cooking spray. From 1 lime, grate 1 teaspoon peel and squeeze 2 teaspoons juice. In small bowl, place juice and 1/2 teaspoon peel. Finely chop 1 tablespoon green onion and add to bowl with lime juice; set aside. Cut remaining green onions into large pieces.

2. In food processor with knife blade attached, place parsley, jalapeño, thyme, allspice, green onion pieces, 1/2 teaspoon salt, and remaining 1/2 teaspoon lime peel. Pulse until finely chopped.

3. In medium bowl, lightly beat egg white; set aside. Remove and discard any bones from cod and cut into 2-inch chunks. Place in food processor with green-onion mixture; pulse just until cod is coarsely chopped. Transfer cod mixture and 2 tablespoons panko to bowl with egg white; stir until well combined.

4. On large sheet of waxed paper, place remaining panko. With measuring cup, scoop out heaping 1/4 cup cod mixture (mixture will be soft); shape by hand into

3″ by 1¹/₂″ stick (about 1-inch thick), then place in panko, patting gently to cover all sides. Place fish stick on prepared baking sheet. Repeat, forming 8 fish sticks in all. Cover loosely; refrigerate for at least 30 minutes or for up to 1 day.

5. Meanwhile, preheat oven to 450°F. Into bowl with lime juice mixture, stir mayonnaise, sour cream, and remaining ¹/₈ teaspoon salt until well blended. If not using right away, cover and refrigerate for up to 1 day. Makes about ¹/₃ cup dipping sauce.

6. Lightly spray fish with cooking spray; bake for 10 to 13 minutes or until opaque throughout. Cut remaining lime into wedges. Arrange spinach on plates; top with fish. Serve with sauce and lime wedges on the side.

Each serving: About 190 calories, 24g protein, 12g carbohydrate, 5g total fat (1g saturated), 5g fiber, 585mg sodium

BAKED SNAPPER WITH PEPPERS AND MUSHROOMS

This fast fish is ultra-low in fat and calories but still bursts with flavor. Sweet peppers and mushrooms are sautéed in white wine and fresh thyme, then baked with the fillets. A squeeze of lemon juice further brightens the flavors.

ACTIVE TIME: 20 minutes   **TOTAL TIME**: 35 minutes

MAKES: 6 main-dish servings

1	tablespoon olive oil
2	orange and/or yellow peppers, thinly sliced
1	onion, chopped
1	package (10 ounces) sliced mushrooms
$1/2$	cup dry white wine
1	teaspoon fresh thyme leaves, chopped, plus more for garnish
Nonstick cooking spray	
6	boneless skinless snapper, sole, or flounder fillets (4 ounces each)
2	tablespoons fresh lemon juice
$1/4$	teaspoon salt
$1/4$	teaspoon ground black pepper

1. Preheat oven to 450°F. In 12-inch skillet, heat oil over medium heat. Add peppers and onion and cook for 10 minutes or until tender, stirring often. Add mushrooms, wine, and thyme; increase heat to medium-high and cook for 3 minutes, stirring frequently.

2. Meanwhile, spray 13" by 9" glass or ceramic baking dish with cooking spray. Arrange fillets in baking dish, folding narrow ends under. Sprinkle with lemon juice, salt, and pepper.

3. Spoon hot vegetable mixture on top of fish. Bake for 15 to 18 minutes or until opaque throughout. (An instant-read thermometer inserted horizontally into center of fish should register 145°F.) Garnish with additional thyme leaves.

Each serving: About 175 calories, 26g protein, 9g carbohydrate, 4g total fat (1g saturated), 2g fiber, 175mg sodium

PAN-ROASTED COD ON CABBAGE AND APPLES

Light and easy to prepare, this fish dinner showcases the cool-weather flavors of tart apple and caraway-scented sautéed cabbage.

ACTIVE TIME: 12 minutes   **TOTAL TIME**: 20 minutes
MAKES: 4 main-dish servings

2	tablespoons butter or margarine
1	small head red cabbage (1¼ pounds), cored and thinly sliced
1	pound Granny Smith or Gala apples (2 to 3 medium), cored and cut into ½-inch chunks
2	tablespoons water
1	tablespoon cider vinegar
½	teaspoon caraway seeds
½	teaspoon salt
4	cod or scrod fillets (6 ounces each)
¼	teaspoon coarsely ground black pepper

1. In deep 12-inch nonstick skillet, melt butter over medium-high heat. Stir in cabbage, apples, water, vinegar, caraway seeds, and ¼ teaspoon salt. Reduce heat to medium; cover skillet and cook cabbage mixture for 8 minutes or until cabbage begins to wilt, stirring occasionally.

2. Top cabbage mixture with cod, folding thin tail end under for even cooking. Sprinkle cod with remaining ¼ teaspoon salt and pepper. Cover skillet and cook for about 10 minutes or until cod turns opaque throughout.

Each serving: About 290 calories, 32g protein, 25g carbohydrate, 8g total fat (1g saturated), 5g fiber, 470mg sodium

ROASTED HALIBUT WITH FENNEL AND POTATOES

Popular brands of anise-flavored liqueur include Pernod and Ricard. A jigger of these spirits subtly enhances the natural licorice flavor found in fennel.

ACTIVE TIME: 15 minutes   **TOTAL TIME**: 1 hour

MAKES: 4 main-dish servings

1	large leek
Nonstick cooking spray	
1	pound Yukon Gold potatoes, unpeeled and thinly sliced
1	medium bulb fennel, cored and thinly sliced, or 4 stalks celery, thinly sliced
1	tablespoon plus 1 teaspoon extra-virgin olive oil
3/4	teaspoon salt
3/8	teaspoon ground black pepper
4	pieces skinless halibut fillet (6 ounces each)
2	tablespoons anise-flavored liqueur or white wine
1	teaspoon fennel seeds
1	lemon, thinly sliced
Fennel fronds (optional)	

1. Cut off roots and trim dark-green top from leek. Discard any tough outer leaves. Thinly slice leek. Rinse leek thoroughly in bowl of cold water; swish to remove any sand. With hands, transfer leek to colander, leaving sand in bottom of bowl. Drain well.

2. Preheat oven to 425°F. Spray 13" by 9" glass baking dish with nonstick cooking spray. To baking dish, add leek, potatoes, fennel, 1 tablespoon oil, 1/2 teaspoon salt, and 1/4 teaspoon pepper; toss to coat, then spread evenly. Roast vegetables for 35 minutes or until tender, stirring once halfway through roasting.

3. Remove baking dish from oven. Place halibut on vegetables; drizzle with liqueur and remaining 1 teaspoon oil. Sprinkle with fennel seeds, 1/4 teaspoon salt, and 1/8 teaspoon pepper. Place lemon slices on halibut; return dish to oven and roast for 10 to 12 minutes or just until halibut turns opaque in center. To serve, sprinkle with fennel fronds, if using.

Each serving: About 365 calories, 39g protein, 33g carbohydrate, 9g total fat (1g saturated), 6g fiber, 570mg sodium

ASIAN-STYLE FLOUNDER BAKED IN PARCHMENT

Baking in parchment packets is a simple nonfat way to seal in the juices and flavor of delicate fish. You can substitute aluminum foil for the parcheat paper.

TOTAL TIME: 25 minutes
MAKES: 4 main-dish servings

2	large green onions
2	tablespoons soy sauce
2	tablespoons seasoned rice vinegar
4	flounder fillets (6 ounces each)
4	sheets cooking parchment or foil (12" by 16" each, folded in half to 12" by 8")
2	teaspoons grated, peeled fresh ginger

1. Preheat oven to 425°F. Cut green onion tops into 2″ by ¼″ strips; reserve for garnish. Thinly slice white part of green onions.

2. In cup, combine soy sauce and vinegar.

3. Place 1 flounder fillet on one side of each opened parchment sheet. Sprinkle with ginger and sliced green onions; drizzle with soy mixture. Fold parchment over fish; beginning at a corner where parchment is folded, make ½-inch-wide folds, overlapping previous folds, until packet is completely sealed. Packet will resemble half circle. Place packets in jelly-roll pan. Bake for 8 minutes (packets will puff up and brown).

4. To serve, cut packets open and garnish fish with reserved green-onion strips.

Each serving: About 170 calories, 33g protein, 3g carbohydrate, 2g total fat (0g saturated), 0g fiber, 802mg sodium

LEMONY CRAB LINGUINE

This light, zesty seafood pasta dish is perfect for time-crunched weeknights; it takes only 20 minutes to prepare, but tastes like it was cooking all day.

TOTAL TIME: 20 minutes
MAKES: 4 servings

1	pound linguine
¼	cup olive oil
3	garlic cloves, thinly sliced
1	tablespoon fresh thyme
8	ounces lump crabmeat

Zest and juice of 1 lemon

½	teaspoon salt
½	teaspoon ground black pepper
⅓	cup sliced pickled peppers

Lemon wedges, for serving

1. In large pot of boiling salted water, cook linguine; before draining, reserve ¼ cup cooking water.

2. In 12-inch nonstick skillet, heat oil over medium heat; add garlic and thyme and cook for 3 minutes, stirring. Add crabmeat, lemon zest and juice, salt, and pepper and cook, stirring often.

3. Toss crab mixture with linguine; add reserved pasta water and peppers and combine. Serve with lemon wedges.

Each serving: About 485 calories, 22g protein, 66g carbohydrate, 15g total fat (2g saturated), 3g fiber, 600mg sodium

TIP

If you can't find crabmeat, no problem—you can sauté a pound of shrimp with the garlic and thyme instead.

TUNA AU POIVRE WITH LEMON-CAPER LENTILS

Lean tuna replaces fattier beef loin steak in this favorite, while a surprise side of lentils—instead of the expected calorie-laden French fries—adds an earthy boost of fiber.

ACTIVE TIME: 10 minutes   **TOTAL TIME**: 35 minutes
MAKES: 4 main-dish servings

2³/₄	cups water
1¹/₃	cups green lentils
1	teaspoon salt
4	tuna steaks, 1-inch thick (6 ounces each)
4	teaspoons cracked black peppercorns
1	tablespoon olive oil
1	medium shallot, finely chopped
1	cup reduced-sodium chicken broth
1	tablespoon capers, chopped
1	tablespoon fresh lemon juice

1. In 2-quart saucepan, combine water, lentils, and ¹/₂ teaspoon salt; heat to boiling over high heat. Reduce heat to low; cover and simmer for 20 to 25 minutes or until lentils are tender. Drain lentils and return to pan; cover to keep warm.

2. Meanwhile, evenly season both sides of tuna with pepper and remaining ¹/₂ teaspoon salt, pressing in pepper. In 12-inch cast-iron skillet, heat oil over medium-high heat until hot. Add tuna and cook for 5 to 8 minutes for medium or until desired doneness, turning over once. Transfer to plate; cover to keep warm.

3. To same skillet, add shallot and cook for 1 minute, stirring. Add broth and capers; heat to boiling. Boil for 3 minutes or until liquid is reduced by half. Add lentils; heat through. Remove from heat; stir in lemon juice. Serve tuna over lentils.

Each serving: About 445 calories, 58g protein, 40g carbohydrate, 6g total fat (1g saturated), 20g fiber, 830mg sodium

FARFALLE LIVORNESE WITH TUNA

Classic tangy and spicy Livornese flavors come alive in this pasta recipe, which makes a filling, easy-to-prepare weeknight dinner.

ACTIVE TIME: 20 minutes   **TOTAL TIME**: 30 minutes

MAKES: 6 main-dish servings

12	ounces farfalle or rotini pasta
8	ounces green beans, trimmed and cut into 1-inch pieces
1	pound tuna steak (1¼-inch thick)
¼	teaspoon salt
1	tablespoon olive oil
1	onion, chopped
1	garlic clove, crushed with press
1	can (14½ ounces) diced tomatoes
2	tablespoons capers, drained and chopped
2	teaspoons grated fresh lemon peel
¼	teaspoon crushed red pepper
¼	cup loosely packed fresh parsley leaves, chopped

Caper berries, for garnish (optional)

1. Cook pasta in boiling salted water as label directs, adding green beans to saucepot 2 minutes before pasta is done.

2. Meanwhile, sprinkle tuna with salt to season both sides. In 12-inch skillet, heat 2 teaspoons oil over medium-high heat until hot. Add tuna and cook for 2 minutes per side. Reduce heat to medium; cover skillet and cook for 5 to 8 minutes longer or until tuna is almost opaque throughout, turning over once halfway through cooking. (An instant-read thermometer inserted horizontally into center of fish should register 145°F.) Transfer tuna to plate.

3. To same skillet, add remaining 1 teaspoon oil. Reduce heat to medium; add onion and garlic, and cook for 6 to 8 minutes or until lightly browned and tender, stirring occasionally. Stir in tomatoes, capers, lemon peel, and crushed red pepper; heat to boiling over medium-high heat. Boil for 1 minute. While vegetables are cooking, with two forks, flake tuna into bite-size pieces.

4. When pasta and beans are done, reserve ¹/₄ cup pasta cooking water. Drain pasta and green beans, and return to saucepot; stir in vegetable mixture from skillet, flaked tuna, chopped parsley, and reserved pasta cooking water and toss to coat. Transfer to warm bowls, and garnish each serving with whole caper berries, if you like.

Each serving: About 335 calories, 28g protein, 50g carbohydrate, 4g total fat (1g saturated), 7g fiber, 585mg sodium

SALT-BAKED FISH

Baking the whole fish in a crust of kosher salt seals in juices and guarantees an exquisitely moist—and surprisingly unsalty—finished product.

ACTIVE TIME: 5 minutes   **TOTAL TIME**: 30 minutes

MAKES: 2 main-dish servings

4	cups kosher salt
1	whole red snapper, striped bass, or porgy (1½ to 2 pounds), cleaned and scaled
1	lemon
3	sprigs rosemary or thyme

1. Preheat oven to 450°F. Line 13" by 9" baking pan with foil; spread 2 cups salt in bottom of pan.

2. Rinse snapper inside and out with cold running water; pat dry with paper towels. From 1 lemon, cut 3 slices. Cut remaining lemon into wedges and set aside.

3. Place lemon slices and rosemary in cavity of fish. Place fish on bed of salt; cover with remaining 2 cups salt. Bake until fish is just opaque throughout when knife is inserted at backbone, about 30 minutes.

4. To serve, tap salt crust to release from top of fish; discard salt. Slide cake server under front section of top fillet and lift off fillet; transfer to platter. Slide server under backbone and lift it away from bottom fillet; discard. Slide server between bottom fillet and skin and transfer fillet to platter. Serve with reserved lemon wedges.

Each serving: About 190 calories, 37g protein, 6g carbohydrate, 3g total fat (1g saturated), 0g fiber, 800mg sodium

STEAMED SCROD FILLETS

These fresh fillets are steamed on a bed of bok choy and ginger-soy-drizzled carrots for added flavor.

ACTIVE TIME: 15 minutes
TOTAL TIME: 25 minutes
MAKES: 4 main-dish servings

3	tablespoons reduced-sodium soy sauce
2	tablespoons seasoned rice vinegar
1	tablespoon finely chopped peeled, fresh ginger
1	garlic clove, crushed with press
1	pound bok choy, coarsely chopped
1³/₄	cups peeled shredded carrots
4	scrod fillets (6 ounces each)
3	green onions, sliced

1. In small bowl, with fork, mix soy sauce, vinegar, ginger, and garlic.

2. In 12-inch skillet, toss bok choy and carrots. Fold thin ends of scrod fillets under to create even thickness; place on top of vegetables. Add soy-sauce mixture and sprinkle with green onions; cover and heat to boiling over high heat. Reduce heat to medium; cook until scrod is just opaque throughout, about 10 minutes.

Each serving: About 200 calories, 34g protein, 12g carbohydrate, 2g total fat (0g saturated), 3g fiber, 820mg sodium

MISO-GLAZED SALMON

For a satisfying low-fat dinner, we spread a sweet and savory sauce on salmon fillets and broil them to make a rich glaze. Serve with a side of aromatic jasmine or basmati rice, or a salad of edamame and sliced radishes.

ACTIVE TIME: 10 minutes   **TOTAL TIME**: 20 minutes
MAKES: 4 main-dish servings

Nonstick cooking spray
¼	cup white miso (see Tip)
5	teaspoons granulated sugar
4	teaspoons seasoned rice vinegar
1	tablespoon water
1	tablespoon minced, peeled fresh ginger
4	salmon fillets, 1-inch thick (5 ounces each)
1	green onion, thinly sliced diagonally

1. Preheat broiler. Lightly spray rack in broiling pan with nonstick cooking spray.

2. In small bowl, mix miso, sugar, vinegar, water, and ginger; set aside.

3. Place salmon fillets on rack in broiling pan. Place pan in broiler at closest position to heat source; broil salmon for 5 minutes. Remove pan from broiler and spread half of miso mixture on salmon; broil for 1 minute longer.

4. Remove pan from broiler; turn salmon over and top with remaining miso mixture. Broil salmon until miso mixture is bubbly and salmon is opaque throughout, 3 to 4 minutes longer. Sprinkle with green onion before serving.

Each serving: About 260 calories, 35g protein, 13g carbohydrate, 7g total fat (1g saturated), 0g fiber, 870mg sodium

 TIP

Miso—a paste made of fermented soybeans—comes in a variety of flavors, colors, and textures that fall into three basic categories: red, which has a strong flavor; golden, which is mild; and white, which is mellow and slightly sweet. Miso can be purchased in health-food stores and Asian markets.

MUSTARD-DILL SALMON WITH HERBED POTATOES

A light and creamy sauce adds piquant flavor to succulent salmon. After you make the sauce, sauté snow peas in a teaspoon of vegetable oil for a healthy side dish.

ACTIVE TIME: 20 minutes   **TOTAL TIME**: 30 minutes

MAKES: 4 main-dish servings

12	ounces small red potatoes, cut into 1-inch chunks	4	pieces salmon fillet (6 ounces each)
12	ounces small white potatoes, cut into 1-inch chunks	2	tablespoons light mayonnaise
1½	teaspoons salt	1	tablespoon white wine vinegar
3	tablespoons chopped fresh dill	2	teaspoons Dijon mustard
½	teaspoon coarsely ground black pepper	¾	teaspoon sugar

1. In a 3-quart saucepan, heat potatoes, 1 teaspoon salt, and enough water to cover to boiling over high heat. Reduce heat to low; cover and simmer until potatoes are fork-tender, about 15 minutes. Drain potatoes and toss with 1 tablespoon dill, ¼ teaspoon salt, and ¼ teaspoon pepper; keep potatoes warm.

2. Meanwhile, preheat boiler. Grease rack in broiling pan. Place salmon on rack; sprinkle with ⅛ teaspoon each salt and pepper. Place broiling pan at closest position to heat source. Broil until salmon is just opaque throughout, 8 to 10 minutes.

3. While salmon is broiling, prepare sauce: In small bowl, mix mayonnaise, vinegar, mustard, sugar, remaining 2 tablespoons dill, and remaining ⅛ teaspoon each salt pepper.

4. Serve salmon with sauce and potatoes.

Each serving: About 335 calories, 37g protein, 31g carbohydrate, 7g total fat (1g saturated), 2g fiber, 655mg sodium

SEAFOOD FRA DIAVOLO

This tempting mix of squid, mussels, and shrimp in a robust tomato sauce just needs garlic bread and a green salad—dinner is ready!

ACTIVE TIME: 25 minutes   **TOTAL TIME**: 1 hour
MAKES: 6 main-dish servings

8	ounces cleaned squid
1	tablespoon olive oil
1	large garlic clove, finely chopped
1/4	teaspoon crushed red pepper
1	can (28 ounces) plum tomatoes
1/2	teaspoon salt
1	dozen mussels, scrubbed and debearded
8	ounces medium shrimp, peeled and deveined
1	package (16 ounces) linguine or spaghetti pasta
1/4	cup chopped fresh parsley leaves

1. Rinse squid and pat dry with paper towels. Slice squid bodies crosswise into 1/4-inch rings. Cut tentacles into several pieces, if large.

2. In nonreactive 4-quart saucepan, heat oil over medium heat. Add garlic and crushed red pepper; cook just until fragrant, about 30 seconds. Stir in tomatoes with their juice and salt, breaking up tomatoes with side of spoon. Heat to boiling over high heat. Add squid and return to boiling. Reduce heat; cover and simmer for 30 minutes, then simmer uncovered for 15 minutes longer.

3. Increase heat to high. Add mussels; cover and cook for 3 minutes. Stir in shrimp; cover and cook until mussels open and shrimp are just opaque throughout, about 2 minutes longer. Discard any mussels that have not opened after 5 minutes.

4. Meanwhile, cook pasta as label directs. Drain. In warm serving bowl, toss pasta with seafood mixture and parsley.

Each serving: About 410 calories, 25g protein, 65g carbohydrate, 5g total fat (1g saturated), 3g fiber, 588mg sodium

SWORDFISH WITH SUMMER SALAD

Here's a tip: To save yourself the half hour needed to soak bamboo skewers in water, use metals skewers instead! Dinner can be on the table that much faster. (See photograph on page 204.)

TOTAL TIME: 20 minutes
MAKES: 4 servings

3	large ears corn, husked
1	pound swordfish steak, skinned and cut into 1-inch chunks
8	bamboo skewers, pre-soaked
3/4	pound zucchini, sliced
2	tablespoons canola oil
2	teaspoons chili powder
3/4	teaspoon salt
2	cans (15 ounces each) chickpeas
1/2	cup packed fresh mint, chopped
3	tablespoons lime juice

1. Prepare outdoor grill for direct grilling over medium-high heat.

2. Place corn on hot grill rack and grill for 12 minutes or until charred in spots, turning occasionally.

3. Thread swordfish chunks onto skewers; brush fish and zucchini with 1 tablespoon oil and sprinkle with chili powder and 1/2 teaspoon salt. Grill fish and zucchini for 6 minutes or until fish is opaque, turning once.

4. Cut corn off cobs, chop zucchini, and toss with chickpeas, mint, lime juice, and remaining 1 tablespoon oil and 1/4 teaspoon salt. Serve with kabobs.

Each serving: About 500 calories, 34g protein, 55g carbohydrate, 19g total fat (3g saturated), 12g fiber, 735mg sodium

LINGUINE WITH RED CLAM SAUCE

Here's a beloved Italian classic. If you can't make it to the fish market for fresh clams, substitute two 10-ounce cans of whole baby clams.

ACTIVE TIME: 20 minutes   **TOTAL TIME**: 1 hour
MAKES: 6 main-dish servings

½	cup dry white wine
2	dozen littleneck clams, scrubbed
12	ounces linguine pasta
3½	cups marinara sauce, store-bought or homemade
1	tablespoon butter or margarine, cut into pieces (optional)
¼	cup chopped fresh parsley

1. In nonreactive 12-inch skillet, heat wine to boiling over high heat. Add clams; cover and cook until clams open, 5 to 10 minutes, transferring clams to bowl as they open. Discard any that have not opened after 10 minutes. Strain clam broth from skillet through sieve lined with paper towels; reserve ¼ cup broth. When cool enough to handle, remove and discard clam shells; coarsely chop clams.

2. Meanwhile, in large saucepot, cook pasta in boiling salted water as label directs. Drain.

3. In same clean 12-inch skillet, combine marinara, reserved clam broth, and clams; cook over low heat until heated through. In warm serving bowl, toss pasta with sauce and butter, if using. Sprinkle with parsley and serve.

Each serving: About 395 calories, 20g protein, 65g carbohydrate, 6g total fat (1g saturated), 3g fiber, 661mg sodium

Pancetta Chicken (page 249)

6 | POULTRY

Chicken is popular for so many reasons, but this stands out: This convenient dinner solution on busy weeknights can also be a lower-fat option. Just select white meat, or remove the skin from dark meat to up the health quotient of the bird. The choice of cooking method is important, too. Many of the recipes here use baking, grilling, or stir frying that require little additional fat.

Another secret to healthy poultry dinners: serving a rainbow of vegetables and fiber-rich whole grains. Some of the recipes that follow include fruits and veggies; if they don't, be sure to serve them on the side. And choose whole-grain couscous, pasta, or brown rice as an accompaniment.

But just as appealing as its health qualities is that fact that you can fix chicken fast. Our skillet dishes paired with flavorful sauces can be made in one pan, and dinner will be on the table in 30 minutes or less. Our duck recipe featuring a tart cherry sauce is just as speedy to prepare, but perfect for special nights when you want to cook to impress. If grilling is your quick-cooking method of choice, then take a look at our Grilled Chicken Bruschetta. And if you prefer to spend a little time up front, and then let the oven work its magic, you'll welcome our recipes for baked "fried" chicken and a turkey shepherd's pie.

CHICKEN BREASTS WITH TWO QUICK SAUCES

Simply sauté boneless chicken breasts, then take your pick from two easy sauces.

TOTAL TIME: 10 to 12 minutes plus time to make sauce

MAKES: 4 main-dish servings

1 teaspoon vegetable oil	Sauce of your choice (see recipes, below)
4 medium boneless skinless chicken breast halves (1¼ pounds total)	

1. In 12-inch nonstick skillet, heat oil over medium heat until hot. Add chicken and cook until chicken is golden brown and loses its pink color throughout, 5 to 6 minutes per side. Transfer chicken to platter; keep warm.

2. Prepare sauce and serve.

CHINESE GINGER SAUCE

After removing chicken from skillet, reduce heat to medium and add **1 teaspoon vegetable oil** to the skillet. Add **1 red pepper**, thinly sliced, and cook until tender-crisp. Add ½ **cup water**, **2 tablespoons soy sauce**, **2 tablespoons seasoned rice vinegar**, and **1 tablespoon grated, peeled fresh ginger**. Heat to boiling; boil for 1 minute. Spoon over chicken and sprinkle with **2 green onions**, chopped.

Each serving with chicken: About 195 calories, 34g protein, 4g carbohydrate, 5g total fat (1g saturated), 1g fiber, 757mg sodium

PROVENÇAL SAUCE

After removing chicken from skillet, reduce heat to medium and add **1 teaspoon olive or vegetable oil** to skillet. Add **1 onion**, chopped, and cook, stirring, until tender. Stir in **1 can (14½ ounces) Italian-style stewed tomatoes**; ½ **cup pitted ripe olives**, each cut in half; **1 tablespoon drained capers**; and ¼ **cup water**. Cook, stirring, until heated through, about 1 minute. Spoon over chicken.

Each serving with chicken: About 255 calories, 35g protein, 11g carbohydrate, 8g total fat (1g saturated), 3g fiber, 785mg sodium

PANCETTA CHICKEN

Simple and sophisticated. Those two words sum up this Italian-inspired meal. (See photograph on page 246.)

ACTIVE TIME: 10 minutes   **TOTAL TIME**: 30 minutes
MAKES: 4 servings

1½   pounds boneless skinless chicken breast halves (about 5 small)
Kosher salt
10   slices pancetta
Ground black pepper
1   pound green beans
2   teaspoons olive oil
Lemon wedges, for serving

1. Preheat oven to 450°F. Line large rimmed baking sheet with foil. Sprinkle chicken breasts with ½ teaspoon salt; drape 2 slices pancetta over each, tucking ends under. Place on prepared baking sheet.

2. On another baking sheet, toss green beans with oil; season with salt and pepper.

3. Place both baking sheets in oven and roast for 30 minutes or until chicken is cooked through (internal temperature registers 165°F). Serve together with lemon wedges.

Each serving: About 265 calories, 38g protein, 10g carbohydrate, 8g total fat (2g saturated), 4g fiber, 520mg sodium

CHICKEN CHILAQUILES

Make sure to use extra-thick tortilla chips—they stay crisp and help maintain the soft-and-crunchy balance in this deliciously spiced skillet dish.

TOTAL TIME: 20 minutes
MAKES: 4 servings

1	can (28 ounces) fire-roasted tomatoes
2	green onions, sliced
1	teaspoon ground cumin
1/4	teaspoon salt
1	tablespoon olive oil
2	cups shredded cooked chicken
6	ounces tortilla chips
1/2	cup sour cream
1	tablespoon lime juice

Sliced radishes, cilantro, and lime wedges, for serving

1. In blender or small food processor, puree tomatoes, green onions, cumin, and salt until smooth.

2. In 12-inch skillet, heat oil over medium heat. Add tomato mixture; partially cover and cook for 8 minutes or until slightly thickened. Stir in shredded chicken and tortilla chips. Cook, uncovered, for 2 minutes.

3. In small bowl, mix together sour cream and lime juice. Place on top of chicken mixture in skillet along with radishes, cilantro, and lime wedges.

Each serving: About 450 calories, 23g protein, 40g carbohydrate, 22g total fat (5g saturated), 4g fiber, 768mg sodium

BASIL-ORANGE CHICKEN WITH COUSCOUS

Marinating the chicken in orange and basil gives it a bright, fresh flavor. Served over whole wheat couscous with steamed sugar snap peas, this light dish is perfect for warmer weather.

ACTIVE TIME: 20 minutes   **TOTAL TIME**: 30 minutes
MAKES: 4 main-dish servings

2	large navel oranges
3	lemons
1/2	cup packed fresh basil leaves, chopped
2	tablespoons olive oil
3/8	teaspoon salt
3/8	teaspoon ground black pepper
4	medium boneless skinless chicken breast halves (1¼ pounds total)
1/2	teaspoon granulated sugar
1	cup whole wheat couscous
1	package (8 ounces) stringless sugar snap peas

1. From 1 orange, grate 1½ teaspoons peel and squeeze 4 tablespoons juice. From 2 lemons, grate 1½ teaspoons peel and squeeze ⅓ cup juice. Cut remaining orange and lemon into slices and set aside.

2. In medium bowl, combine 1 teaspoon of each peel and 1 tablespoon orange juice with half of basil, 1 tablespoon olive oil, ¼ teaspoon salt, and ¼ teaspoon pepper.

3. Place chicken breasts between two sheets of plastic wrap and, with flat side of meat mallet, pound to an even ½-inch thickness. Add chicken to citrus mixture, turning to coat; set aside.

4. In small pitcher or bowl, combine sugar, remaining $^1/_8$ teaspoon each salt and pepper, citrus peels, citrus juices, basil, and oil; set aside. (Dish can be made to this point up to 8 hours ahead. Cover chicken and citrus sauce and refrigerate.)

5. Preheat large ridged grill pan or prepare outdoor grill for direct grilling over medium-high heat. Meanwhile, prepare couscous as label directs. In 4-quart saucepan filled with $^1/_2$-inch water, place a vegetable steamer. Heat to boiling over high heat.

6. Add chicken to hot grill pan or grate; cook for 4 minutes. Turn chicken over and cook for 3 to 4 minutes longer or until no longer pink in center. Grill reserved citrus slices as well.

7. While chicken is cooking on second side, add snap peas to steamer; cook for 2 to 3 minutes or until tender-crisp. Fluff couscous and spoon onto large platter; top with chicken and snap peas. Drizzle sauce over all. Garnish with grilled citrus slices.

Each serving: About 400 calories, 46g protein, 33g carbohydrate, 9g total fat (1g saturated), 6g fiber, 365mg sodium

Chicken Breast Savvy

The demand for chicken breasts has increased with consumers' growing commitment to cutting back on fat (see "The Skinny on Poultry," page 275). Now companies market several variations. Boneless, skinless breast halves may be labeled exactly that, or they may be called boneless, skinless split breasts or portions. If the label doesn't indicate that the breast is cut into two pieces, it could be whole—the clues to look for are the terms "halves," "split," or "portions."

Poultry companies also package tenderloins (the narrow pieces of chicken from the underside of breasts). These could be labeled tenders or fillets—either way, they are boneless, very tender, and perfect for chicken fingers, stir-fries, and salads. Thin-sliced chicken breast cutlets are breast halves cut horizontally for quicker cooking. They're great in place of pounded chicken breasts, or instead of veal for a lower-fat take on veal scaloppine.

CHICKEN BOLOGNESE

This delicious twist on a beloved pasta dish trims the calories and fat without sacrificing the richly satisfying flavor.

ACTIVE TIME: 25 minutes   **TOTAL TIME**: 40 minutes
MAKES: 6 main-dish servings

12	ounces linguine or fettuccine
4	teaspoons olive oil
1	pound ground chicken breast
1/2	teaspoon salt
2	carrots, peeled and chopped
2	stalks celery, chopped
1	large onion (12 ounces), chopped
1	garlic clove, crushed with press
1	can (28 ounces) crushed tomatoes
1/4	teaspoon ground black pepper
1/2	cup reduced-fat (2%) milk
1/3	cup freshly grated Parmesan cheese
1/4	cup loosely packed fresh parsley leaves, chopped

1. In large saucepot, cook pasta as label directs.

2. Meanwhile, in 12-inch nonstick skillet, heat 2 teaspoons oil over medium heat for 1 minute. Add ground chicken to skillet; sprinkle with 1/4 teaspoon salt. Cook chicken for 8 to 9 minutes, or until no longer pink, stirring occasionally. Transfer chicken along with any juices to bowl.

3. To same skillet, add remaining 2 teaspoons oil with carrots, celery, onion, and garlic; cook for 10 to 12 minutes or until vegetables are lightly browned and tender, stirring occasionally. Stir in tomatoes with their juice, remaining 1/4 teaspoon salt, and pepper; heat to boiling. Reduce heat to medium-low and simmer, uncovered, for 10 minutes, stirring occasionally. Stir in cooked chicken and milk; heat through.

4. Reserve 1/4 cup pasta cooking water. Drain pasta and return to saucepot; stir in sauce from skillet, Parmesan, parsley, and reserved cooking water, and toss to coat.

Each serving: About 410 calories, 29g protein, 59g carbohydrate, 6g total fat (2g saturated), 5g fiber, 800mg sodium

RED-COOKED CHICKEN, SLOW-COOKER STYLE

Traditional Chinese "red cooked" chicken involves slowly cooking it in a soy sauce–based liquid, which gives the dish a deep red color. Here, the slow cooker makes it ready when you are.

ACTIVE TIME: 20 minutes   **SLOW-COOK TIME**: 8 hours on Low or 4 hours on High
MAKES: 4 main-dish servings

1/2	cup dry sherry
1/3	cup reduced-sodium soy sauce
1/4	cup packed brown sugar
2	tablespoons grated, peeled fresh ginger
1	teaspoon Chinese five-spice powder
3	garlic cloves, crushed with press
1	bunch green onions, white parts cut into 2-inch pieces and green parts chopped
3	pounds bone-in chicken thighs, skin and fat removed
1	bag (16 ounces) fresh vegetables for stir-fry (i.e., snow peas, carrots, broccoli, peppers)

1. In 5- to 6-quart slow-cooker bowl, combine sherry, soy sauce, sugar, ginger, five-spice powder, garlic, and white parts of green onions. (Keep remaining chopped green parts refrigerated until serving time.) Add chicken thighs and toss to coat with sherry mixture. Cover slow cooker and cook for 8 hours on Low or 4 hours on High.

2. Just before serving, place vegetables in microwave-safe medium bowl and cook in microwave as label directs.

3. With tongs, transfer chicken thighs to deep platter. Stir vegetables into sauce in slow cooker. Spoon vegetable mixture around chicken. Sprinkle with reserved green onions.

Each serving: About 410 calories, 41g protein, 24g carbohydrate, 8g total fat (2g saturated), 2g fiber, 930mg sodium

GRILLED CHICKEN BRUSCHETTA

Add grilled chicken breasts to this popular appetizer and you have a lean dinner—rich in fiber and vitamin C—that's good for your heart *and* your taste buds.

ACTIVE TIME: 20 minutes   **TOTAL TIME**: 25 minutes
MAKES: 4 main-dish servings

3	garlic cloves, peeled
3	teaspoons extra-virgin olive oil
³/₈	teaspoon salt
³/₈	teaspoon ground black pepper
4	boneless skinless chicken breast halves (6 ounces each)
1³/₄	pounds tomatoes, chopped
1	small shallot, finely chopped
¹/₄	cup packed fresh basil leaves, finely chopped
2	tablespoons red wine vinegar
1	loaf round crusty whole wheat bread (8 ounces), sliced

1. Preheat outdoor grill for covered direct grilling over medium heat. Crush 2 garlic cloves with press.

2. In 9-inch pie plate, mix crushed garlic, 1 teaspoon oil, and ¹/₄ teaspoon each salt and pepper, then rub all over chicken.

3. In large bowl, combine tomatoes, shallot, basil, vinegar, 1 teaspoon oil, and ¹/₈ teaspoon each salt and pepper. Let stand.

4. Grill chicken, covered, for 10 to 13 minutes or until juices run clear when thickest part of chicken is pierced, turning once. Transfer to cutting board. Let rest for 10 minutes; slice.

5. Brush bread with remaining 1 teaspoon oil. Grill for 1 minute, turning once. Cut remaining garlic clove in half. Rub cut sides all over bread. Divide bread and chicken among serving plates; top with tomato mixture.

Each serving: About 365 calories, 45g protein, 31g carbohydrate, 7g total fat (1g saturated), 5g fiber, 325mg sodium

NUTTY CHICKEN NOODLES

This recipe turns popular Chinese sesame noodles into a meal.

TOTAL TIME: 20 minutes

MAKES: 4 servings

1	tablespoon olive oil
12	ounces boneless skinless chicken breasts, thinly sliced
3	cups sliced red cabbage
1	cup shredded carrots
2	garlic cloves, chopped
¼	cup cider vinegar
¼	cup peanut butter or other nut butter
¼	cup soy sauce
¼	cup chicken broth
8	ounces rice noodles or Chinese egg noodles, cooked

Chopped peanuts and cilantro leaves, for topping

1. In large skillet, heat oil over medium-high heat. Add chicken, red cabbage, carrots, and garlic; cook for 5 minutes or until chicken is cooked through, stirring.

2. In small bowl, whisk together vinegar, peanut butter, soy sauce, and chicken broth; add to skillet along with cooked noodles. Top with peanuts and cilantro.

Each serving: About 520 calories, 28g protein, 61g carbohydrate, 19g total fat (3g saturated), 3g fiber, 1,040mg sodium

TIP

If you can't eat peanuts, try this sauce alternative: Whisk together ¼ cup fish sauce, ¼ cup lime juice, 1 crushed garlic clove, and 1 tablespoon brown sugar. You can use this sauce on grilled meats, slaws, and salads, too!

CHICKEN ADOBO OVER GINGERY RICE

A blend of garlic, soy sauce, vinegar, and spices makes this Filipino dish super tasty without any oil.

ACTIVE TIME: 5 minutes **TOTAL TIME**: 1 hour

MAKES: 4 servings

1	cup reduced-sodium soy sauce
3/4	cup rice wine vinegar
1	medium onion, chopped
1/4	cup brown sugar
2	tablespoons lime juice
1	tablespoon fresh ginger, grated
3	garlic cloves, smashed
3	bay leaves
2	teaspoons pepper
2	pounds boneless skinless chicken thighs

RICE

1	cup long-grain brown rice
1	tablespoon grated ginger
1	bay leaf
Pinch salt	
1/2	teaspoon pepper

GREEN BEANS

1	pound green beans
1	tablespoon garlic, minced
Lime juice	

1. In 5-quart saucepot, mix soy sauce, vinegar, onion, brown sugar, lime juice, ginger, garlic, bay leaves, and pepper. Add chicken thighs. Cover; heat to simmering over high heat. Reduce heat; simmer for 1 hour.

2. Serve with long-grain brown rice (cooked as label directs, with ginger, bay leaf, salt, and pepper) and green beans (steamed with garlic and lime juice).

Each serving: About 370 calories, 32g protein, 33g carbohydrate, 12g total fat (3g saturated), 4g fiber, 305mg sodium

TANGERINE CHICKEN STIR-FRY

Toss stir-fried chicken and mixed vegetables with a citrus-infused sauce for a quick and delicious meal.

ACTIVE TIME: 20 minutes   **TOTAL TIME**: 30 minutes

MAKES: 4 main-dish servings

3	tangerines
¼	cup dry sherry
1	tablespoon grated, peeled fresh ginger
1	teaspoon Asian sesame oil
1	teaspoon plus 1 tablespoon cornstarch
2	tablespoons reduced-sodium soy sauce
1½	pounds boneless skinless chicken breast halves, cut into ½-inch-wide strips
1	cup quick-cooking (10-minute) brown rice
4	teaspoons vegetable oil
1	bag (12 ounces) broccoli florets
2	carrots, peeled and thinly sliced diagonally
3	green onions, cut into 1-inch pieces
⅓	cup water

1. From 1 tangerine, with vegetable peeler, remove peel in strips. Using small knife, remove and discard any white pith from peel; set peel aside. Into 1-cup liquid measuring cup, squeeze ½ cup juice from tangerines. Stir in sherry, ginger, sesame oil, and 1 teaspoon cornstarch; set juice mixture aside.

2. In medium bowl, combine soy sauce and remaining 1 tablespoon cornstarch. Add chicken and toss to coat; set chicken mixture aside.

3. Cook rice as label directs. Meanwhile, in 12-inch skillet, heat 2 teaspoons vegetable oil over medium-high heat until hot. Add peel and cook for 1 minute or until lightly browned. With tongs or slotted spoon, transfer peel to large bowl.

4. To same skillet, add broccoli, carrots, and green onions; stir to coat with oil. Add water; cover and cook for 4 minutes, stirring once. Uncover and cook for 1 minute longer or until vegetables are tender-crisp, stirring frequently (stir-frying). Transfer vegetables to bowl with peel.

5. To same skillet, add remaining 2 teaspoons vegetable oil; reduce heat to medium. Add chicken mixture and cook for 6 to 7 minutes or until chicken is golden and loses its pink color throughout, stirring frequently. Transfer chicken to bowl with cooked vegetables.

6. Add juice mixture to skillet and heat to boiling over medium-high heat; boil for 1 minute, stirring until browned bits are loosened. Return chicken and vegetables to skillet and cook for 1 minute to heat through, stirring. To serve, spoon brown rice into four shallow dinner bowls; top with chicken and vegetables.

Each serving: About 390 calories, 45g protein, 32g carbohydrate, 9g total fat (1g saturated), 5g fiber, 420mg sodium

LEMON-OREGANO CHICKEN

This fresh-flavored chicken dish is perfect for outdoor grilling on one of those surprisingly warm days in early spring. For even cooking, it's a good idea to pound chicken breasts to a uniform thickness with a meat mallet.

ACTIVE TIME: 15 minutes   **TOTAL TIME**: 30 minutes
MAKES: 4 main-dish servings

3	medium zucchini (8 ounces each)
2	tablespoons olive oil
1/2	teaspoon salt
1/2	cup loosely packed fresh mint leaves, chopped
4	medium boneless skinless chicken breast halves (1 1/2 pounds total)
3	lemons
1	tablespoon chopped fresh oregano
1/2	teaspoon coarsely ground black pepper

1. Prepare outdoor grill for covered direct grilling over medium heat.

2. With mandolin or sharp knife, slice zucchini very thinly lengthwise. In large bowl, toss zucchini with 1 tablespoon oil, 1/4 teaspoon salt, and half of mint.

3. Place chicken breasts between two sheets of plastic wrap and, with meat mallet, pound to uniform 1/4-inch thickness. From 2 lemons, grate 1 tablespoon peel and squeeze 2 tablespoons juice. Cut remaining lemon into 4 wedges; set aside. In medium bowl, combine lemon peel and juice with oregano, pepper, and remaining 1 tablespoon oil and 1/4 teaspoon salt. Add chicken to bowl and toss until evenly coated.

4. Place zucchini slices, in batches, on hot grill rack and cook until grill marks appear and zucchini is tender, 2 to 4 minutes, turning over once. Remove zucchini from grill; place on large platter and sprinkle with remaining mint.

5. Place chicken on hot grill rack. Cover and cook until juices run clear when chicken is pierced with tip of knife, 6 to 8 minutes, turning over once. Transfer chicken to platter with zucchini; serve with lemon wedges.

Each serving: About 280 calories, 42g protein, 8g carbohydrate, 9g total fat (2g saturated), 3g fiber, 390mg sodium

CHICKEN NOODLE STIR-FRY

Dark, slender soba noodles are a Japanese specialty. We love their nutty flavor combined with stir-fried chicken, bok choy, and red pepper.

ACTIVE TIME: 15 minutes   **TOTAL TIME**: 30 minutes
MAKES: 4 main-dish servings

1	package (about 8 ounces) soba noodles	1	medium head bok choy (about 1½ pounds), cut crosswise into ½-inch-wide ribbons
2	tablespoons vegetable oil		
1	pound boneless skinless chicken breasts, cut lengthwise into ½-inch-wide strips	1	cup low-sodium chicken broth
		2	garlic cloves, crushed with press
2	tablespoons reduced-sodium soy sauce	1	tablespoon grated, peeled fresh ginger
3	green onions, thinly sliced	1	tablespoon seasoned rice vinegar
1	large red pepper, cut lengthwise into ¼-inch-wide strips	2	teaspoons cornstarch
		1	teaspoon granulated sugar

1. Cook soba noodles as label directs. Drain noodles; rinse under cold running water and drain again. Set aside.

2. Meanwhile, in 12-inch nonstick skillet, heat 1 tablespoon oil over medium-high heat until hot. Add chicken and 1 tablespoon soy sauce, and cook until chicken loses its pink color throughout, about 5 minutes, stirring often (stir-frying). Transfer chicken to plate.

3. Add remaining 1 tablespoon oil to skillet; add green onions and red pepper, and cook for 3 minutes, stirring often (stir-frying). Add bok choy and cook until vegetables are tender-crisp, about 3 minutes longer.

4. Meanwhile, in 2-cup glass measuring cup, whisk together broth, garlic, ginger, vinegar, cornstarch, sugar, and remaining 1 tablespoon soy sauce.

5. Add noodles and sauce mixture to bok choy mixture and heat to boiling; cook for 1 minute, stirring to coat noodles. Add chicken and toss just until heated through.

Each serving: About 440 calories, 34g protein, 54g carbohydrate, 11g total fat (1g saturated), 7g fiber, 684mg sodium

CHICKEN THIGHS PROVENÇAL

The quintessentially Mediterranean combination of thyme, basil, fennel, and orange makes for sensational chicken.

ACTIVE TIME: 30 minutes   **TOTAL TIME**: 1 hour 45 minutes

MAKES: 8 main-dish servings

2	pounds boneless skinless chicken thighs, fat removed and cut into quarters
³/₄	teaspoon salt
3	teaspoons olive oil
2	red peppers, cut into ¹/₄-inch-wide strips
1	yellow pepper, cut into ¹/₄-inch-wide strips
1	jumbo onion (1 pound), thinly sliced
3	garlic cloves, crushed with press
1	can (28 ounces) plum tomatoes
¹/₄	teaspoon dried thyme
¹/₄	teaspoon fennel seeds, crushed
3	strips (3" by 1" each) orange peel
¹/₂	cup loosely packed fresh basil leaves, chopped

1. Sprinkle chicken with ¹/₂ teaspoon salt. In nonreactive 5-quart Dutch oven, heat 1 teaspoon oil over medium-high heat until very hot. Add half of chicken and cook until golden brown, about 5 minutes per side. With tongs, transfer chicken pieces to bowl as they are browned. Repeat with 1 teaspoon oil and remaining chicken pieces.

2. Reduce heat to medium. To drippings in Dutch oven, add remaining 1 teaspoon oil, red and yellow peppers, onion, and remaining ¹/₄ teaspoon salt. Cook, stirring frequently, until vegetables are tender and lightly browned, about 20 minutes. Add garlic; cook for 1 minute longer.

3. Return chicken to Dutch oven. Add tomatoes with their juice, thyme, fennel seeds, and orange peel; heat to boiling, breaking up tomatoes with side of spoon. Reduce heat; cover and simmer until chicken loses its pink color throughout, about 15 minutes. Transfer to serving bowl and sprinkle with basil to serve.

Each serving: About 215 calories, 24g protein, 12g carbohydrate, 7g total fat (1g saturated), 3g fiber, 480mg sodium

Eat Your Peppers

Bell peppers come in a rainbow of rich colors, and while they're all healthy, some are nutritional standouts. Red peppers pack the most powerful antioxidant punch, but yellow and orange peppers are close behind, say researchers from Louisiana State University. Yellow peppers are also the vitamin C champs: Just one delivers 340 milligrams of the vitamin—more C than you'd get in three 8-ounce glasses of orange juice. Green peppers, which haven't matured to their final color, also haven't developed their full array of nutrients. Still, eating one will ensure that you meet your 60-milligram vitamin C quota for the day.

SWEET AND STICKY CHICKEN WITH SNOW PEAS

This delicious dinner is mostly prepared in the oven instead of on the stove, giving you some extra minutes for other tasks.

TOTAL TIME: 35 minutes
MAKES: 4 servings

2½	pounds chicken drumsticks and thighs
¼	cup hoisin sauce
Salt	
½	teaspoon ground black pepper
1	pound snow peas
½	teaspoon crushed red pepper
2	teaspoons toasted sesame oil
Chopped cilantro, for garnish	

1. Preheat oven to 450°F. Line a rimmed baking sheet with foil.

2. Toss chicken drumsticks and thighs with hoisin sauce, ½ teaspoon salt, and pepper. Arrange on the prepared baking sheet. Roast for 30 minutes or until cooked through (165°F).

3. Bring saucepan of water to a boil. Add snow peas and cook for 5 minutes or until tender. Drain and toss with crushed red pepper, sesame oil, and pinch salt.

4. Serve chicken over snow peas, garnished with cilantro.

Each serving: About 370 calories, 38g protein, 16g carbohydrate, 16g total fat (4g saturated), 4g fiber, 680mg sodium

SLOW-COOKER SESAME-GARLIC CHICKEN

Twenty minutes of prep time in the morning is all it takes to come home to this fragrant, filling chicken dinner.

ACTIVE TIME: 20 minutes   **SLOW-COOK TIME**: 5 to 6 hours
MAKES: 6 servings

⅓	cup rice wine or mirin
⅓	cup soy sauce
⅓	cup toasted sesame oil
1	tablespoon brown sugar
2	pounds boneless skinless chicken breasts
8	garlic cloves, peeled
1	piece fresh ginger (1-inch), sliced into thin coins
4	cups frozen cooked white rice, warmed
1	pound broccoli florets, steamed

Sliced green onions and red chiles, for garnish

1. In small bowl, whisk together rice wine, soy sauce, toasted sesame oil, and brown sugar.

2. In 6-quart slow-cooker bowl, layer chicken breasts, soy mixture, garlic, and ginger. Cover bowl with lid and cook on low for 5 to 6 hours, until chicken is tender. Transfer chicken to cutting board; shred and return to slow-cooker bowl.

3. Serve chicken mixture with rice and broccoli. Garnish with green onions and red chiles.

Each serving: About 510 calories, 41g protein, 51g carbohydrate, 16g total fat (2g saturated), 3g fiber, 720mg sodium

HONEY-MUSTARD CHICKEN AND POTATOES

Everything for this meal cooks in the oven at the same time. If you'd like to add something green, steamed fresh green beans make a delicious accompaniment.

ACTIVE TIME: 10 minutes   **TOTAL TIME**: 1 hour 35 minutes
MAKES: 4 main-dish servings

1½	pounds small red potatoes, cut into quarters
1	jumbo onion (1 pound), cut into 8 wedges
6	teaspoons olive oil
¾	teaspoon salt
¼	teaspoon coarsely ground black pepper
4	medium chicken breast halves, skin removed
2	tablespoons honey mustard

1. Preheat oven to 450°F. In small roasting pan (13" by 9"), toss potatoes and onion with 4 teaspoons oil, salt, and pepper. Place pan on middle rack and roast for 25 minutes.

2. Meanwhile, place chicken breasts in separate small roasting pan (13" by 9"); coat chicken with 1 teaspoon oil. In cup, mix remaining 1 teaspoon oil with honey mustard; set aside.

3. After potatoes and onions have baked for 25 minutes, remove pan from oven and carefully turn pieces with metal spatula. Return to oven, placing pan on lower oven rack. Place chicken on upper rack.

4. After chicken has baked for 10 minutes, remove from oven and brush with honey-mustard mixture. Continue baking chicken, along with potatoes and onions, for 12 to 15 minutes longer, until juices run clear when thickest part of chicken is pierced with a knife and potatoes and onions are golden and tender. Serve hot.

Each serving: About 380 calories, 31g protein, 44g carbohydrate, 10g total fat (1g saturated), 3g fiber, 630mg sodium

THE SKINNY ON POULTRY

The breast is the tenderest part of the bird—and also the leanest. A 3½-ounce portion of breast meat without skin has about 4 grams of fat. The same amount of skinless dark meat has about 10 grams of fat.

And, whether you're eating chicken, turkey, duck, or Cornish hen, keep in mind that removing poultry skin slashes the amount of fat by almost half. However, cooking poultry with the skin on keeps the moisture in—so simply remove the skin before eating. The fat reduction is practically the same as if you removed the skin before cooking, but the resulting bird will be juicier and more flavorful.

MOROCCAN OLIVE AND ORANGE CHICKEN

Take a quick trip to North Africa for dinner with this bright, flavorful, and effortless dish.

TOTAL TIME: 20 minutes
MAKES: 4 servings

3	tablespoons olive oil
1	pound thin chicken breast cutlets
1/4	teaspoon salt
1/4	teaspoon ground black pepper
1/4	cup all-purpose flour
1	small red onion, sliced
2	large navel oranges, sliced in half
1/2	cup green olives, pitted and halved
1/4	cup water
	Chopped fresh flat-leaf parsley, for garnish
2	cups cooked rice pilaf

1. In 12-inch skillet, heat oil over medium-high heat. Sprinkle chicken with salt and pepper and dredge in flour. Add to skillet and cook for 3 to 4 minutes or until browned, turning once. Transfer to plate.

2. Reduce heat to medium. To same skillet, add onion and cook for 2 minutes or until browned, stirring once. Squeeze juice from 3 orange halves into skillet. Thinly slice remaining orange half and add to skillet along with olives and water.

3. Return chicken to skillet. Cook for 3 minutes, scraping browned bits off bottom of pan. Garnish with parsley and serve over rice pilaf.

Each serving: About 440 calories, 31g protein, 40g carbohydrate, 18g total fat (3g saturated), 3g fiber, 790mg sodium

TIP

For perfectly golden cutlets, set a timer and sear each one for at least 2 minutes before turning.

HEALTHY MAKEOVER FRIED CHICKEN

The crunchy coating is what seals in the juices, giving traditional Southern fried chicken its finger-licking flavor. Too bad it also absorbs so much fat! By stripping the bird of its skin, baking instead of frying, and ditching the batter for panko crumbs, our crispy cheat carves off 240 calories and 22 grams of fat per serving.

ACTIVE TIME: 10 minutes **TOTAL TIME**: 45 minutes plus marinating
MAKES: 4 main-dish servings

1½	cups buttermilk
½	teaspoon cayenne (ground red) pepper
¾	teaspoon salt
1	cut-up chicken (3 pounds; 8 pieces), skin removed from all pieces except wings
	Nonstick cooking spray
1½	cups panko (Japanese-style bread crumbs)
1	teaspoon grated fresh lemon peel

1. In large zip-tight plastic bag, place buttermilk, cayenne, and salt; add chicken pieces, turning to coat. Seal bag, pressing out excess air. Refrigerate chicken for at least 1 hour or preferably overnight, turning bag over once.

2. Preheat oven to 425°F. Spray 15½" by 10½" jelly-roll pan with nonstick spray. In large bowl, combine panko and lemon peel.

3. Remove chicken from marinade, shaking off excess. Discard marinade. Add chicken pieces, a few at a time, to panko mixture, turning to coat. Place chicken in prepared pan.

4. Bake for 30 to 35 minutes or until coating is crisp and juices run clear when thickest part of chicken is pierced with tip of knife. For browner coating, preheat broiler after chicken is cooked. Broil chicken 5 to 6 inches from heat source for 1 to 2 minutes or until golden brown.

Each serving: About 305 calories, 36g protein, 16g carbohydrate, 9g total fat (3g saturated), 1g fiber, 370mg sodium

CRISPY CHICKEN TENDERS WITH BBQ SAUCE

Chinese five-spice powder—a robust blend of cinnamon, cloves, fennel seed, star anise, and Szechuan peppercorns—is a handy helper when you want to keep ingredients to a minimum. It is available in Asian markets and most supermarkets.

TOTAL TIME: 30 minutes

MAKES: 4 main-dish servings

³/₄	cup panko (Japanese-style bread crumbs)
2	tablespoons sesame seeds
1	large egg white
1	teaspoon Chinese five-spice powder
¹/₂	teaspoon salt
1	pound chicken breast tenders
1	tablespoon olive oil
1	small onion, chopped
¹/₂	cup ketchup
1	tablespoon brown sugar
1¹/₂	teaspoons cider vinegar
1¹/₂	teaspoons Worcestershire sauce

1. Preheat oven to 475°F. In 10-inch skillet, toast panko and sesame seeds over high heat, stirring frequently, until golden, about 5 minutes. Transfer panko mixture to plate. Do not wash skillet.

2. In medium bowl, with wire whisk or fork, mix egg white, ¹/₂ teaspoon five-spice powder, and salt until foamy. Dip chicken tenders in egg-white mixture, then in panko mixture to coat. Place tenders on baking sheet. Bake tenders, without turning, until they lose their pink color throughout, 13 to 15 minutes.

3. Meanwhile, in same skillet, heat oil over medium heat until hot. Add onion and cook until soft and lightly browned, 8 to 10 minutes. Remove skillet from heat; stir in ketchup, brown sugar, vinegar, Worcestershire, and remaining ¹/₂ teaspoon five-spice powder. Pour sauce into small bowl and serve with tenders.

Each serving: About 280 calories, 30g protein, 23g carbohydrate, 8g total fat (1g saturated), 1g fiber, 775mg sodium

CHICKEN AND APPLE MEATLOAVES

Easy-to-prepare chicken meatloaves, spiced with fennel seeds, parsley, and brushed with an apple jelly and mustard sauce, make for a scrumptious and calorie-saving main dish.

ACTIVE TIME: 25 minutes   **TOTAL TIME**: 1 hour
MAKES: 4 main-dish servings

1	slice whole wheat bread
1/4	cup low-fat (1%) milk
4	medium Golden Delicious apples
1	pound ground dark-meat chicken
1/2	cup finely chopped onion
1/4	cup packed fresh flat-leaf parsley leaves, finely chopped
1	large egg, lightly beaten
1 1/2	teaspoons fennel seeds
1/2	teaspoon salt
1/2	teaspoon ground black pepper
1	tablespoon vegetable oil
1/4	cup apple jelly
1	tablespoon Dijon mustard with seeds

Green beans, for serving (optional)

1. Preheat oven to 450°F. In food processor with knife blade attached, pulse bread into fine crumbs. Transfer to large bowl and stir in milk; let crumbs soak. Meanwhile, grate half of 1 apple on large holes of box grater. Cut remaining apple half and remaining 3 apples into wedges, removing and discarding cores; set aside.

2. To bowl with crumbs, add chicken, onion, parsley, egg, grated apple, 1/2 teaspoon fennel seeds, salt, and pepper. With hands, mix until well combined. Divide mixture into 4 equal pieces. On 18" by 12" jelly-roll pan, form each piece into 4 1/2" by 2 1/2" loaf, spacing 3 inches apart.

3. In large bowl, toss apples wedges, oil, and remaining 1 teaspoon fennel seeds until well combined; scatter in even layer around meatloaves. Roast for 10 minutes.

4. Meanwhile, stir together apple jelly and mustard until well blended. Brush or spoon thick layer of mixture onto meatloaves. Roast for 10 minutes or until tops are browned and temperature on meat thermometer inserted into center of meatloaves reaches 165°F. Transfer apples and meatloaves to serving plates. Serve with green beans, if you like.

Each serving: About 380 calories, 27g protein, 44g carbohydrate, 11g total fat (2g saturated), 6g fiber, 515mg sodium

★ Chicken – Easy, good!

TURKEY SHEPHERD'S PIE

Here's a good way to use up those Thanksgiving leftovers: a turkey-meat filling topped with leftover mashed potatoes. Although canned chicken broth works well, the dish is even better if you use the turkey carcass to make a flavorful homemade turkey broth.

ACTIVE TIME: 30 minutes   **TOTAL TIME**: 1 hour
MAKES: 4 main-dish servings

1	tablespoon olive oil
2	carrots, peeled and finely chopped
1	onion, finely chopped
1	celery stalk, finely chopped
2	cups mashed potatoes
³/₄	cup milk
2	tablespoons all-purpose flour
1	cup canned chicken or homemade turkey broth
8	ounces cooked turkey meat, cut into bite-size pieces (2 cups)
1	cup frozen peas
¼	teaspoon salt
⅛	teaspoon coarsely ground black pepper

Pinch dried thyme

1. In 5- to 6-quart Dutch oven, heat oil over medium heat. Add carrots, onion, and celery; cook until vegetables are tender and lightly browned, about 15 minutes.

2. Meanwhile, in small bowl, stir mashed potatoes with ¼ cup milk until combined.

3. Preheat oven to 450°F. In cup, with fork, mix flour with broth and remaining ½ cup milk until blended. Pour broth mixture into Dutch oven with vegetables. Cook over high heat, stirring often, until mixture boils and thickens slightly. Boil for 1 minute. Reduce heat to medium; add turkey, frozen peas, salt, pepper, and thyme; heat through.

4. Place four 1½-cup ramekins or soufflé dishes on 15½" by 10½" jelly-roll pan for easier handling. Spoon warm turkey mixture into ramekins; top with potato mixture. Bake until hot, bubbly, and potatoes are lightly browned, 30 minutes.

Each serving: About 320 calories, 25g protein, 33g carbohydrate, 10g total fat (3g saturated), 3g fiber, 615mg sodium

ROSEMARY ROAST TURKEY BREAST

When a whole turkey is too much, just use the breast. It will make white-meat fans very happy.

ACTIVE TIME: 20 minutes **TOTAL TIME**: 2 hours 35 minutes
MAKES: 10 main-dish servings

1	bone-in turkey breast (6 to 7 pounds)
1½	teaspoons dried rosemary, crumbled
1	teaspoon salt
¾	teaspoon coarsely ground black pepper
1	cup canned or homemade chicken broth (see recipe, page 137)

1. Preheat oven to 350°F. Rinse turkey breast with cold running water and drain well; pat dry with paper towels. In cup, combine rosemary, salt, and pepper. Rub rosemary mixture on both inside and outside of turkey breast.

2. Place turkey, skin-side up, on rack in small roasting pan (13" by 9"). Cover turkey with loose tent of foil; roast for 1½ hours. Remove foil; roast, occasionally basting with pan drippings, for 45 to 60 minutes longer. Start checking for doneness during last 30 minutes of cooking. Turkey breast is done when temperature on meat thermometer inserted into thickest part of breast (not touching bone) reaches 170°F and juices run clear when thickest part of breast is pierced with tip of knife.

3. Transfer turkey to warm platter. Let stand for 15 minutes to set juices for easier carving.

4. Meanwhile, pour broth into drippings in hot roasting pan; heat to boiling, stirring until browned bits are loosened from bottom of pan. Strain mixture through sieve into 1-quart saucepan; let stand for 1 minute. Skim and discard fat. Heat over medium heat until hot; serve with turkey. Remove skin before eating.

Each serving (without skin or pan juices): About 250 calories, 55g protein, 0g carbohydrate, 2g total fat (0g saturated), 0g fiber, 428mg sodium

PROSCIUTTO TURKEY CUTLETS WITH MELON

When buying turkey cutlets for this recipe, make sure to avoid ones that are very thinly sliced.

ACTIVE TIME: 20 minutes   **TOTAL TIME**: 30 minutes

MAKES: 4 servings

2	limes
1½	cups chopped, peeled cantaloupe
1½	cups chopped, peeled honeydew melon
1	small Kirby cucumber, shredded (½ cup)
1	jalapeño chile, seeded and finely chopped
¼	cup loosely packed fresh basil leaves, chopped
¼	teaspoon salt
4	turkey breast cutlets (1 pound total)
¼	teaspoon coarsely ground black pepper
4	ounces thinly sliced prosciutto

1. Grease grill rack. Prepare outdoor grill for direct grilling over medium heat.

2. From 1 lime, grate 1 teaspoon peel and squeeze 2 tablespoons juice. Cut remaining lime into 4 wedges and set aside. In bowl, combine lime juice, cantaloupe, melon, cucumber, jalapeño, basil, and salt. Makes about 3 cups salsa.

3. Sprinkle turkey cutlets with lime peel and pepper. Wrap turkey cutlets with prosciutto, pressing prosciutto firmly onto turkey.

4. Place turkey on hot grill rack and cook until it loses its pink color throughout, 5 to 7 minutes, turning over once. Transfer turkey to plate; serve with salsa and lime wedges.

Each serving turkey: About 185 calories, 35g protein, 0g carbohydrate, 4g total fat (1g saturated), 0g fiber, 815mg sodium

Each ¼-cup serving salsa: About 10 calories, 0g protein, 3g carbohydrate, 0g total fat, 0g fiber, 50mg sodium

TURKEY CUTLETS WITH PEARS AND TARRAGON

This good-for-you recipe contains lean protein (turkey) and green veggies (spinach). The best pears for this recipe are Anjou and Bosc, which are juicy and keep their shape when cooked.

ACTIVE TIME: 15 minutes   **TOTAL TIME**: 25 minutes
MAKES: 4 main-dish servings

1	tablespoon olive oil	1	cup chicken broth
4	turkey breast cutlets (about 1 pound total)	1/4	cup dried tart cherries or cranberries
1/4	teaspoon salt	2	tablespoons Dijon mustard with seeds
1/8	teaspoon ground black pepper		
2	large firm ripe pears, peeled, cored, and cut into 1/2-inch-thick wedges (see Tip)	1/2	teaspoon dried tarragon
		1	bag (9 ounces) microwave-in-bag spinach

1. In 12-inch skillet, heat oil over high heat until hot. Sprinkle turkey breast cutlets with salt and pepper. Add cutlets to skillet and cook, turning once, until turkey is golden brown on both sides and has just lost its pink color throughout, 3 to 4 minutes. Transfer cutlets to plate; keep warm.

2. To same skillet, add pears. Reduce heat to medium-high and cook pears, turning occasionally, until browned, about 3 minutes. Add broth, cherries, Dijon mustard, and tarragon to skillet. Increase heat to high and cook, stirring occasionally, until sauce thickens slightly and pears are tender, 4 to 5 minutes.

3. Meanwhile, in microwave, cook spinach in bag as label directs.

4. Return cutlets to skillet; heat through, spooning pear sauce over cutlets. To serve, spoon spinach onto four dinner plates. Top with turkey, pears, and sauce.

Each serving: About 255 calories, 31g protein, 20g carbohydrate, 6g total fat (1g saturated), 8g fiber, 565mg sodium

TIP

Peel and cut the pears just before you are ready to use them; like cut apples, they discolor. If you want to prep them in advance, place them in a bowl of cold water with 1 teaspoon lemon juice. Drain and pat dry before using.

"SPAGHETTI" AND MEATBALLS

The "spaghetti" in this recipe isn't spaghetti at all—it's spaghetti squash! But once it's tossed with tomatoes and turkey meatballs, you won't be able to tell the difference.

ACTIVE TIME: 15 minutes   **TOTAL TIME**: 35 minutes

MAKES: 4 main-dish servings

2	medium spaghetti squash (about 4 pounds total)	1/4	teaspoon ground black pepper
1	pound lean (93%) ground turkey	2	tablespoons olive oil
		1	medium eggplant, chopped
2	small zucchini, grated and squeezed dry	1	medium onion, finely chopped
4	garlic cloves, crushed with press	1	can (24 ounces) crushed tomatoes
1/2	teaspoon smoked paprika	1	tablespoon sherry vinegar
3/8	teaspoon salt	1	bag (5 ounces) baby arugula

1. With sharp paring knife, pierce squash all over. Place on microwave-safe platter or baking dish. Microwave on high for 5 minutes per pound, about 20 minutes total. Cool for 10 minutes.

2. Meanwhile, in medium bowl, combine turkey, zucchini, garlic, paprika, 1/4 teaspoon salt, and pepper. Form into 1 1/2-inch meatballs; place on large platter. In deep 12-inch skillet, heat oil over medium-high heat. Add meatballs to skillet and cook for 5 to 7 minutes or until browned on bottoms. With thin spatula, gently transfer meatballs back to platter. Reduce heat to medium.

3. To same skillet, add eggplant and onion and cook for 3 to 5 minutes or until beginning to soften, stirring and scraping up browned bits. Stir in tomatoes, vinegar, and remaining 1/8 teaspoon salt. Nestle meatballs in sauce. Cook for 8 to 10 minutes or until meatballs are cooked through, gently stirring occasionally.

4. While meatballs cook, when squash are cool enough to handle, cut in half lengthwise. With spoon, scrape out and discard seeds. With fork, scrape pulp to separate strands. Toss strands with arugula. Serve meatballs and sauce over squash mixture.

Each serving: About 455 calories, 30g protein, 50g carbohydrate, 19g total fat (4g saturated), 14g fiber, 615mg sodium

SPICY TURKEY SAUSAGE JAMBALAYA

This hearty Creole classic gets slimmed down with chicken tenders and turkey sausage. Brown rice boosts the fiber, while peppers and tomatoes deliver half the recommended daily amount of vitamin C—and it's all cooked in one skillet!

ACTIVE TIME: 10 minutes   **TOTAL TIME**: 25 minutes
MAKES: 4 main-dish servings

8	ounces turkey andouille sausage, sliced ¼-inch thick
1	green or yellow pepper, chopped
1	can (14½ ounces) stewed tomatoes
1	cup quick-cooking (10-minute) brown rice
8	ounces chicken tenders, cut crosswise in half
½	cup water
¼	teaspoon salt
1	bunch green onions, sliced

1. Heat 12-inch skillet over medium heat. Add sausage and pepper and cook for 5 minutes, stirring occasionally.

2. Stir in tomatoes with their juice, rice, chicken, water, and salt; heat to boiling over high heat. Reduce heat to low; cover and simmer for 10 minutes or until rice is just tender. Remove skillet from heat and stir in green onions.

Each serving: About 265 calories, 26g protein, 30g carbohydrate, 6g total fat (2g saturated), 4g fiber, 830mg sodium

CRISPY DUCK BREASTS WITH TART CHERRY SAUCE

This streamlined classic recipe is also great with pork. You can substitute two 6-ounce, ¾-inch-thick boneless pork loin chops for the duck. In step 2, season the chops and cook them in 1 teaspoon vegetable oil over medium heat for about 8 minutes, turning them once. Then proceed as directed.

ACTIVE TIME: 25 minutes   **TOTAL TIME**: 30 minutes

MAKES: 4 main-dish servings

1	package (6 ounces) white-and-wild rice blend (optional)	²/₃	cup port wine
4	small duck breast halves (6 ounces each; see Tip)	2	cans (14½ ounces each) tart cherries in water, well drained
½	teaspoon salt	¼	cup granulated sugar
½	teaspoon ground black pepper		Steamed green beans, for serving (optional)

1. If desired, prepare rice blend as label directs. Keep warm.

2. Meanwhile, pat duck breasts dry with paper towels. Make several ¼-inch-deep diagonal slashes in duck skin. Place breasts, skin-side down, in 10-inch nonstick skillet; sprinkle with salt and pepper. Cook over medium heat until skin is deep brown, about 12 minutes; turn breasts and cook 3 minutes longer for medium. Transfer breasts, skin-side down, to cutting board; let stand 5 minutes for easier slicing. Discard fat from skillet but do not wash. Add port to skillet; heat to boiling over medium heat. Boil until reduced by half, about 5 minutes. Add cherries and sugar and simmer, stirring occasionally, until most of liquid has evaporated, 3 to 4 minutes.

3. To serve, slice breasts crosswise. Transfer slices, skin-side up, to four dinner plates. Spoon cherry sauce over duck. Serve with rice and green beans, if you like.

Each serving: About 320 calories, 23g protein, 36g carbohydrate, 10g total fat (3g saturated), 1g fiber, 380mg sodium

---

TIP

If you can only find the larger duck breasts, which weigh about 12 to 13 ounces each, buy two and cook them on medium-low for 20 minutes, skin-side down; turn them over and continue cooking for 4 minutes longer. Slice to serve, as in step 3, and divide among four dinner plates.

Sautéed Beef and Pepper Skillet with Fries (page 303)

7 | LEAN RED MEAT

If you're trying to cut back on red meat to lower your intake of saturated fat, you're not alone. The good news: You don't have to completely eliminate beef, pork, or even lamb (unless your doctor suggests it). Simply serve small portions of lean cuts like flank steak and pork tenderloin, and explore lower-fat cooking methods, including grilling and roasting. In this chapter, we've rounded up lots of recipes for lean but flavorful meaty mains—many of them accompanied by wholesome veggies or grains. So fire up your grill or preheat that oven: It's time to enjoy a little meat.

If you love steak and chops, our steak- and pepper-filled fajitas, flank steak sandwiches, and Brazilian-style pork chops allow you to indulge. See "The Skinny on Grilled Meat" on page 299 for other lean cuts you can sink your teeth into. Or heat up a skillet and stir-fry slices of meat with mixed vegetables; our Orange Pork and Asparagus Stir-Fry and Sesame Pork Stir-Fry are winners.

We also offer low-maintenance roasts that make it easy for you to put a hot, home-cooked meal on the dinner table. Try our Beef Eye Round au Jus, served with new potatoes and carrots, or Sweet and Savory Pork, which gets sweetness from prunes and saltiness from olives and capers.

Pasta with meat sauce is a classic combination. We provide recipes for a whole wheat penne with a zesty beef and picadillo sauce and even a lighter take on the classic beef stroganoff. Your family will leave the table satisfied!

PASTRAMI-SPICED FLANK STEAK SANDWICHES

Although our pastrami isn't smoked, it is similarly coated with spices. Serve it on sliced rye with a side of coleslaw, deli-style.

ACTIVE TIME: 15 minutes   **TOTAL TIME**: 30 minutes plus marinating

MAKES: 6 sandwiches

1 tablespoon coriander seeds	½ teaspoon crushed red pepper
1 tablespoon paprika	3 garlic cloves, crushed with press
1 tablespoon cracked black pepper	1 beef flank steak (about 1½ pounds), well-trimmed
2 teaspoons ground ginger	12 slices rye bread
1½ teaspoons salt	Deli-style mustard, for serving
1 teaspoon granulated sugar	

1. In mortar with pestle or in zip-tight plastic bag with rolling pin, crush coriander seeds. In cup, mix coriander, paprika, black pepper, ginger, salt, sugar, and crushed red pepper.

2. Rub garlic on both sides of steak, then pat with spice mixture. Place steak in large zip-tight plastic bag; seal bag, pressing out excess air. Place bag on plate; refrigerate for at least 2 hours or up to 24 hours.

3. Prepare outdoor grill for direct grilling over medium heat.

4. Remove steak from bag. Place steak on hot grill rack and grill, turning once, 13 to 15 minutes for medium-rare or until desired doneness.

5. Place bread slices on grill rack and toast, without turning, just until grill marks appear on underside of bread.

6. Transfer steak to cutting board and let stand for 10 minutes to allow juices to set for easier slicing. Thinly slice steak across the grain and serve mounded on grilled rye bread with mustard alongside.

Each sandwich: About 380 calories, 33g protein, 35g carbohydrate, 12g total fat (4g saturated), 3g fiber, 1,015mg sodium

TIP
Crushing whole spices in a mortar with a pestle releases their flavorful oils, which makes the steak even tastier.

STEAK AND OVEN FRIES

While the potatoes are baking, you can pan-fry the steak, make the red-wine-and-shallot sauce, and even whip up a salad with dressing. This dish pairs nicely with a simple salad, such as romaine tossed with a light vinaigrette.

ACTIVE TIME: 15 minutes   **TOTAL TIME**: 40 minutes
MAKES: 4 main-dish servings

Oven Fries (see recipe, page 418)
1   beef flank steak (1 pound)
¼   teaspoon coarsely ground black pepper
2   teaspoons olive oil
1   large shallot, finely chopped
½   cup dry red wine
½   cup canned or homemade chicken broth (see recipe, page 137)
2   tablespoons chopped fresh parsley

1. Prepare Oven Fries.

2. Meanwhile, pat steak dry with paper towels; sprinkle with pepper on both sides. Heat 12-inch nonstick skillet over medium heat until hot. Add steak and cook, turning once, 7 minutes per side for medium-rare, or until desired doneness. Transfer steak to cutting board; keep warm.

3. To drippings in skillet, add olive oil; heat over medium heat. Add shallot and cook, stirring occasionally, until golden, about 2 minutes. Increase heat to medium-high. Add wine and broth; heat to boiling. Cook for 3 to 4 minutes. Stir in parsley.

4. To serve, hold knife blade almost parallel to cutting surface and slice steak crosswise into thin slices. Spoon red-wine sauce over steak slices and serve with Oven Fries.

Each serving with oven fries: About 390 calories, 31g protein, 40g carbohydrate, 11g total fat (4g saturated), 4g fiber, 455mg sodium

STEAK AND PEPPER FAJITAS

Arrange the meat and condiments in pretty dishes and let everyone assemble their own fajitas.

ACTIVE TIME: 10 minutes   **TOTAL TIME**: 30 minutes
MAKES: 4 main-dish servings

1	beef top round steak, 1-inch thick (¾ pound), well-trimmed
1	jar (8 ounces) medium-hot chunky salsa
1	tablespoon light corn-oil spread (56% to 60% fat)
1	red onion, thinly sliced
1	green pepper, thinly sliced
1	red pepper, thinly sliced
2	tablespoons chopped fresh cilantro leaves
8	low-fat flour tortillas (6-inch), warmed
1	container (8 ounces) fat-free sour cream
8	ounces fat-free sharp Cheddar cheese, shredded (2 cups)

Chile peppers, lime wedges, and cilantro sprigs, for garnish

1. Preheat broiler. Place steak on rack in broiling pan; spread ¼ cup salsa on top. Place pan in broiler at closest position to heat source; broil steak for 8 minutes. Turn steak over and spread ¼ cup salsa on top; broil 8 minutes longer for medium-rare or until desired doneness.

2. Meanwhile, in 12-inch nonstick skillet, melt corn-oil spread over medium heat. Add onion and peppers and cook until vegetables are tender-crisp. Stir in chopped cilantro. Spoon mixture into serving bowl.

3. Slice steak crosswise into thin slices. Serve with pepper mixture, tortillas, sour cream, shredded cheese, and remaining salsa. Garnish with chile peppers, lime wedges, and cilantro.

Each serving: About 450 calories, 45g protein, 55g carbohydrate, 7g total fat (1g saturated), 6g fiber, 1,060mg sodium

The Skinny on Grilled Meat

Grilling lends mouthwatering flavor to even the leanest cuts of meat. Try these options the next time you fire up your grill.

BEEF: Look for round or loin (eye or top round, tenderloin, or flank steak).

PORK: Choose loin or leg (tenderloin, loin, or sirloin chops).

LAMB: The leanest cuts are loin chops, boneless leg shank halves, or leg and shoulder cubes for kabobs.

VEAL: Get cutlets from leg or loin chops.

All of these cuts are 185 calories or less and have just 3 to 9 grams of fat per trimmed, cooked, 3-ounce serving. When selecting meat, keep in mind that ribs are high in fat, as is ground (except if specifically labeled 90% lean or higher). If you're craving burgers, preparing turkey or chicken patties is a smart, low-fat alternative.

STEAK AND OVEN FRIES

While the potatoes are baking, you can pan-fry the steak, make the red-wine-and-shallot sauce, and even whip up a salad with dressing. This dish pairs nicely with a simple salad, such as romaine tossed with a light vinaigrette.

ACTIVE TIME: 15 minutes   **TOTAL TIME**: 40 minutes
MAKES: 4 main-dish servings

Oven Fries (see recipe, page 418)
1	beef flank steak (1 pound)
¼	teaspoon coarsely ground black pepper
2	teaspoons olive oil
1	large shallot, finely chopped
½	cup dry red wine
½	cup canned or homemade chicken broth (see recipe, page 137)
2	tablespoons chopped fresh parsley

1. Prepare Oven Fries.

2. Meanwhile, pat steak dry with paper towels; sprinkle with pepper on both sides. Heat 12-inch nonstick skillet over medium heat until hot. Add steak and cook, turning once, 7 minutes per side for medium-rare, or until desired doneness. Transfer steak to cutting board; keep warm.

3. To drippings in skillet, add olive oil; heat over medium heat. Add shallot and cook, stirring occasionally, until golden, about 2 minutes. Increase heat to medium-high. Add wine and broth; heat to boiling. Cook for 3 to 4 minutes. Stir in parsley.

4. To serve, hold knife blade almost parallel to cutting surface and slice steak crosswise into thin slices. Spoon red-wine sauce over steak slices and serve with Oven Fries.

Each serving with oven fries: About 390 calories, 31g protein, 40g carbohydrate, 11g total fat (4g saturated), 4g fiber, 455mg sodium

Cooking with Wine

Wine adds fat-free flavor and body to quick pan sauces, stews, and poached fruit desserts. Because the success of any dish is determined by the quality of its ingredients, it is important to cook with good wine. Avoid the cooking wines sold in supermarkets; they're high in salt and low in flavor. Instead, consider using the leftovers from a bottle of wine served the night before or some of the wine you'll serve with the dish.

BEEF EYE ROUND AU JUS

Roast some herbed new potatoes while you prepare the beef. And for the tenderest results, do not roast this cut to more than medium-rare.

ACTIVE TIME: 30 minutes   **TOTAL TIME**: 1 hour 40 minutes
MAKES: 12 main-dish servings

1½	teaspoons salt
½	teaspoon dried thyme
¼	teaspoon ground black pepper
1	beef eye round roast (4½ pounds), trimmed
2	tablespoons olive oil
1	bag (16 ounces) carrots, peeled and cut into 2" by ¼" matchstick strips
1	pound leeks (3 medium), white and light green parts only, cut into 2" by ¼" matchstick strips
4	garlic cloves, thinly sliced
1¼	cups dry red wine
½	cup water
1	bay leaf

1. Preheat oven to 450°F. In small bowl, combine salt, thyme, and pepper; use to rub on roast. In 12-inch skillet, heat oil over medium-high heat until very hot. Add beef and cook until browned on all sides, about 10 minutes. Transfer beef to nonreactive medium roasting pan (14" by 10").

2. Add carrots, leeks, and garlic to skillet and cook, stirring occasionally, until carrots are tender, about 7 minutes. Arrange vegetable mixture around beef.

3. Roast beef for 25 minutes. Add wine, water, and bay leaf to roasting pan. Turn down oven temperature to 325°F and roast until meat thermometer inserted in center of roast reaches 140°F, about 45 minutes longer. Internal temperature of meat will rise to 145°F (medium) upon standing, or roast until desired doneness. Remove and discard bay leaf.

4. When roast is done, transfer to warm large platter and let stand for 15 minutes to set juices for easier slicing. To serve, cut roast into thin slices and serve with vegetables.

Each serving: About 230 calories, 33g protein, 6g carbohydrate, 8g total fat (2g saturated), 1g fiber, 358mg sodium

SAUTÉED BEEF AND PEPPER SKILLET WITH FRIES

French fries give this quick and easy dinner a Peruvian flair. (See photograph on page 294.)

ACTIVE TIME: 20 minutes   **TOTAL TIME**: 50 minutes
MAKES: 4 servings

1	pound beef sirloin, trimmed and thinly sliced into bite-size pieces
3	tablespoons soy sauce
2	tablespoons cider vinegar
3	garlic cloves, crushed with press
1	tablespoon grated, peeled fresh ginger
1	teaspoon ground cumin
12	ounces frozen French fries
3	tablespoons vegetable oil
1	large yellow pepper, seeded and thinly sliced
1	small red onion, thinly sliced
2	plum tomatoes, halved and thinly sliced

Chopped fresh parsley, for garnish

1. In large resealable plastic bag, combine beef, soy sauce, vinegar, garlic, ginger, and cumin. Seal bag and let stand for 20 minutes or up to overnight. Cook French fries as label directs.

2. In 12-inch skillet, heat oil over medium-high heat until hot. Drain beef, discarding marinade; add to skillet (oil may spatter). Cook for 3 minutes or until browned, stirring twice. Transfer beef to plate.

3. To same skillet, add pepper and onion; cook for 5 minutes or until almost tender, stirring occasionally. Add tomatoes and beef; cook for 2 minutes. Remove from heat. Fold in fries and garnish with parsley. Serve immediately.

Each serving: About 390 calories, 26g protein, 28g carbohydrate, 19g total fat (3g saturated), 3g fiber, 605mg sodium

PARMESAN AND SAUSAGE BOLOGNESE

Whip up this simple but satisfying pasta dish for unexpected dinner guests or for yourself when you're craving something hearty.

TOTAL TIME: 20 minutes

MAKES: 6 main-dish servings

12	ounces spicy Italian sausage, casings removed
3	garlic cloves, crushed with press
2	tablespoons tomato paste
1	can (28 ounces) crushed tomatoes
1	tablespoon red wine vinegar
½	teaspoon salt
½	cup finely grated Parmesan cheese
¼	cup heavy cream
1	pound rigatoni pasta, cooked

1. In large skillet over medium-high heat, cook sausage for 5 minutes or until browned, breaking up meat with spoon. With slotted spoon, transfer sausage to bowl. Discard all but 1 tablespoon fat in skillet.

2. Return sausage to skillet along with garlic. Cook for 30 seconds. Stir in tomato paste and cook for 2 minutes, then stir in crushed tomatoes, red wine vinegar, and salt and heat to simmering.

3. Cook for 7 minutes or until thickened slightly. Stir in Parmesan and heavy cream. Serve over rigatoni with more Parmesan cheese, if desired.

Each serving: About 500 calories, 20g protein, 69g carbohydrate, 17g total fat (5g saturated), 5g fiber, 865mg sodium

BEEF AND BARLEY WITH MUSHROOMS

This is a hearty dinner of sautéed beef tossed with a rich barley-and-mushroom pilaf. Because top round steak is a very lean cut, it must be thinly sliced across the grain—otherwise, it may be tough.

ACTIVE TIME: 30 minutes **TOTAL TIME**: 1 hour 10 minutes
MAKES: 6 main-dish servings

3	cups boiling water
1	package (1/2 ounce) dried porcini mushrooms
1	beef top round steak, 3/4-inch thick (about 1 1/2 pounds)
1	teaspoon olive oil
1	tablespoon soy sauce
1	package (8 ounces) sliced white mushrooms
2	carrots, peeled and cut lengthwise in half, then crosswise into 1/4-inch-thick slices
1	onion, finely chopped
1/2	teaspoon salt
1/4	teaspoon ground black pepper
1/4	teaspoon dried thyme
1 1/2	cups pearl barley
1	can (14 1/2 ounces) chicken broth, or 1 3/4 cups homemade (see recipe, page 137)
1/2	cup loosely packed fresh parsley leaves

1. In medium bowl, pour boiling water over porcini; let stand for 10 minutes.

2. Meanwhile, cut steak lengthwise in half. With knife blade held in slanted position, almost parallel to cutting surface, slice each half of steak crosswise into 1/8-inch-thick slices (see Tip, opposite).

3. In deep 12-inch nonstick skillet, heat oil over medium heat until hot. Add half of steak slices and cook until they just lose their pink color, about 2 minutes, stirring constantly. Transfer steak to medium bowl; repeat with remaining steak. Toss steak slices with soy sauce; set aside.

4. To same skillet, add mushrooms, carrots, onion, salt, pepper, and thyme; cook over medium-high heat until vegetables are tender-crisp, about 12 minutes, stirring occasionally.

5. While vegetables are cooking, with slotted spoon, remove porcini from soaking water, reserving liquid. Rinse porcini to remove any sand; coarsely chop. Strain soaking water through sieve lined with paper towel into medium bowl.

6. Add barley, broth, porcini, and mushroom soaking water to vegetables in skillet; heat mixture to boiling over medium-high heat. Reduce heat to medium-low; cover and simmer until barley and vegetables are tender and most of the liquid has evaporated, 35 to 40 minutes, stirring occasionally. Stir in steak mixture and parsley; heat through.

Each serving: About 320 calories, 47g carbohydrate, 20g protein, 7g total fat (2g saturated), 10g fiber, 695mg sodium

TIP

To cut raw beef into thin, even slices for stir-fries, first freeze the beef for about 15 minutes until it is firm. Then be sure to choose a sharp knife for slicing. By the time you finish cutting, the meat will have lost its chill, and you can proceed with the recipe as directed.

SLOW-BRAISED BEEF RAGU

Hearty, rich beef ragu is a classic sauce that pairs perfectly with satisfying egg noodles or pappardelle.

ACTIVE TIME: 15 minutes   **SLOW-COOK TIME**: 10 hours on Low
MAKES: 8 servings

3	stalks celery, cut into large chunks	1/2	teaspoon pepper
1	medium carrot, cut into large chunks	1/4	cup tomato paste
1	medium onion, cut into large chunks	1	can (14 ounces) diced tomatoes, drained
4	garlic cloves, peeled	1	cup dry red wine
1	tablespoon olive oil	2	sprigs fresh rosemary
1	beef chuck roast (3 to 4 pounds), trimmed and cut into quarters	1	pound pappardelle or curly egg noodles, cooked
3/4	teaspoon salt		Grated Parmesan cheese and finely chopped fresh parsley, for garnish

1. In food processor, pulse celery, carrot, onion, and garlic until finely chopped, scraping down side of bowl occasionally.

2. In large skillet, heat oil over medium-high heat until hot. Sprinkle beef all over with salt and pepper. Add beef to skillet; cook for 6 to 8 minutes or until browned on all sides, turning occasionally. Transfer beef to 6- to 7-quart slow-cooker bowl.

3. To same skillet, add vegetable mixture and 1/4 teaspoon salt. Reduce heat to medium. Cook for 5 minutes, stirring occasionally. Add tomato paste; cook for 1 minute, stirring. Stir in diced tomatoes and wine. Cook for 2 minutes, stirring and scraping up browned bits. Pour mixture over beef. Add rosemary. Cover and cook on low for 10 hours or until very tender.

4. Transfer beef to cutting board. Skim and discard fat from cooking liquid. Remove and discard chunks of fat from beef. Shred beef into bite-size chunks and return to cooking liquid. Serve tossed with pappardelle; garnish with parsley and Parmesan, if desired.

Each serving: About 510 calories, 48g protein, 49g carbohydrate, 12g total fat (3g saturated), 4g fiber, 400mg sodium

THAI NOODLES
WITH BEEF AND BASIL

Why spring for takeout when you can toss together a healthier noodle stir-fry for a fraction of the cost?

ACTIVE TIME: 20 minutes   **TOTAL TIME**: 25 minutes
MAKES: 4 main-dish servings

1	package (7 to 8 ounces) rice stick noodles
1	tablespoon vegetable oil
4	garlic cloves, thinly sliced
1	piece fresh ginger (3-inch), peeled and cut into thin slivers
1	onion, thinly sliced
12	ounces lean (90%) ground beef
½	cup canned or homemade chicken broth (see recipe, page 137)
3	tablespoons Asian fish sauce
1	teaspoon granulated sugar
¾	teaspoon crushed red pepper
¼	cup chopped fresh cilantro
¼	cup sliced fresh basil
1	small cucumber, cut lengthwise in half and thinly sliced crosswise
½	cup bean sprouts, rinsed and drained
¼	cup unsalted peanuts, chopped
1	lime, cut into wedges

1. In large bowl, soak rice stick noodles in enough hot water to cover for 15 minutes. (Do not soak longer or noodles may become too soft.) Drain well.

2. Meanwhile, heat oil in 12-inch skillet over medium heat. Add garlic, ginger, and onion; cook, stirring occasionally, until golden, 8 to 10 minutes. Stir in beef; cook, stirring and breaking up beef with spoon until meat is no longer pink, about 5 minutes. Stir in broth, fish sauce, sugar, and crushed red pepper; simmer, uncovered, until thickened slightly, about 5 minutes.

3. Add drained noodles, cilantro, and basil to beef mixture; cook, stirring, until heated through. Divide noodle mixture among four bowls; top each with cucumber, bean sprouts, and peanuts. Serve with lime wedges.

Each serving: About 450 calories, 25g protein, 60g carbohydrate, 14g total fat (3g saturated), 4g fiber, 720mg sodium

LEAN BEEF STROGANOFF

This comfort food favorite typically contains a lot of calories and fat. We offer a skinnier version that gets its creaminess from nonfat sour cream.

ACTIVE TIME: 20 minutes   **TOTAL TIME**: 30 minutes
MAKES: 6 main-dish servings

1	boneless beef top sirloin steak, $^3/_4$-inch thick (1 pound), well-trimmed
	Olive-oil nonstick cooking spray
3	teaspoons olive oil
1	pound mushrooms, trimmed and thickly sliced
1	onion, chopped
1	teaspoon cornstarch
1	cup beef broth
$^1/_2$	cup chili sauce
2	tablespoons spicy brown mustard
2	tablespoons plus $^1/_4$ cup water
12	ounces sugar snap or snow peas, strings removed
2	bags (6 ounces each) radishes, halved if large
$^1/_2$	teaspoon salt
1	package (12 ounces) extra-wide curly noodles, cooked
6	tablespoons nonfat sour cream
2	tablespoons chopped fresh parsley leaves

1. Holding knife blade almost parallel to cutting surface, slice steak crosswise into very thin slices.

2. Spray 12-inch nonstick skillet lightly with cooking spray and heat over medium heat. Add half of meat and cook, stirring quickly and constantly, until meat loses its pink color, about 2 minutes. Transfer to bowl. Without using more nonstick spray, repeat with remaining meat.

3. In same skillet, heat 2 teaspoons olive oil over medium heat. Add mushrooms and onion and cook, stirring, until tender. In cup, mix cornstarch and beef broth; stir into mushroom mixture with chili sauce and mustard. Cook, stirring, until mixture boils and thickens slightly. Return beef to skillet; heat through.

4. Meanwhile, in 10-inch nonstick skillet, heat remaining 1 teaspoon olive oil and 2 tablespoons water over medium heat until hot. Add sugar snap peas and cook until tender-crisp, 5 to 7 minutes. Transfer to bowl. In same skillet, pour remaining ¼ cup water and cook radishes over medium-high heat until tender-crisp, 5 to 7 minutes. Add sugar snap peas and salt to radishes; heat through.

5. Spoon noodles onto six dinner plates. Spoon beef mixture over noodles; top each serving with 1 tablespoon sour cream and sprinkle with parsley. Serve with sugar snap peas and radishes.

Each serving: About 430 calories, 30g protein, 58g carbohydrate, 9g total fat (2g saturated), 5g fiber, 740mg sodium

PENNE RIGATE WITH PICADILLO SAUCE

Pasta gets a Spanish twist in this dish, with a meat sauce similar to the filling you might find in empanadas.

ACTIVE TIME: 10 minutes   **TOTAL TIME**: 25 minutes

MAKES: 6 main-dish servings

1	package (16 ounces) whole wheat penne rigate, bow ties (farfalle), or radiatore pasta	3/4	pound lean (90%) ground beef
2	teaspoons olive oil	1/2	teaspoon salt, plus more for seasoning
1	small onion (4 to 6 ounces), finely chopped	1	can (14 1/4 ounces) reduced-sodium tomatoes in puree
2	garlic cloves, crushed with press	1/2	cup dark seedless raisins
1/4	teaspoon ground cinnamon	1/4	cup salad olives or chopped pimiento-stuffed olives, drained
1/8 to 1/4 teaspoon cayenne (ground red) pepper		Chopped fresh parsley, for garnish	

1. In large saucepot, cook pasta as label directs.

2. Meanwhile, in 12-inch nonstick skillet, heat oil over medium heat until hot. Add onion and cook, stirring frequently, until tender, about 5 minutes. Stir in garlic, cinnamon, and cayenne; cook for 30 seconds. Add beef and salt and cook, stirring frequently, until beef begins to brown, about 8 minutes. Spoon off excess fat as necessary. Stir in tomatoes with their puree, raisins, and olives, breaking up tomatoes with side of spoon, and cook until sauce thickens slightly, about 5 minutes longer.

3. When pasta has reached desired doneness, remove 1 cup pasta cooking water; set aside. Drain pasta and return to saucepot. Add beef mixture and reserved cooking water; toss well to coat pasta. Season with salt to taste. Garnish with parsley to serve.

Each serving: About 450 calories, 22g protein, 67g carbohydrate, 12g total fat (3g saturated), 9g fiber, 175mg sodium

TIP

Unless the label says 100% whole wheat, the product is actually a whole wheat blend, which still provides a higher fiber content than regular pasta.

PORK TENDERLOIN WITH MELON SALSA

This fruity and earthy dish is just a quick pop in the oven away.

ACTIVE TIME: 10 minutes
TOTAL TIME: 25 minutes
MAKES: 4 main-dish servings

1	whole pork tenderloin (1¼ pounds)
1	tablespoon olive oil
¼	teaspoon salt
2	cups finely chopped cantaloupe
¼	cup fresh cilantro, finely chopped
¼	cup orange segments
2	tablespoons lime juice
½	teaspoon chili powder
¼	teaspoon salt

1. Preheat oven to 450°F.

2. On baking sheet, brush pork tenderloin with oil; season with salt. Roast for 30 minutes or until cooked.

3. Combine cantaloupe, cilantro, orange segments, lime juice, chili powder, and salt.

4. Slice pork and serve over mixed greens topped with melon salsa.

Each serving: About 220 calories, 28g protein, 10g carbohydrate, 7g total fat (2g saturated), 1g fiber, 410mg sodium

PORK TENDERLOIN WITH ROASTED-LEMON ORZO

This tangy pork dish pairs perfectly with a crisp glass of Chardonnay.

TOTAL TIME: 20 minutes
MAKES: 6 main-dish servings

2	lemons, halved and thinly sliced
2	pork tenderloins (1 pound each)
4	teaspoons plus 1 tablespoon canola oil
½	teaspoon salt
½	teaspoon ground black pepper
2	garlic cloves, chopped
2	bunches Swiss chard, chopped
1	pound orzo, cooked

1. Preheat oven to 450°F. Line a large rimmed baking sheet with parchment paper.

2. Toss lemon slices and pork tenderloins with 4 teaspoons oil; surround pork with lemon slices on prepared baking sheet. Sprinkle with salt and pepper. Roast for 30 minutes or until cooked through (145°F).

3. In large saucepot, heat 1 tablespoon oil over medium heat. Add garlic and cook for 2 minutes. Add chard and cook, covered, for 7 minutes or until tender.

4. Toss chard with cooked orzo and roasted lemon slices; serve with sliced pork.

Each serving: About 510 calories, 41g protein, 63g carbohydrate, 11g total fat (2g saturated), 5g fiber, 505mg sodium

SOY-HONEY PORK WITH SWEET POTATOES

Honey-soy glaze unites sweet potatoes and pork tenderloin for a very tasty meal. Let the oven do the work for you and enjoy your hassle-free dinner in only 40 minutes.

ACTIVE TIME: 15 minutes   **TOTAL TIME**: 40 minutes
MAKES: 4 main-dish servings

1/4	cup reduced-sodium soy sauce
2	tablespoons hoisin sauce
2	tablespoons honey
1	tablespoon rice vinegar
1	teaspoon grated, peeled fresh ginger
2	garlic cloves, crushed with press
1	whole pork tenderloin (1 1/4 pounds)
1 1/2	pounds sweet potatoes
1	tablespoon vegetable oil
1/4	teaspoon salt
1/8	teaspoon ground black pepper
2	green onions, cut into slivers

1. Preheat oven to 475°F. In small bowl, whisk soy sauce, hoisin, honey, vinegar, ginger, and half of garlic until well blended. Pour into gallon-size zip-tight plastic bag. Add pork; seal bag and turn until pork is well coated. Set aside.

2. Meanwhile, peel sweet potatoes. Cut each into 1/2-inch-thick rounds. In large bowl, combine oil and remaining garlic. Add sweet potatoes, salt, and pepper. Toss until well coated.

3. Transfer pork from marinade to center of 18" by 12" jelly-roll pan, shaking off any excess marinade into bag. Tuck tapered ends under pork to ensure even cooking. Arrange sweet potato rounds in single layer on pan around pork. Roast for 10 minutes.

4. Meanwhile, transfer marinade to 2-quart saucepan. Heat to boiling over medium-high heat. Boil for 3 minutes or until thickened and syrupy. Transfer half of marinade to small serving bowl; set aside. Turn over sweet potatoes and pork. Brush remaining marinade on pork. Roast for 10 to 15 minutes longer or until sweet potatoes are browned and temperature on meat thermometer

inserted into thickest part of pork registers 155°F. Cover pork loosely with foil and let stand for 5 minutes.

5. Cut pork into ¹/₂-inch-thick slices.

6. Transfer pork and sweet potatoes to large platter. Garnish with green onions and serve with reserved marinade.

Each serving: About 430 calories, 44g protein, 45g carbohydrate, 9g total fat (2g saturated), 4g fiber, 875mg sodium

SWEET AND SAVORY PORK

Salty olives and capers interplay with sweet prunes to create a mouth-watering sauce.

ACTIVE TIME: 15 minutes   **TOTAL TIME**: 25 minutes

MAKES: 4 main-dish servings

2	tablespoons brown sugar
3	garlic cloves, crushed with press
³/₄	teaspoon salt
¹/₄	teaspoon ground black pepper
1	whole pork tenderloin (1 pound), patted dry and cut crosswise into 1-inch-thick slices
2	teaspoons olive oil
¹/₂	cup dry white wine
2	tablespoons red wine vinegar
1	teaspoon cornstarch
¹/₄	teaspoon dried oregano
¹/₂	cup pitted prunes, coarsely chopped
¹/₄	cup pitted green olives, coarsely chopped
2	tablespoons capers, drained

1. On waxed paper, combine brown sugar, garlic, salt, and pepper; use to coat pork.

2. In 12-inch nonstick skillet, heat oil over medium heat until hot. Add pork and cook until slices are lightly browned and lose their pink color throughout, about 3 minutes per side. Transfer pork to plate.

3. In cup, blend wine, vinegar, cornstarch, and oregano. Stir cornstarch mixture into skillet. Heat to boiling, stirring. Return pork to skillet. Add prunes, olives, and capers; heat through.

Each serving: About 270 calories, 25g protein, 22g carbohydrate, 7g total fat (2g saturated), 2g fiber, 892mg sodium

HOT AND SPICY PORK NOODLES

This dish is quicker than take-out—and healthier, too.

TOTAL TIME: 20 minutes

MAKES: 4 main-dish servings

12	ounces lo mein or linguine noodles
2	teaspoons oil
12	ounces ground pork
3	tablespoons reduced-sodium soy sauce
2	tablespoons balsamic vinegar
2	tablespoons Sriracha hot sauce
2	bags (5 ounces each) baby spinach

1. Cook lo mein or linguine as label directs.

2. In 12-inch skillet, heat oil over medium-high heat until hot. Add ground pork; cook for 5 to 7 minutes or until browned, breaking up meat with back of wooden spoon.

3. Whisk together soy sauce, vinegar, and Sriracha; add to skillet with pork, along with both bags baby spinach. Cook for 2 minutes or until pork is cooked through and spinach has wilted, stirring occasionally. Toss pork mixture with cooked noodles and serve.

Each serving: About 485 calories, 32g protein, 75g carbohydrate, 7g total fat (2g saturated), 6g fiber, 755mg sodium

PORK TENDERLOIN WITH ROASTED GRAPES

If you've never had roasted grapes, try this recipe. They are absolutely delicious and a perfect match for the pork.

ACTIVE TIME: 15 minutes   **TOTAL TIME**: 30 minutes
MAKES: 4 main-dish servings

1	teaspoon fennel seeds, crushed
½	teaspoon salt
½	teaspoon coarsely ground black pepper
1	whole pork tenderloin (1 pound)
2	teaspoons extra-virgin olive oil
3	cups seedless red and green grapes (about 1 pound)
½	cup canned or homemade chicken broth (see recipe, page 137)

1. Preheat oven to 475°F. In cup, with fork, stir fennel seeds, salt, and pepper. Rub mixture all over pork.

2. In 12-inch skillet with oven-safe handle, heat oil over medium-high heat until very hot. Add pork and cook for 5 minutes, turning to brown all sides of tenderloin.

3. Add grapes and broth to skillet; heat to boiling. Cover and place in oven. Roast until meat thermometer inserted in center of roast reaches 150°F, 15 to 18 minutes. Internal temperature of meat will rise to 160°F upon standing. Transfer pork to warm platter.

4. Meanwhile, heat grape mixture to boiling over high heat; boil until liquid has thickened slightly, about 1 minute. Slice pork; serve with grapes and pan juices.

Each serving: About 245 calories, 25g protein, 22g carbohydrate, 7g total fat (2g saturated), 2g fiber, 475mg sodium

PORK STEAK WITH PLUM GLAZE

For this recipe, we butterfly pork tenderloin, then pound it for quick, even cooking. A meat mallet is a handy tool for this job, but a small heavy skillet or a rolling pin will work, too.

ACTIVE TIME: 25 minutes   **TOTAL TIME**: 30 minutes
MAKES: 4 main-dish servings

1	whole pork tenderloin (1 pound), trimmed	1	tablespoon fresh lemon juice
1	teaspoon salt	1/2	teaspoon ground cinnamon or Chinese five-spice powder
1/4	teaspoon coarsely ground black pepper	2	garlic cloves, crushed with press
1/2	cup plum jam or preserves	4	large plums (1 pound total), cut in half and pitted
1	tablespoon brown sugar		Cooked white rice, for serving (optional)
1	tablespoon grated, peeled fresh ginger		

1. Prepare grill for covered direct grilling over medium heat, or preheat ridged grill pan over medium heat until very hot.

2. Holding knife blade parallel to cutting surface and against long side of tenderloin, cut pork lengthwise almost in half, being careful not to cut all the way through. Open tenderloin like a book and spread flat. With meat mallet, pound pork to even 1/4-inch thickness (or place pork between two sheets of plastic wrap and pound with rolling pin). Cut tenderloin crosswise into 4 steaks; season with salt and pepper.

3. In small bowl, with fork, mix jam, sugar, ginger, lemon juice, cinnamon, and garlic. Brush one side of each pork steak and cut side of each plum half with plum glaze.

4. Place steaks and plums, glaze-side down, on grill. Cover and cook for 3 minutes. Brush steaks and plums with remaining glaze; turn steaks and plums and grill until steaks are browned on both sides and just lose their pink color throughout and plums are tender, about 3 minutes longer. Serve with rice, if desired.

Each serving: About 310 calories, 25g protein, 42g carbohydrate, 5g total fat (1g saturated), 2g fiber, 524mg sodium

HOISIN PORK TENDERLOIN WITH GRILLED PINEAPPLE

When choosing a pineapple, pick one that is slightly soft with a deep, sweet fragrance. Pineapples are harvested ripe and will not get any sweeter with time.

ACTIVE TIME: 10 minutes   **TOTAL TIME**: 30 minutes
MAKES: 4 main-dish servings

¼	cup hoisin sauce
1	tablespoon honey
1	tablespoon grated, peeled fresh ginger
1	teaspoon Asian sesame oil
1	whole pork tenderloin (1¼ pounds), trimmed
½	medium pineapple
2	tablespoons brown sugar

1. Prepare outdoor grill for covered direct grilling over medium heat. In small bowl, combine hoisin sauce, honey, ginger, and sesame oil.

2. Place pork on hot grill rack. Cover and cook until an instant-read meat thermometer inserted in thickest part of tenderloin registers 155°F, 18 to 20 minutes, turning occasionally. Pork will be browned on the outside and still slightly pink in the center.

3. Meanwhile, with serrated knife, cut pineapple half into 4 wedges. Rub cut sides of pineapple with brown sugar.

4. Grill pineapple on rack with pork until browned on both sides, about 5 minutes, turning over once. While pineapple is grilling, brush pork with hoisin-honey glaze and turn frequently.

5. Transfer pork to cutting board; let stand for 5 minutes to allow juices to set for easier slicing. Transfer pineapple to platter. Thinly slice pork and serve with pineapple wedges.

Each serving: About 275 calories, 31g protein, 23g carbohydrate, 6g total fat (2g saturated), 2g fiber, 245mg sodium

PORK, CABBAGE, AND APPLE SAUTÉ

A splash of cider vinegar adds tang to this hearty skillet supper of pan-browned pork chops, shredded cabbage, sliced apples, red potatoes, and caramelized onions.

ACTIVE TIME: 15 minutes   **TOTAL TIME**: 55 minutes
MAKES: 4 main-dish servings

1	teaspoon olive oil
4	bone-in pork loin chops, ³/₄-inch thick (about 6 ounces each), trimmed
³/₄	teaspoon salt
¹/₄	teaspoon ground black pepper
1	large onion (12 ounces), thinly sliced
1	bag (16 ounces) shredded cabbage mix for coleslaw
2	large Golden Delicious or Gala apples (8 ounces each), cored and cut into ¹/₂-inch-thick slices
12	ounces red potatoes, cut into 1-inch pieces
³/₄	cup apple cider
¹/₄	teaspoon dried thyme
1	tablespoon cider vinegar

1. In 12-inch nonstick skillet, heat oil over medium heat until hot. Add pork chops; sprinkle with ¹/₄ teaspoon salt and ¹/₈ teaspoon pepper. Cook chops until golden on the outside and still slightly pink inside, about 4 minutes per side. Transfer chops to a plate; keep warm.

2. Add onion to skillet and cook over medium heat, covered, stirring occasionally, until tender and golden, 8 to 10 minutes. Gradually stir in the cabbage mix and cook until wilted, about 5 minutes. Add apples, potatoes, apple cider, thyme, and remaining ¹/₂ teaspoon salt and ¹/₈ teaspoon pepper; heat to boiling. Reduce heat to medium-low, and simmer, covered, until potatoes are tender, about 15 minutes.

3. Stir in vinegar. Tuck chops into cabbage mixture and heat through.

Each serving: About 380 calories, 26g protein, 46g carbohydrate, 11g total fat (3g saturated), 8g fiber, 535mg sodium

ORANGE PORK AND ASPARAGUS STIR-FRY

Slices of lean pork tenderloin are quickly cooked with fresh asparagus and juicy orange pieces.

ACTIVE TIME: 20 minutes   **TOTAL TIME**: 25 minutes
MAKES: 4 main-dish servings

2	navel oranges	¼	teaspoon ground black pepper
1	teaspoon olive oil	1½	pounds thin asparagus, trimmed and each stalk cut crosswise in half
1	whole pork tenderloin (about ¾ pound), trimmed and thinly sliced diagonally		
¾	teaspoon salt	1	garlic clove, crushed with press
		¼	cup water

1. From 1 orange, grate 1 teaspoon peel and squeeze ¼ cup juice. Remove peel and white pith from remaining orange. Cut orange into ¼-inch-thick slices; cut each slice into quarters.

2. In 12-inch nonstick skillet, heat ½ teaspoon oil over medium heat until hot. Add half the pork, and sprinkle with ¼ teaspoon salt and ⅛ teaspoon pepper; cook, stirring frequently, until pork just loses its pink color, 2 minutes. Transfer pork to plate. Repeat with remaining pork, again using ½ teaspoon oil, ¼ teaspoon salt, and remaining ⅛ teaspoon pepper. Transfer pork to same plate.

3. To the same skillet, add asparagus, garlic, grated orange peel, remaining ¼ teaspoon salt, and water; cover and cook, stirring occasionally, until asparagus is tender-crisp, about 3 minutes. Return pork to skillet. Add reserved orange juice and orange pieces; heat through, stirring often.

Each serving: About 165 calories, 24g protein, 8g carbohydrate, 4g total fat (1g saturated), 2g fiber, 495mg sodium

Eat Your Asparagus

Fresh asparagus is a great source of folic acid, which protects against heart disease and birth defects, so women of child-bearing years should add it to their menu. Steam up a handful (it takes less than 10 minutes), sprinkle lightly with salt or a little grated Parmesan cheese, and enjoy. At 3 calories per spear, you can afford to eat a whole bunch.

SESAME PORK STIR-FRY

So gingery good—and this one-dish meal is only 375 calories per serving.

ACTIVE TIME: 20 minutes   **TOTAL TIME**: 40 minutes

MAKES: 4 main-dish servings

Aromatic Brown Rice (see recipe, page 402)

1 cup loosely packed watercress leaves, coarsely chopped

1 whole pork tenderloin (12 ounces), trimmed and thinly sliced

2 tablespoons soy sauce

1 tablespoon minced, peeled fresh ginger

1 teaspoon Asian sesame oil

1 garlic clove, crushed with press

3/4 cup canned or homemade chicken broth (see recipe, page 137)

1 1/4 teaspoons cornstarch

2 teaspoons olive oil

3 carrots, peeled and cut into 2" by 1/4" matchstick strips

1 red pepper, cut into 1/4-inch-wide strips

1 tablespoon water

1 medium zucchini (about 8 ounces), cut into 2" by 1/4" matchstick strips

1. Prepare Aromatic Brown Rice. Stir in watercress and keep warm.

2. Meanwhile, in medium bowl, toss pork, soy sauce, ginger, sesame oil, and garlic. In cup, mix broth and cornstarch; set aside.

3. In 12-inch nonstick skillet, heat 1 teaspoon olive oil over medium heat until hot. Add carrots and red pepper; cook, stirring frequently (stir-frying), until lightly browned, about 5 minutes. Add water and stir-fry until vegetables are tender-crisp, 3 to 5 minutes longer. Transfer to bowl.

4. In same skillet, heat remaining 1 teaspoon olive oil. Add zucchini; stir-fry until tender-crisp, about 3 minutes. Transfer zucchini to bowl with other vegetables.

5. To same skillet, add pork mixture and stir-fry until pork just loses its pink color. Stir cornstarch mixture; add to pork. Stir in vegetables; heat to boiling. Boil until sauce thickens, 1 minute. Serve stir-fry with watercress rice.

Each serving: About 375 calories, 23g protein, 48g carbohydrate, 10g total fat (2g saturated), 3g fiber, 975mg sodium

BRAZILIAN PORK CHOPS

An excellent example of Brazilian-influenced cuisine, this spicy dish with a hint of citrus is accompanied by black beans.

ACTIVE TIME: 15 minutes   **TOTAL TIME**: 30 minutes

MAKES: 4 main-dish servings

4	boneless pork loin chops, ³/₄-inch thick (5 ounces each), trimmed
¹/₂	teaspoon ground cumin
¹/₂	teaspoon ground coriander
¹/₄	teaspoon dried thyme
¹/₈	teaspoon ground allspice
¹/₂	teaspoon salt
1	teaspoon olive oil
1	onion, chopped
3	garlic cloves, crushed with press

1	can (15 to 19 ounces) black beans, rinsed and drained
¹/₂	cup canned or homemade chicken broth (see recipe, page 137)
1	tablespoon fresh lime juice
¹/₄	teaspoon coarsely ground black pepper
¹/₄	cup packed fresh cilantro leaves, chopped
	Fresh orange wedges, for serving (optional)

1. Pat pork chops dry with paper towels. In cup, mix cumin, coriander, thyme, allspice, and ¹/₄ teaspoon salt. Rub both sides of pork chops with spice mixture.

2. Heat 12-inch nonstick skillet over medium heat until hot. Add pork chops and cook until lightly browned outside and still slightly pink inside, about 4 minutes per side. Transfer pork to platter; keep warm.

3. In same skillet, heat oil over medium heat. Add onion and cook, stirring frequently, until golden, about 5 minutes. Add the garlic and cook, stirring, for 1 minute longer. Add beans, broth, lime juice, pepper, and remaining ¹/₄ teaspoon salt; heat through.

4. To serve, spoon bean mixture over pork; sprinkle with cilantro. Serve with orange wedges, if you like.

Each serving: About 340 calories, 42g protein, 25g carbohydrate, 11g total fat (3g saturated), 10g fiber, 760mg sodium

BALSAMIC ROASTED PORK WITH BERRY SALAD

We've paired roasted pork loin with bright berries, licorice-flavored fennel, and baby spinach for a colorful and satisfying no-fuss meal.

ACTIVE TIME: 25 minutes   **TOTAL TIME**: 35 minutes

MAKES: 4 main-dish servings

1/4	cup balsamic vinegar	1	small red onion, thinly sliced
2	tablespoons extra-virgin olive oil	1	whole pork tenderloin (1 pound)
1	tablespoon Dijon mustard	5/8	teaspoon salt
2	teaspoons packed fresh oregano leaves, finely chopped	1/8	teaspoon ground black pepper
2	medium fennel bulbs (12 ounces each), each cut into 1/4-inch-thick slices	1	pound strawberries
		1/4	cup packed fresh basil leaves
		1	bag (5 ounces) baby spinach
		1/2	pint blackberries

1. Preheat oven to 450°F.

2. In large bowl, with wire whisk, stir together 3 tablespoons vinegar, 1 tablespoon oil, 2 teaspoons mustard, and oregano. Add fennel, tossing until well coated. Transfer fennel to 18″ by 12″ jelly-roll pan, arranging on outer edges; leave remaining dressing in bowl. Add onions to bowl and toss until well coated. Transfer onions to center of pan. Add pork to same bowl and toss until coated; place on top of onions.

3. Sprinkle pork and vegetables with 1/4 teaspoon salt and pepper. Roast for 18 to 22 minutes or until instant-read thermometer inserted in thickest part of pork registers 140°F. Let pork stand for 5 minutes.

4. While pork roasts, hull and slice strawberries. Finely chop basil; place in large bowl.

5. In bowl with basil, whisk together remaining 1 tablespoon vinegar, 1 tablespoon oil, 1 teaspoon mustard, and remaining 1/8 teaspoon salt until well combined. Thinly slice pork. Add fennel, onion, spinach, and strawberries to bowl with dressing, tossing until well mixed. Divide among serving plates. Top with blackberries and pork.

Each serving: About 315 calories, 26g protein, 30g carbohydrate, 11g total fat (2g saturated), 10g fiber, 480mg sodium

CARAMELIZED BRISKET WITH GLAZED SHIITAKES

This tender Asian-inspired brisket, cooked low and slow, is sure to become a family favorite!

ACTIVE TIME: 30 minutes   **TOTAL TIME**: 3 hours 30 minutes

MAKES: 10 servings

3	tablespoons canola or vegetable oil	1/4	cup granulated sugar
1	beef brisket (about 4 pounds), trimmed	1/4	cup rice vinegar
		2	whole star anise
1	teaspoon salt	1/2	teaspoon five-spice powder
1/2	teaspoon ground black pepper	1 1/2	pounds shiitake mushrooms, stems removed
1	large onion, chopped		Finely chopped fresh parsley, for garnish
4	garlic cloves, smashed		
3/4	cup reduced-sodium soy sauce		Steamed white rice, for serving (optional)
1/2	cup molasses		

1. Preheat oven to 325°F. In 7- to 9-quart wide-bottomed Dutch oven or heavy saucepot, heat oil over medium-high heat until hot. Season brisket all over with salt and pepper; add to pot. Cook for 10 minutes or until browned on both sides, turning over halfway through cooking. Transfer to large plate.

2. To same pot, add onion and garlic and cook for 3 minutes, stirring. Add soy sauce, molasses, sugar, vinegar, star anise, and five-spice powder, scraping up any browned bits from bottom of pot. Return brisket to pot; heat to boiling over high heat. Cover; place in oven and bake for 2 hours.

3. To same pot, add shiitakes; re-cover and bake for another 1 to 1 1/2 hours or until brisket is very tender. Transfer brisket to cutting board and shiitakes to serving dish. Pour cooking liquid through fine-mesh strainer set over medium bowl or fat separator; discard solids and fat. Serve brisket with shiitakes and cooking liquid; garnish with parsley. Serve with rice, if desired.

Each serving: About 375 calories, 36g protein, 25g carbohydrate, 14g total fat (4g saturated), 2g fiber, 675mg sodium

MAPLE-GLAZED SAUSAGES AND FIGS

Here's an easy Italian meal that combines both sweet and savory. You can prepare the side of chard in the microwave.

ACTIVE TIME: 30 minutes   **TOTAL TIME**: 40 minutes

MAKES: 4 main-dish servings

2 tablespoons maple syrup	1/2 large sweet onion (12 ounces), chopped
2 tablespoons balsamic vinegar	
8 fully-cooked chicken and roasted garlic sausages (two 12-ounce packages; see Tip)	1 1/2 pounds Swiss chard, stems sliced and leaves chopped
	2 teaspoons olive oil
8 ripe fresh figs, cut lengthwise in half	1/4 teaspoon salt
	1/4 teaspoon ground black pepper

1. Preheat oven to 450°F and line baking sheet with foil. In small bowl, stir syrup and 1 tablespoon vinegar until blended. Place sausages and figs in single layer on prepared baking sheet, and lightly brush with half of syrup mixture.

2. Roast sausages and figs for 8 to 10 minutes or until heated through and golden, turning over and brushing with remaining syrup mixture halfway through roasting.

3. Meanwhile, place onion in large microwave-safe bowl. Cover with vented plastic wrap and microwave on high for 3 minutes. Add chard to bowl; cover and microwave for 9 minutes or until vegetables are tender, stirring once. Stir in oil, salt, pepper, and remaining 1 tablespoon vinegar.

4. Place 2 sausages on each plate and serve chard and figs alongside.

Each serving: About 450 calories, 34g protein, 42g carbohydrate, 17g total fat (4g saturated), 7g fiber, 1,455mg sodium

TIP

To lower the sodium in this recipe by 650 milligrams (and cut some calories, too), serve one sausage per person instead of two.

OSSO BUCO WITH GREMOLATA

This aromatic recipe from northern Italy is a wonderful choice for company. Risotto is the traditional accompaniment, or for a lower-calorie meal, pair the veal with broccoli rabe tossed with a little balsamic vinegar.

ACTIVE TIME: 40 minutes   **TOTAL TIME**: 2 hours 40 minutes
MAKES: 4 main-dish servings

4	meaty veal shank cross cuts (osso buco), each about 2 inches thick (1 pound total)
½	teaspoon salt
¼	teaspoon ground black pepper
1	tablespoon olive oil
2	onions, chopped
3	carrots, peeled and chopped
2	stalks celery, chopped
4	garlic cloves, finely chopped
1	can (14½ to 16 ounces) tomatoes in puree
1	cup dry white wine
1	cup canned or homemade chicken broth (see recipe, page 137)
1	bay leaf
2	tablespoons chopped fresh parsley
½	teaspoon freshly grated lemon peel

1. Preheat oven to 350°F. Sprinkle shanks with salt and pepper. In nonreactive 5-quart Dutch oven, heat oil over medium-high heat until very hot. Add shanks and cook until browned on both sides, about 10 minutes, transferring shanks to plate as they are browned.

2. Add onions to Dutch oven and cook over medium heat, stirring occasionally, until slightly browned, about 5 minutes. Add carrots, celery, and three-fourths of garlic and cook for 2 minutes longer.

3. Return veal to Dutch oven. Stir in tomatoes with their puree, wine, broth, and bay leaf; heat to boiling over high heat. Cover and place in oven. Bake until veal is tender when pierced with fork, about 2 hours.

4. Meanwhile, prepare gremolata: In small bowl, mix parsley, lemon peel, and remaining garlic. Cover and refrigerate until ready to serve.

5. Transfer veal to platter. Heat sauce in Dutch oven to boiling over high heat; boil until it has reduced to 4 cups, about 10 minutes. Pour sauce over veal and sprinkle with gremolata.

Each serving: About 375 calories, 53g protein, 20g carbohydrate, 8g total fat (2g saturated), 4g fiber, 874mg sodium

Let's Talk Gremolata

A finishing touch, gremolata is a classic Italian herb mixture best known as a garnish for braised veal shanks (osso buco). It can also be stirred into sauces or sprinkled over grilled fish, roast chicken, and bean dishes just before serving. You can make gremolata from mint, parsley, or equal parts parsley and cilantro. Other variations: Try orange or lime zest instead of lemon.

8 VEGGIE & WHOLE-GRAIN MAINS

Looking to incorporate more greens and grains into your family's diet, and cut back on saturated fat? We have the perfect solution: Go meatless for a couple of nights a week. The great-tasting vegetarian meals in this chapter are sure to keep your family satisfied, and you'll feel good knowing that they're getting lots of heart-protecting antioxidants and cholesterol-lowering soluble fiber.

Start with familiar favorites: Serve our hearty black bean burgers with a side of oven fries. Or simmer a big pot of our spicy vegetarian chili made special with white beans and tomatillos. Hankering for Indian food? Our vegetable stew and cauliflower curry are fresh and healthy.

If vegetables for dinner sound boring, try stuffing them for a fun new twist. Our artichokes filled with couscous make a complete meal. Or bake our gingery napa cabbage and bulgur casserole for a hot, satisfying dish on a cold night.

And, of course, we haven't forgotten the noodles. Our Whole Wheat Penne Genovese icludes beans for extra protein. Other options include our lasagna toss (with tomato-spinach sauce and ricotta cheese) and broccoli pesto pasta. To learn why you should swap in whole wheat or multigrain pasta, see the box on page 373.

SWEET POTATO CAKES WITH KALE AND BEAN SALAD

If you're a fan of potato pancakes, try this healthier take on those traditional patties.

TOTAL TIME: 30 minutes

MAKES: 4 servings

Nonstick cooking spray

3	sweet potatoes, peeled and shredded
2	green onions, thinly sliced
1/4	teaspoon salt
1/4	teaspoon ground black pepper
1/4	cup light mayonnaise
2	tablespoons lime juice
1	tablespoon soy sauce
1	bag (5 ounces) baby kale
2	cans (14 ounces each) no-salt-added black beans, rinsed and drained
2	cups shelled frozen (thawed) edamame

1. Preheat oven to 450°F. Spray baking sheet with cooking spray.

2. In large bowl, toss shredded sweet potatoes with green onions, salt, and pepper. With 1/4-cup measure, scoop packed sweet potatoes onto prepared baking sheet to form 12 mounds, spacing 2 inches apart. Flatten slightly. Spray tops with cooking spray. Bake for 25 minutes or until browned at edges.

3. Meanwhile, in large bowl, whisk together mayonnaise, lime juice, and soy sauce.

4. When cakes are cooked, add baby kale, black beans, and edamame to dressing. Toss until coated. Serve cakes over salad.

Each serving: About 375 calories, 21g protein, 56g carbohydrate, 9g total fat (1g saturated), 16g fiber, 530mg sodium

WHITE-BEAN AND TOMATILLO CHILI

This spicy vegetarian chili is made with fresh tomatillos—the tart, green, tomato-like fruits (with papery husks) that are a staple in Southwestern cuisine. Serve with warm tortillas and a dollop of plain yogurt.

ACTIVE TIME: 25 minutes   **TOTAL TIME**: 45 minutes

MAKES: 4 main-dish servings

2	tablespoons olive oil
3	garlic cloves, crushed with press
1	small onion, cut in half and thinly sliced
1	jalapeño chile, seeded and minced
1	teaspoon ground cumin
1	pound tomatillos, husked, rinsed, and coarsely chopped
1¼	teaspoons salt
½	teaspoon granulated sugar
1	can (14½ ounces) low-sodium vegetable broth, or 1¾ cups homemade (see recipe, page 136)
1	can (4 ounces) chopped mild green chiles
1	cup water
2	cans (15 to 19 ounces each) low-sodium white kidney beans (cannellini), rinsed, drained, and coarsely mashed
1	cup loosely packed fresh cilantro leaves, chopped

1. In 10-inch nonstick skillet, heat oil over medium heat until hot. Add garlic, onion, jalapeño, and cumin and cook until lightly golden, 7 to 10 minutes, stirring often.

2. Meanwhile, in 5- to 6-quart saucepot, heat tomatillos, salt, sugar, broth, green chiles and their liquid, and water to boiling over high heat. Reduce heat to low. Stir onion mixture into saucepot; cover and simmer for 15 minutes.

3. Stir in beans and cilantro; heat through.

Each serving: About 300 calories, 12g protein, 42g carbohydrate, 10g total fat (1g saturated), 12g fiber, 966mg sodium

CORN FRITTERS WITH BLACK BEAN SALAD

This hearty vegetarian dish combines all the best tastes of the Southwest.

ACTIVE TIME: 20 minutes   **TOTAL TIME**: 40 minutes
MAKES: 4 main-dish servings

2	cans (15 ounces each) black beans, rinsed and drained
1	large avocado, cut into small cubes
1/2	cup packed fresh cilantro leaves
1/4	small red onion, very thinly sliced
3	tablespoons lime juice
3/4	teaspoon salt
4	cups fresh corn kernels
1/2	cup all-purpose flour
2	large eggs, beaten
2	garlic cloves, finely chopped
1	teaspoon ground cumin
3/4	cup vegetable oil

1. In large bowl, combine beans, avocado, cilantro, onion, lime juice, and 1/4 teaspoon salt, tossing.

2. In another large bowl, combine corn, flour, eggs, garlic, cumin, and remaining 1/2 teaspoon salt until well mixed.

3. In 12-inch skillet, heat oil over medium-high heat until very hot. Add batter to oil by 1/4-cupfuls, forming 4 mounds; gently press tops to flatten. Cook for 4 to 5 minutes or until browned on each side, turning over once. (Be careful: Oil will splatter.) Transfer to baking sheet in 225°F oven to keep warm. Repeat with remaining batter, reducing heat to medium, if necessary to maintain temperature. Serve with bean salad.

Each serving: About 615 calories, 23g protein, 79g carbohydrate, 29g total fat (4g saturated), 19g fiber, 880mg sodium

BLACK BEAN BURGERS

Spicy cumin and coriander flavor these healthy, meat-free, bean burgers.

ACTIVE TIME: 15 minutes **TOTAL TIME**: 20 minutes
MAKES: 4 burgers

¼	cup dried bread crumbs
¼	teaspoon ground cumin
¼	teaspoon ground coriander
2	cans (15 ounces each) low-sodium black beans, rinsed and drained, or 3 cups cooked black beans
4	tablespoons light mayonnaise
¼	teaspoon salt
¼	teaspoon ground black pepper
2	large stalks celery, finely chopped
Nonstick cooking spray	
1	chipotle chile in adobo, finely chopped
4	green-leaf lettuce leaves
4	whole wheat hamburger buns, toasted
4	slices ripe tomato

1. In food processor with knife blade attached, pulse bread crumbs, cumin, coriander, two-thirds of beans, 2 tablespoons mayonnaise, salt, and pepper until well blended. Transfer to large bowl. Stir in celery and remaining whole beans until well combined. Divide into 4 portions and shape into patties.

2. Lightly coat 12-inch nonstick skillet with cooking spray. Heat over medium heat for 1 minute, then add patties. Cook for 10 to 12 minutes or until browned on both sides, turning once.

3. Meanwhile, in small bowl, combine chipotle chile and remaining 2 tablespoons mayonnaise until well mixed. Place 1 lettuce leaf on bottom of each bun; top with patty, then tomato slice. Divide chipotle mayonnaise among burgers and replace tops of buns to serve.

Each burger: About 370 calories, 18g protein, 59g carbohydrate, 8g total fat (1g saturated), 14g fiber, 725mg sodium

MOROCCAN SWEET-POTATO STEW

This fragrant stew, served on top of couscous, is loaded with vegetables and spices.

ACTIVE TIME: 15 minutes **TOTAL TIME**: 45 minutes
MAKES: 4 main-dish servings

2	teaspoons olive oil
1	yellow onion, chopped
3	garlic cloves, crushed with press
1½	teaspoons curry powder
1½	teaspoons ground cumin
¼	teaspoon ground allspice
1	can (14½ ounces) diced tomatoes
1	can (14½ ounces) reduced-sodium vegetable broth
1	cup no-salt-added canned garbanzo beans, rinsed and drained
1	large sweet potato (1 pound), peeled and cut into ¾-inch chunks
2	small zucchini (6 ounces each), cut into ¾-inch chunks
1	cup whole-grain couscous (Moroccan pasta)
¼	cup loosely packed fresh mint leaves, chopped

1. In 12-inch nonstick skillet, heat oil over medium heat until hot. Add onion and cook until tender and lightly browned, 8 to 10 minutes, stirring occasionally. Stir in garlic, curry powder, cumin, and allspice; cook for 30 seconds.

2. Add tomatoes, broth, beans, and sweet potato; cover and heat to boiling over medium-high heat. Reduce heat to medium and cook for 10 minutes.

3. Stir in zucchini; cover and cook until vegetables are tender, about 10 minutes.

4. Meanwhile, prepare couscous as label directs.

5. Just before serving, stir mint into stew. Serve stew with couscous.

Each serving: About 360 calories, 14g protein, 70g carbohydrate, 5g total fat (1g saturated), 13g fiber, 670mg sodium

POLENTA WITH GARLICKY GREENS

This is a nutritious meal of soft cornmeal, with a tasty topping of sautéed Swiss chard, raisins, and pine nuts. We simplified and reduced the total prep time by microwaving the polenta. (Stir just once instead of constantly.)

ACTIVE TIME: 30 minutes **TOTAL TIME**: 50 minutes
MAKES: 4 main-dish servings

2	bunches Swiss chard (3½ pounds total)
1	tablespoon olive oil
3	garlic cloves, thinly sliced
¼	teaspoon crushed red pepper
1	teaspoon salt
⅓	cup plus 4½ cups water
¼	cup golden raisins
1½	cups yellow cornmeal
2	cups skim milk
2	tablespoons freshly grated Parmesan or Romano cheese, plus more for serving
1	tablespoon pine nuts (pignoli), toasted and chopped

1. Cut off and discard bottom 3 inches of Swiss-chard stems. Cut remaining stems into ½-inch-thick slices; coarsely chop leaves. Rinse stems and leaves separately and dry with paper towels; place in separate bowls.

2. In 12-inch nonstick skillet, heat oil, garlic, and crushed red pepper over medium heat until garlic is lightly golden, about 2 minutes, stirring occasionally.

3. Add sliced chard stems to skillet and cook for 8 minutes, stirring occasionally. Gradually add chard leaves and ½ teaspoon salt, stirring until leaves wilt; stir in ⅓ cup water. Cover skillet and simmer until stems and leaves are tender, about 5 minutes; stir in raisins and set aside.

4. Meanwhile, prepare polenta in microwave: In 4-quart microwave-safe bowl or casserole, combine cornmeal, remaining $^1/_2$ teaspoon salt, milk, and remaining $4^1/_2$ cups water. Cover and cook on high for 12 to 15 minutes, until thickened, stirring once.

5. To serve, stir Parmesan into polenta. Spoon polenta onto platter; top with Swiss-chard mixture and sprinkle with pine nuts. Serve with additional Parmesan to sprinkle over each serving, if you like.

Each serving: About 415 calories, 16g protein, 76g carbohydrate, 7g total fat (1g saturated), 10g fiber, 995mg sodium

FARRO RISOTTO WITH BUTTERNUT SQUASH

The firm, chewy texture of farro resembles Arborio rice but boasts the nutritional characteristics of spelt. Italians have enjoyed this grain since the days of the Roman Empire.

ACTIVE TIME: 20 minutes   **TOTAL TIME**: 55 minutes
MAKES: 4 main-dish servings

1	tablespoon olive oil
1	small onion, finely chopped
1/2	teaspoon salt
1/4	teaspoon ground black pepper
1 1/2	cups farro (emmer wheat)
1/2	cup dry white wine
1 1/4	cups water
1	can (14 1/2 ounces) vegetable broth, or 1 3/4 cups homemade (see recipe, page 136)
1/8	teaspoon dried thyme
1/8	teaspoon dried rosemary, crushed
1	butternut squash (2 pounds), peeled and cut into 1/2-inch pieces
1/2	cup freshly grated Parmesan cheese, plus more for serving
1/4	cup loosely packed fresh parsley leaves, chopped

1. In deep 12-inch nonstick skillet, heat oil over medium heat until hot. Add onion, salt, and pepper and cook for 5 to 7 minutes or until onion is tender and lightly browned. Add farro and cook for 2 to 3 minutes or until lightly browned, stirring constantly. Add wine and cook for about 1 minute or until absorbed.

2. To farro mixture in skillet, add water, broth, thyme, and rosemary; cover skillet and heat to boiling over high heat. Stir in squash; reduce heat to medium-low. Cover and simmer for about 20 minutes longer or until farro is just tender (mixture will still be soupy).

3. Uncover and cook for 1 to 2 minutes longer over high heat, stirring constantly, until most liquid is absorbed. Remove skillet from heat and stir in Parmesan and parsley. Serve with additional Parmesan, if you like.

Each serving: About 415 calories, 16g protein, 74g carbohydrate, 9g total fat (3g saturated), 6g fiber, 925mg sodium

BROWN-RICE RISOTTO WITH BUTTERNUT SQUASH

Prepare recipe as instructed, substituting **1¹/₂ cups regular long-grain brown rice** for farro. In step 2, add **2¹/₂ cups water** and cook rice for 45 minutes (instead of 20 minutes) over medium-low heat, once pot is covered and simmering.

Each serving: About 445 calories, 13g protein, 80g carbohydrate, 9g total fat (3g saturated), 6g fiber, 930mg sodium

RISOTTO PUTTANESCA

Creamy risotto gets kicked up a notch with the rich tang of tomato paste and the briny flavors of olives and capers.

ACTIVE TIME: 20 minutes   **TOTAL TIME**: 1 hour
MAKES: 4 main-dish servings

1	quart lower-sodium chicken or vegetable broth
7	cups water
2	tablespoons olive oil
1	medium onion, finely chopped
1	pound Arborio or Carnaroli rice
1	can (6 ounces) tomato paste
1	cup pitted Kalamata olives, chopped
¼	cup fresh parsley leaves, chopped
3	tablespoons capers, drained
2	tablespoons butter, at room temperature
1	teaspoon salt
½	teaspoon ground black pepper

1. In 3-quart saucepan, combine broth with water; cover and heat to simmering over high heat. Reduce heat to low.

2. In 5- to 6-quart saucepot, heat oil over medium heat. Add onion and cook for 5 minutes or until translucent, stirring occasionally. Add rice; cook for 1 minute, stirring. Add 2 ladlefuls of broth to rice; stir until most of liquid is absorbed before adding another ladleful. Reduce heat to medium-low. Continue adding broth and stirring until about 1 cup broth remains in saucepan; whisk tomato paste into broth. Add tomato broth to rice, stirring until liquid is absorbed and rice is tender.

3. Gently fold olives, parsley, capers, butter, salt, and pepper into rice. Reserve 3 cups risotto for another use. Serve remaining risotto immediately.

Each serving: About 445 calories, 11g protein, 69g carbohydrate, 15g total fat (4g saturated), 5g fiber, 825mg sodium

WHEAT-BERRY PILAF WITH GREEN BEANS

Make this tasty veggie-flecked combination of brown rice and wheat berries the centerpiece of a vegetarian meal.

ACTIVE TIME: 30 minutes   **TOTAL TIME**: 1 hour 30 minutes

MAKES: 4 main-dish or 8 side-dish servings

1	cup wheat berries (whole wheat kernels)
4	cups water
1/2	cup long-grain brown rice
3	teaspoons olive oil
4	carrots, peeled and cut into 1/2-inch dice
2	stalks celery, cut into 1/2-inch dice
1	large onion (12 ounces), cut into 1/2-inch dice
1	can (14 1/2 ounces) vegetable broth, or 1 3/4 cups homemade (see recipe, page 136)
8	ounces green beans, trimmed and cut into 1 1/2-inch pieces
3/4	teaspoon salt
1/2	teaspoon freshly grated orange peel
1/4	teaspoon coarsely ground black pepper
1/4	teaspoon dried thyme
3/4	cup dried cranberries

1. In 3-quart saucepan, heat wheat berries and water to boiling over high heat. Reduce heat to low; cover and simmer until wheat berries are firm to the bite but tender enough to eat, about 50 minutes; drain and set aside.

2. Meanwhile, in 2-quart saucepan, prepare brown rice as label directs, but do not add butter or salt.

3. While wheat berries and brown rice are cooking, in deep 12-inch skillet, heat 2 teaspoons oil over medium heat until hot. Add carrots and celery; cook until almost tender, about 10 minutes, stirring occasionally. Add onion and remaining 1 teaspoon oil; cook until vegetables are lightly browned, 12 to 15 minutes longer, stirring occasionally.

4. Increase heat to high; add broth, green beans, salt, orange peel, pepper, and thyme and heat to boiling. Reduce heat to medium-high; cook until green beans are just tender, about 5 minutes, stirring often.

5. Add cranberries, wheat berries, and brown rice to skillet; stir to combine.

Each main-dish serving: About 425 calories, 14g protein, 84g carbohydrate, 6g total fat (1g saturated), 12g fiber, 790mg sodium

Get Your Grains:
WHEAT BERRIES

Whole wheat is a nutritional powerhouse, containing thirteen B vitamins, vitamin E, protein, and essential fatty acids. Wheat berries are unmilled kernels of wheat; they are chewy with a pleasant nutty taste that makes them a great choice for salads. The coarsely crushed kernels of wheat are sold as cracked wheat. Because the kernels have been split open, cracked wheat cooks more quickly than wheat berries, so use it when you need to get whole-grain goodness fast!

CABBAGE AND BULGUR CASSEROLE

We layered napa cabbage with a gingery grain filling and topped it all with tangy-sweet tomatoes.

ACTIVE TIME: 45 minutes   **TOTAL TIME**: 1 hour 25 minutes
MAKES: 6 main-dish servings

2	cups water
1½	cups bulgur
1	tablespoon vegetable oil
2	carrots, peeled and diced
2	stalks celery, diced
1	red pepper, diced
½	small head napa (Chinese) cabbage, cored and cut crosswise into 2-inch strips (about 12 cups)
3	garlic cloves, crushed with press
3	green onions, sliced
2	tablespoons minced, peeled fresh ginger
2	tablespoons plus 1 teaspoon soy sauce
2	tablespoons seasoned rice vinegar
1	can (14½ ounces) diced tomatoes
2	tablespoons brown sugar
2	tablespoons chopped fresh parsley, for garnish

1. Preheat oven to 350°F.

2. In 2-quart saucepan, heat 1½ cups water to boiling over high heat; stir in bulgur. Remove saucepan from heat; cover and set aside.

3. In 5-quart Dutch oven, heat oil over medium-high heat. Add carrots, celery, and red pepper; cook for 5 minutes. Add cabbage stems and cook until vegetables are tender, 7 minutes longer. Reduce heat to low; add garlic, green onions, and ginger and cook for 1 minute longer, stirring.

4. Add remaining ½ cup water; heat to boiling over high heat. Reduce heat to low; simmer for 1 minute, stirring. Remove Dutch oven from heat; stir in 2 tablespoons soy sauce, 1 tablespoon vinegar, and cooked bulgur.

5. In small bowl, combine tomatoes with their juice, brown sugar, and remaining 1 teaspoon soy sauce and 1 tablespoon vinegar.

6. In 3-quart casserole, place half of cabbage leaves; top with bulgur mixture, then remaining cabbage leaves. Spoon tomato mixture over top. Cover casserole and bake until hot in center and top layer of cabbage leaves is wilted, about 40 minutes. Sprinkle with parsley before serving.

Each serving: About 220 calories, 7g protein, 43g carbohydrate, 3g total fat (0g saturated), 12g fiber, 800mg sodium

BULGUR AND CASHEW STUFFED EGGPLANT

There may be no meat or dairy, but there's plenty of flavor (curry, golden raisins) in this heart-healthy meal.

TOTAL TIME: 30 minutes

MAKES: 4 servings

3	tablespoons olive oil
3	garlic cloves, crushed with press
1/2	cup golden raisins
1/2	teaspoon curry powder
3/4	teaspoon salt
1	cup quick-cooking bulgur
2	cups water
2	medium eggplants
1/2	cup cashews, chopped

Chopped fresh mint, for garnish

1. Preheat broiler. Line large baking sheet with foil.

2. In small saucepot, heat 1 tablespoon oil over medium heat. Add garlic, raisins, curry powder, and 1/4 teaspoon salt; cook for 2 minutes, stirring. Add bulgur and water; heat to simmering. Cover and simmer for 15 minutes or until bulgur is tender.

3. Meanwhile, cut eggplants in half lengthwise; scoop out seeds. Arrange on prepared baking sheet, cut-sides up. Brush with remaining 2 tablespoons oil and sprinkle with remaining 1/2 teaspoon salt. Broil on high, 6 inches from heat source, for 7 minutes or until tender. Remove from oven; cover with foil.

4. With fork, fluff bulgur; stir in cashews. Stuff each eggplant with bulgur mixture and garnish with mint.

Each serving: About 460 calories, 11g protein, 69g carbohydrate, 19g total fat (3g saturated), 16g fiber, 450mg sodium

Eat Your Eggplant

It's worth the effort to learn to like eggplant: That bitter taste comes, in part, from chlorogenic acid, which helps prevent cancer and can also keep heart-threatening plaque from building up. What's more, lab studies show that eating eggplant lowers LDL cholesterol and helps artery walls relax, which can cut your risk for high blood pressure. To mellow eggplant's flavor, try grilling or slow-roasting it. (Salting it and letting it stand for 30 minutes also helps draw out some of the bitterness. Rinse off the salt before proceeding with your recipe.)

BEAN AND CORN-STUFFED SWEET POTATOES

This dish is a perfect, easy weeknight dinner for the whole family. Packed with healthy veggies like spinach and fiber-loaded beans, it's a great alternative to a boring baked potato.

ACTIVE TIME: 10 minutes   **TOTAL TIME**: 20 minutes
MAKES: 4 main-dish servings

4	sweet potatoes, pricked with fork
1	tablespoon olive oil
1	medium onion, sliced
1	can (15 ounces) black beans, rinsed and drained
2	cups packed baby spinach
1	cup corn
½	cup sliced green onions
1	tablespoon chopped chipotle chiles in adobo
1	garlic clove, crushed with press
2	teaspoons salt
4	tablespoons shredded low-fat Mexican-blend cheese

1. Microwave sweet potatoes on high for 10 minutes or until tender, turning over once.

2. Meanwhile, heat olive oil in 12-inch skillet over medium-high heat. Add sliced onion and cook for 6 to 7 minutes or until soft, stirring frequently.

3. Add black beans, spinach, corn, green onions, chopped chipotle chiles, garlic, and salt. Cook for 2 minutes or until spinach wilts.

4. Split sweet potatoes and fill with bean mixture. Sprinkle each with 1 tablespoon shredded cheese.

Each serving: About 265 calories, 10g protein, 50g carbohydrate, 5g total fat (2g saturated), 12g fiber, 555mg sodium

TIP
For a vegan recipe, just substitute soy cheese for the Mexican-blend cheese or omit it altogether.

BBQ TOFU SANDWICHES

Here's a quick and easy way to flavor tofu.

ACTIVE TIME: 20 minutes   **TOTAL TIME**: 25 minutes

MAKES: 4 sandwiches

1	package (16 ounces) extra-firm tofu	1/8	teaspoon cayenne (ground red) pepper
Nonstick cooking spray		2	garlic cloves, crushed with press
1/4	cup ketchup	2	teaspoons sesame seeds
2	tablespoons Dijon mustard	8	slices whole-grain bread, toasted
2	tablespoons reduced-sodium soy sauce		
1	tablespoon molasses	Sliced ripe tomatoes, sliced red onion, and lettuce leaves, for topping (optional)	
1	tablespoon grated, peeled fresh ginger		

1. Drain tofu; wrap in clean dish towel. Place wrapped tofu in pie plate; top with a dinner plate. Place 1 to 2 heavy cans on top of plate to weight down tofu to extract excess water; set aside for about 15 minutes.

2. Meanwhile, preheat broiler. Coat rack in broiling pan with nonstick cooking spray.

3. In small bowl, combine ketchup, mustard, soy sauce, molasses, ginger, cayenne, and garlic, stirring until blended.

4. Remove plate and cans, unwrap tofu, and place on cutting board. Cut tofu lengthwise into 8 slices.

5. Place slices on rack in broiling pan; brush with half of ketchup mixture. Place in broiler about 5 inches from heat source and broil tofu until ketchup mixture looks dry, about 3 minutes. With metal spatula, turn slices over; brush with remaining ketchup mixture and sprinkle with sesame seeds. Broil tofu for 3 minutes longer.

6. To serve, place 2 tofu slices on 1 slice of toasted bread. Top with tomato, onion, and lettuce, if you like. Top with another slice of bread. Repeat with remaining tofu and bread.

Each sandwich: About 230 calories, 14g protein, 35g carbohydrate, 5g total fat (0g saturated), 2g fiber, 975mg sodium

BROCCOLI PESTO SPAGHETTI

The pesto is best made in a food processor; a blender will make the mixture too creamy. Serve with breadsticks and a green salad splashed with balsamic vinegar.

TOTAL TIME: 15 minutes
MAKES: 4 main-dish servings

1	package (16 ounces) spaghetti or thin spaghetti
1	bag (16 ounces) frozen chopped broccoli
1	cup vegetable broth
2	cups freshly grated Parmesan cheese
2	tablespoons olive oil
1	small garlic clove
¼	teaspoon salt

Ground black pepper

1. In large saucepot, cook pasta as label directs. In saucepan, prepare broccoli as label directs.

2. In food processor with knife blade attached, puree cooked broccoli, broth, Parmesan, oil, garlic, and salt until smooth, stopping processor occasionally to scrape down sides.

3. Drain pasta; transfer to warm serving bowl. Add broccoli pesto to pasta; toss well. Sprinkle with pepper and serve.

Each serving: About 550 calories, 22g protein, 81g carbohydrate, 11g total fat (3g saturated), 8g fiber, 615mg sodium

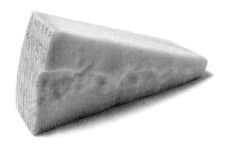

SKILLET VEGETABLE CURRY

As the vegetables simmer, toast some naan or pita bread. A sprinkle of flaked coconut and mustard seeds add South Indian flair to this vegan-friendly dish.

ACTIVE TIME: 15 minutes   **TOTAL TIME**: 35 minutes

MAKES: 4 main-dish servings

³/₄	pound cauliflower florets	1	teaspoon mustard seeds
1	large all-purpose potato (about 8 ounces), peeled and cut into 1-inch pieces	1¹/₂	teaspoons ground cumin
		1¹/₂	teaspoons ground coriander
1	large sweet potato (about 12 ounces), peeled and cut into 1-inch pieces	3	teaspoons cayenne (ground red) pepper
		2	medium tomatoes, chopped
2	tablespoons lightly packed sweetened flaked coconut	1	cup frozen peas, thawed
		¹/₂	teaspoons salt
2	teaspoons olive oil	¹/₂	cup loosely packed fresh cilantro leaves, chopped
1	medium onion (8 ounces), finely chopped		

1. In 4-quart saucepan, combine cauliflower, potato, sweet potato, and enough water to cover; heat to boiling over high heat. Reduce heat to low; cover and simmer until vegetables are tender, 8 to 10 minutes. Drain well, reserving ³/₄ cup cooking water.

2. Meanwhile, in dry 12-inch nonstick skillet, cook coconut over medium heat, stirring constantly, until lightly browned, about 3 minutes; transfer to small bowl.

3. In same skillet, heat oil over medium heat until hot; add onion and cook for 5 minutes. Add mustard seeds, cumin, coriander, and cayenne; cover and cook, shaking skillet frequently, until onion is tender and lightly browned and seeds start to pop, 5 minutes longer.

4. Spoon cauliflower mixture into skillet. Add tomatoes, peas, salt, and reserved cooking water; heat through. Sprinkle with cilantro to serve.

Each serving: About 230 calories, 8g protein, 43g carbohydrate, 4g total fat (1g saturated), 7g fiber, 735mg sodium

FAST FRIED RICE

The secrets to this dish are quick-cooking brown rice, pre-cut frozen vegetables, and ready-to-use stir-fry sauce.

ACTIVE TIME: 5 minutes   **TOTAL TIME**: 20 minutes
MAKES: 4 main-dish servings

1½	cups quick-cooking brown rice
1	pound firm tofu, drained and cut into 1-inch cubes
6	teaspoons olive oil
1	package (16 ounces) frozen vegetables for stir-fry
2	large eggs, lightly beaten
⅓	cup stir-fry sauce
¼	cup water

1. Prepare rice as label directs.

2. Meanwhile, in medium bowl, place 3 layers of paper towels. Place tofu on towels and top with 3 more layers of paper towels. With your hand, gently press tofu to extract excess moisture.

3. In 12-inch nonstick skillet, heat 2 teaspoons oil over medium-high heat until hot. Add frozen vegetables; cover and cook, stirring occasionally, for 5 minutes. Transfer vegetables to bowl; keep warm.

4. In same skillet, heat remaining 4 teaspoons oil until hot. Add tofu and cook, stirring gently, for 5 minutes. Stir in cooked rice and cook for 4 minutes longer.

5. With spatula, push rice mixture around edge of skillet, leaving space in center. Add eggs to center of skillet; cook, stirring eggs until scrambled, about 1 minute. Add stir-fry sauce, vegetables, and water; cook, stirring, for 1 minute.

Each serving: About 360 calories, 17g protein, 41g carbohydrate, 15g total fat (2g saturated), 5g fiber, 760mg sodium

TIP
If you have more time, chop a combo of carrots, broccoli, onion, and celery to make a total of 3 to 4 cups, and cook as in step 3.

INDIAN CAULIFLOWER STEW

This easy-to-make vegetarian stew owes its complex flavor to spicy, fresh ginger and traditional Indian curry powder.

ACTIVE TIME: 25 minutes
TOTAL TIME: 50 minutes
MAKES: 8 main-dish servings

1	tablespoon olive oil
3	carrots, peeled and chopped
1	onion, chopped
1½	cups brown rice
1	tablespoon finely chopped, peeled fresh ginger
1	tablespoon curry powder
¾	teaspoon salt
2½	cups canned or homemade vegetable broth (see recipe, page 136)
1	medium head cauliflower (2 pounds), cut into small florets
2	cans (15 to 19 ounces each) garbanzo beans (chickpeas), rinsed and drained
½	cup loosely packed fresh cilantro leaves, chopped
¼	cup plain low-fat yogurt, plus more for serving

1. In 6-quart Dutch oven, heat oil over medium-high heat until hot. Add carrots and onion and cook for 10 to 12 minutes or until vegetables are lightly browned and tender, stirring frequently.

2. Meanwhile, prepare rice as label directs; keep warm.

3. Stir ginger, curry, and salt into carrot mixture; cook for 3 minutes, stirring constantly. Add broth; cover and heat to boiling over high heat. Stir in cauliflower and garbanzo beans; cover and cook over medium heat for 15 to 20 minutes longer, gently stirring every 5 minutes until cauliflower is tender.

4. To serve, stir chopped cilantro and ¼ cup yogurt into cauliflower stew. Spoon rice into serving bowls; top with stew. Serve cauliflower stew with additional yogurt to dollop on top.

Each serving: About 360 calories, 12g protein, 68g carbohydrate, 5g total fat (1g saturated), 10g fiber, 650mg sodium

Get Your Grains:
BROWN RICE

Consider making brown rice a staple in your diet. It has all its bran layers intact (only the inedible outer husk is removed) and therefore all its nutrients—including 3.5 grams of fiber per cup—are present and accounted for. It is an excellent source of manganese (a mineral that helps produce energy from protein and carbohydrates) and selenium (key to a healthy immune system). Experiment with long-, medium-, and short-grain options. Note: White rice has only a shadow of brown rice's nutritional value. Even though it's often enriched, it's been stripped of its bran and germ.

COUSCOUS-STUFFED ARTICHOKES

Instead of topping your grains with veggies, fill your veggies with whole-grain goodness.

ACTIVE TIME: 1 hour   **TOTAL TIME**: 1 hour 15 minutes
MAKES: 4 main-dish or 8 side-dish servings

4	large artichokes
1	tablespoon lemon juice
3	tablespoons olive oil
2	carrots, peeled and diced
2	garlic cloves, minced
1/4	cup chopped fresh mint
3	tablespoons chopped fresh parsley
1	cup whole wheat couscous (Moroccan pasta)
1 1/2	cups canned or homemade vegetable broth (see recipe, page 136)
1/2	teaspoon salt
1/4	teaspoon coarsely ground black pepper

Lemon wedges and parsley sprigs, for garnish

1. Prepare and cook artichokes: With sharp knife, cut off 1 inch straight across top of each artichoke. Cut off stems; peel and reserve them. Pull off outer dark green leaves and trim any thorny tips. Spread artichokes open and carefully cut around and remove chokes. In a 5-quart saucepot, heat lemon juice and 1 inch water to boiling over high heat. Set artichokes on stem ends in boiling water along with peeled stems; heat to boiling. Reduce heat to low; cover and simmer until a knife inserted in center goes through bottom easily, 30 to 40 minutes. Drain.

2. Meanwhile, preheat oven to 400°F.

3. In 10-inch nonstick skillet, heat 1 tablespoon oil over medium heat until hot. Add carrots and cook until tender, about 10 minutes, stirring occasionally. Stir in garlic; cook for 1 minute longer. Remove to medium bowl. Dice artichoke stems; add to carrot mixture with mint and parsley.

4. Prepare couscous as label directs but use 1 cup broth in place of 1 cup water. When couscous is done, stir in salt, pepper, carrot mixture, and remaining 2 tablespoons oil.

5. Pour remaining ½ cup broth into shallow baking dish large enough to hold all artichokes (13″ by 9″); arrange cooked artichokes in dish. Spoon couscous mixture between artichoke leaves and into center cavities. Bake until artichokes are heated through, 15 to 20 minutes.

6. Serve artichokes with lemon wedges and garnish with parsley sprigs.

Each main-dish serving: About 350 calories, 11g protein, 54g carbohydrate, 11g total fat (2g saturated), 12g fiber, 600mg sodium

Get Your Grains:
COUSCOUS

Originally from North Africa, this grain-like pasta is made from semolina wheat flour. The packaged, precooked version is ready to eat in just 5 minutes and is widely available in supermarkets. Look for whole wheat couscous, which is similar in taste and texture to regular couscous, but delivers a whopping 8 grams of fiber per serving.

WHOLE WHEAT PENNE GENOVESE

An onion-flecked white bean sauté adds heft to this fresh and healthy pesto pasta dish, making it light yet satisfying.

ACTIVE TIME: 15 minutes   **TOTAL TIME**: 30 minutes

MAKES: 6 main-dish servings

12	ounces whole wheat penne or rotini pasta
1¹/₂	cups packed fresh basil leaves
1	garlic clove, peeled
3	tablespoons water
3	tablespoons extra-virgin olive oil
¹/₄	teaspoon salt
¹/₄	teaspoon ground black pepper
¹/₂	cup grated Parmesan cheese
1	small onion (4 to 6 ounces), chopped
1	can (15 to 19 ounces) white kidney beans (cannellini), rinsed and drained
1	pint grape tomatoes (red, yellow, and orange mix, if available), cut into quarters

1. In large saucepot, cook pasta as label directs.

2. Meanwhile, make pesto: In food processor with knife blade attached, blend basil, garlic, water, 2 tablespoons oil, salt, and pepper until pureed, stopping processor occasionally and scraping bowl with rubber spatula. Add Parmesan; pulse to combine. Set aside.

3. In 12-inch skillet, heat remaining 1 tablespoon oil over medium heat until very hot; add onion and cook for 5 to 7 minutes or until beginning to soften. Stir in white beans and cook for 5 minutes longer, stirring occasionally.

4. Reserve ¹/₄ cup pasta cooking water. Drain pasta and return to saucepot; stir in white bean mixture, pesto, tomatoes, and reserved cooking water. Toss to coat.

Each serving: About 375 calories, 15g protein, 59g carbohydrate, 10g total fat (2g saturated), 9g fiber, 435mg sodium

SPAGHETTI WITH ROASTED SWEET POTATO

This simple pasta is perfect for weeknight cooking and loaded with healthy, vitamin A-rich sweet potatoes.

ACTIVE TIME: 10 minutes **TOTAL TIME**: 35 minutes
MAKES: 4 main-dish servings

2	sweet potatoes, cubed
3	tablespoons olive oil
3	sprigs fresh rosemary
3/4	teaspoon salt
12	ounces spaghetti
1/3	cup pine nuts
2/3	cup finely grated Parmesan cheese

1. Preheat oven to 475°F. On parchment paper–lined jelly-roll pan, toss sweet potatoes, 1 tablespoon oil, rosemary, and 1/2 teaspoon salt. Roast for 15 minutes or until tender.

2. Meanwhile, heat large covered saucepot of salted water to boiling over high heat. Add spaghetti; cook as label directs.

3. Place pine nuts in medium bowl. Microwave on high for 1 to 2 minutes or until lightly toasted.

4. Drain pasta, reserving 1/4 cup cooking water. In large bowl, toss pasta, sweet potatoes, pine nuts, Parmesan, remaining 2 tablespoons oil, remaining 1/4 teaspoon salt, and reserved cooking water.

Each serving: About 605 calories, 20g protein, 80g carbohydrate, 24g total fat (5g saturated), 6g fiber, 780mg sodium

TIP

Omit the Parmesan cheese in this pasta (or substitute with nutritional yeast) to make it vegan.

BACON AND BRUSSELS SPROUT PENNE

This hearty pasta is full of an array of bright textures and flavors, from salty bacon to sweet raisins.

TOTAL TIME: 20 minutes
MAKES: 4 main-dish servings

1	pound penne pasta
6	slices bacon, chopped
12	ounces Brussels sprouts, quartered
1/2	teaspoon salt
1/2	teaspoon ground black pepper
2	medium shallots, thinly sliced
1/2	cup golden raisins
1/2	cup dry white wine

1. Cook penne as label directs, reserving 1/2 cup cooking water before draining.

2. Meanwhile, in 5-quart saucepan, cook bacon over medium-high heat for 5 minutes or until crisp, stirring. Transfer to plate.

3. To same pan, add Brussels sprouts, salt, and pepper; cover and cook for 5 minutes (do not stir). Reduce heat to medium. Add shallots and raisins; cook for 2 minutes, stirring occasionally. Add wine and cook for 2 minutes, scraping up browned bits from bottom of pan. Add bacon, pasta, and reserved cooking water; toss to combine and serve.

Each serving: About 465 calories, 16g protein, 74g carbohydrate, 12g total fat (4g saturated), 5g fiber, 400mg sodium

TIP
Don't have wine? No problem! Substitute 1 tablespoon lemon juice and enough water to equal 1/2 cup.

SOBA NOODLES PRIMAVERA WITH MISO

This is a quick and easy Asian-inspired pasta primavera made with packaged broccoli florets and shredded carrots. For a nutritional boost, we used soba noodles and miso (concentrated soybean paste).

ACTIVE TIME: 20 minutes   **TOTAL TIME**: 40 minutes
MAKES: 4 main-dish servings

1	package (8 ounces) soba noodles	1	package (16 ounces) extra-firm tofu, drained, patted dry and cut into 1-inch chunks
1	tablespoon olive oil		
1	medium red pepper (4 to 6 ounces), thinly sliced	1	bag (16 ounces) broccoli florets, cut into 1½-inch pieces
1	large onion (12 ounces), sliced	1	bag (10 ounces) shredded carrots
2	garlic cloves, crushed with press	¼	cup water
1	tablespoon grated, peeled fresh ginger	¼	cup red (dark) miso paste
¼	teaspoon crushed red pepper	2	green onions, thinly sliced

1. In large saucepot, prepare noodles as label directs.

2. Meanwhile, in nonstick 5- to 6-quart Dutch oven, heat oil over medium heat until hot. Add red pepper and onion; cook until golden, about 10 minutes, stirring occasionally. Add garlic, ginger, crushed red pepper, and tofu; cook for 1 minute, stirring. Add broccoli, carrots, and water; heat to boiling over medium-high heat. Reduce heat to medium; cover and cook until vegetables are tender, about 7 minutes.

3. When noodles have cooked to desired doneness, drain, reserving ³/₄ cup cooking water. Return noodles to saucepot.

4. With wire whisk, mix miso paste into reserved noodle cooking water until blended.

5. To serve, toss noodles with tofu mixture, green onions, and miso-paste mixture.

Each serving: About 450 calories, 26g protein, 68g carbohydrate, 11g total fat (2g saturated), 11g fiber, 1,290mg sodium

VEGGIE LO MEIN

This spin on a Chinese takeout classic is crazy healthy.

TOTAL TIME: 20 minutes
MAKES: 4 servings

8	ounces whole-grain spaghetti
10	ounces frozen chopped broccoli
1½	cups frozen shelled edamame
2	cups shredded carrots
10	ounces baby spinach
2	tablespoons toasted sesame oil
1	large onion, thinly sliced
2	teaspoons peeled, grated fresh ginger
¼	cup plus 1 teaspoon reduced-sodium soy sauce
2	tablespoons balsamic vinegar
4	large eggs, beaten

1. Cook spaghetti in large pot of boiling water as label directs. Just before draining, add broccoli, edamame, carrots, and spinach. Drain well; set aside.

2. In same pot, heat toasted sesame oil over medium-high heat. Add onion and cook for 5 minutes. Add ginger, soy sauce, and balsamic vinegar and cook for 1 minute. Add eggs and cook for 2 minutes without stirring. Add noodle mixture; cook, tossing, for 2 minutes or until heated through.

Each serving: About 460 calories, 25g protein, 63g carbohydrate, 15g total fat (3g saturated), 15g fiber, 785mg sodium

9 ON THE SIDE

In previous chapters, we've served up recipes for our favorite low-fat mains. Now it's time to share some simple low-fat sides to accompany them! There are hearty recipes for whole grains and low-cal, low-fat ways to prepare everyone's favorite—potatoes. We have them mashed and oven-roasted. We've also tackled trendy veggies like beets and greens (kale, Swiss chard) that younger members of your family may be reluctant to eat. Try our Basil and Balsamic Beets or our delicious Kale "Chips"—simply spray the leaves with nonstick cooking spray, sprinkle with sea salt, and bake for a healthy alternative to potato chips that even kids will embrace.

We know you may not have time to make a special vegetable dish every night, so we've provided instructions for a number of easy ways to top a wide range of steamed or boiled vegetables. And if your main dish doesn't include any grains, serve up our brown rice or wild rice pilaf, or prepare one of our sweet and savory stuffings—there's pear with cornbread, brown rice and cranberry, and then some!

APPLE CIDER-BRAISED GREENS

These easy greens make an excellent side dish for holidays or any day.

ACTIVE TIME: 30 minutes   **TOTAL TIME**: 1 hour 5 minutes
MAKES: 8 cups or 16 side-dish servings

1½	pounds mustard greens	1¼	cups apple cider
1½	pounds collard greens	1	tablespoon cider vinegar
1½	pounds Swiss chard	1½	teaspoons salt
2	tablespoons olive oil	2	red cooking apples such as Gala or Rome Beauty, unpeeled and cut into ¾-inch chunks
3	large garlic cloves, thinly sliced		

1. Remove stems from mustard greens; discard stems. Trim stem ends from collard greens and Swiss chard; remove stems from leaves. Cut stems into 1-inch pieces; cut leaves into 2-inch pieces. Rinse leaves and stems; drain well.

2. In 8-quart saucepot, heat oil over high heat until hot. Add garlic and cook for about 1 minute or until golden, stirring constantly. Add as many leaves and stems as possible, cider, vinegar, and salt, stirring to wilt greens. Add remaining greens in batches.

3. Reduce heat to medium. Cover saucepot and cook greens for 15 minutes. Stir in apples; cook, partially covered, for 10 minutes longer or until stems are very tender and most of liquid evaporates, stirring occasionally. With slotted spoon, transfer to serving bowl.

Each serving: About 60 calories, 2g protein, 10g carbohydrate, 2g total fat (0g saturated), 3g fiber, 310mg sodium

TIP

To make this dish ahead, spoon cooked greens into microwave-safe bowl; cover with plastic wrap and refrigerate for up to 2 days. When ready to serve, vent plastic wrap and microwave on high for 8 minutes or until hot, stirring halfway through.

SAUTÉED SWISS CHARD WITH GOLDEN RAISINS AND CAPERS

This simple side also makes a delicious pasta partner. Toss with a pound of your favorite pasta and ½ cup pasta cooking water for a spectacular main course.

ACTIVE TIME: 30 minutes   **TOTAL TIME**: 50 minutes
MAKES: 4 side-dish servings

2	pounds Swiss chard
1	tablespoon olive oil
1	small onion, chopped
⅓	cup golden raisins
2	tablespoons capers, drained

1. Trim tough stem ends from Swiss chard. Cut stems crosswise into 1-inch pieces; cut leaves into 2-inch pieces, keeping stems and leaves separate. Rinse leaves and stems; drain well.

2. In 12-inch nonstick skillet, heat oil over medium heat. Add onion and cook for about 6 minutes or until onion begins to brown. Add chard stems and cook, covered, for 5 to 7 minutes or until tender. Stir in raisins. Add leaves and stems in batches, covering skillet after each batch; cook for 7 to 10 minutes total or until leaves are tender and wilted and most of liquid evaporates, stirring often. Remove from heat; stir in capers.

Each serving: About 120 calories, 4g protein, 20g carbohydrate, 4g total fat (1g saturated), 5g fiber, 555mg sodium

KALE "CHIPS"

Our crispy kale "chips" are virtually fat-free—perfect for guiltless snacking.

ACTIVE TIME: 10 minutes **TOTAL TIME**: 25 minutes
MAKES: 6 side-dish servings

1	bunch kale (10 ounces), rinsed and dried well

Nonstick cooking spray
½   teaspoon kosher salt

Preheat oven to 350°F. From kale, remove and discard thick stems and tear leaves into large pieces. Spread leaves in single layer on two large baking sheets. Spray leaves with nonstick cooking spray to coat lightly; sprinkle with salt. Bake for 12 to 15 minutes or just until crisp but not browned. Cool on baking sheets on wire racks.

Each 1-cup serving: About 15 calories, 1g protein, 3g carbohydrate, 0g total fat, 1g fiber, 175mg sodium

TARRAGON PEAS AND PEARL ONIONS

Fresh tarragon adds a perky licorice flavor to these lightly cooked peas and pearl onions.

ACTIVE TIME: 5 minutes   **TOTAL TIME**: 15 minutes
MAKES: 8 side-dish servings

1	tablespoon butter or margarine
1	bag (16 ounces) frozen pearl onions
1	bag (16 ounces) frozen peas
¼	cup water
½	teaspoon salt
¼	teaspoon ground black pepper
1	tablespoon chopped fresh tarragon leaves

1. In 12-inch nonstick skillet, heat butter over medium heat until melted. Add frozen pearl onions and cook for 7 to 9 minutes or until browned.

2. Add frozen peas, water, salt, and pepper to skillet; stir to combine. Cover and cook for 3 to 4 minutes longer or until onions and peas are tender. Stir tarragon into vegetables and spoon into serving bowl.

Each serving: About 75 calories, 3g protein, 12g carbohydrate, 2g total fat (0g saturated), 4g fiber, 202mg sodium

GREEN BEANS WITH CARAMELIZED ONIONS

Caramelized onions make everything better. And this green-bean side dish—a lighter take on a beloved holiday casserole—is no exception.

ACTIVE TIME: 30 minutes   **TOTAL TIME**: 1 hour 10 minutes

MAKES: 14 cups or 16 side-dish servings

3	pounds green beans, trimmed
1½	pounds red onions (about 3 medium), cut in half and sliced
3	tablespoons butter or margarine
1	tablespoon fresh thyme leaves, chopped
1½	teaspoons salt
½	teaspoon ground black pepper

1. Fill large bowl with ice water to cool beans quickly after cooking; set aside. Heat 6- to 8-quart saucepot of salted water to boiling over high heat. Add beans in two batches and cook each batch for 4 minutes or until beans are tender-crisp, making sure water returns to boiling before adding each batch of beans. With slotted spoon or sieve, transfer beans to bowl of ice water. Drain beans thoroughly.

2. In 12-inch nonstick skillet, combine onions, butter, thyme, salt, and pepper. Cook over medium heat for 15 minutes or until onions start to brown, stirring occasionally. Reduce heat to medium-low and cook for 5 to 7 minutes longer or until onions turn dark brown, stirring frequently. Stir beans into onion mixture; heat through before serving.

Each serving: About 60 calories, 2g protein, 9g carbohydrate, 2g total fat (0g saturated), 3g fiber, 250mg sodium

TIP

If you want to make this dish ahead (up to two days in advance), blanch, cool, and drain beans. Cook onion mixture and cool. Refrigerate each component separately in sealed plastic bags. To reheat, toss beans and onion mixture into 4-quart microwave-safe glass bowl. Microwave on high for about 8 minutes, stirring once halfway through.

MIXED PEA POD STIR-FRY

This sweet and tender-crisp medley celebrates the glorious flavor of fresh green vegetables.

TOTAL TIME: 15 minutes
MAKES: 4 side-dish servings

4	cups water
1	teaspoon salt
8	ounces green beans, trimmed
2	teaspoons vegetable oil
4	ounces snow peas, trimmed and strings removed
4	ounces sugar snap peas, trimmed and strings removed
1	garlic clove, finely chopped
1	tablespoon soy sauce

1. In 12-inch skillet, combine water and salt; heat to boiling over high heat. Add green beans and cook for 3 minutes. Drain; wipe skillet dry with paper towels.

2. In same skillet, heat oil over high heat. Add green beans and cook, stirring frequently (stir-frying), until they begin to brown, 2 to 3 minutes. Add snow peas, sugar snap peas, and garlic; stir-fry until snow peas and sugar snap peas are tender-crisp, about 1 minute longer. Stir in soy sauce and remove from heat.

Each serving: About 65 calories, 3g protein, 8g carbohydrate, 2g total fat (0g saturated), 3g fiber, 844mg sodium

BASIC COUSCOUS

Couscous is the perfect side for a busy weeknight meal, taking all of 10 minutes to put together. Pair any of these variations with a simple vegetable stew or stir-fry for a meal with fewer than 450 calories.

ACTIVE TIME: 5 minutes   **TOTAL TIME**: 10 minutes plus standing
MAKES: 4 side-dish servings

1	cup whole wheat couscous (Moroccan pasta)
1¼	cups water
½	teaspoon salt

Prepare couscous as the label directs, adding seasoning to the water before boiling. Do not add butter or margarine.

Each serving: About 105 calories, 4g protein, 23g carbohydrate, 0g total fat, 4g fiber, 405mg sodium

LIME COUSCOUS

Add **1 tablespoon fresh lime juice** and **1 teaspoon freshly grated lime peel** to water when preparing couscous.

Each serving: About 110 calories, 4g protein, 23g carbohydrate, 0g total fat, 4g fiber, 405mg sodium

MOROCCAN COUSCOUS

Add ¼ **cup golden raisins**, ¼ **teaspoon ground cinnamon**, ¼ **teaspoon ground turmeric**, and ¼ **teaspoon ground cumin** to water when preparing couscous.

Each serving: About 200 calories, 6g protein, 43g carbohydrate, 0g total fat, 4g fiber, 405mg sodium

SUN-DRIED TOMATO AND GREEN ONION COUSCOUS

Add **1 medium green onion**, sliced, and **5 sun-dried tomato halves**, chopped, to water when preparing couscous.

Each serving: About 185 calories, 7g protein, 38g carbohydrate, 0g total fat, 4g fiber, 500mg sodium

CAULIFLOWER "POPCORN"

This movie snack has blockbuster health benefits—lots of immune-boosting vitamin C, potassium, cancer-fighting phytonutrients, and 2 grams of fiber per cup. Add some extra pop with one of the tasty flavor combos.

TOTAL TIME: 30 minutes

MAKES: 5 cups

8	cups small cauliflower florets (about 1¼ pounds), stems trimmed
1½	tablespoons olive oil
¼	cup grated Parmesan cheese
1	teaspoon garlic powder
½	teaspoon turmeric
½	teaspoon salt

Preheat oven to 475°F. On large rimmed baking sheet, toss cauliflower florets with olive oil, Parmesan, garlic powder, turmeric, and salt. Roast for 25 to 30 minutes or until browned and tender. Serve immediately.

Each 1-cup serving: About 90 calories, 3g protein, 7g carbohydrate, 6g total fat (1g saturated), 2g fiber, 303mg sodium

TRUFFLE "POPCORN"

Omit Parmesan, garlic, powder, and turmeric. Toss roasted cauliflower with **2 tablespoons truffle butter** and **½ teaspoon pepper** before serving.

CHILI-LIME "POPCORN"

Substitute **1 teaspoon chili powder** for Parmesan and turmeric. Grate **zest of 1 lime** over roasted cauliflower before serving.

TIP

Leftover stems? Peel and slice them for a crunchy snack with hummus, or use them to make quick pickles.

LIGHT MASHED POTATOES

Fat-free half-and-half gives these potatoes the same silky texture you'd get with heavy cream, but without the fat and cholesterol.

ACTIVE TIME: 15 minutes   **TOTAL TIME**: 30 minutes

MAKES: 6 side-dish servings

2	pounds Yukon Gold potatoes, peeled and cut into 1-inch pieces
1	tablespoon butter or margarine
³/₄	teaspoon salt
¹/₂	cup fat-free half-and-half, warmed

1. In 4-quart saucepan, combine potatoes and enough water to cover; heat to boiling over high heat. Reduce heat to low; cover and simmer 8 to 10 minutes or until potatoes are fork-tender. Reserve ¹/₄ cup cooking water; drain potatoes.

2. Return potatoes to saucepan. Mash with butter and salt. Gradually add warm half-and-half, continuing to mash potatoes until smooth and well blended; add reserved cooking water, if necessary.

Each serving: About 145 calories, 3g protein, 29g carbohydrate, 2g total fat (0g saturated), 2g fiber, 345mg sodium

MASHED SWEET POTATOES

You don't have to wait until the holidays to enjoy this delectable side dish. A few tablespoons of soy sauce add a salty, earthy flavor to our rendition of this favorite.

ACTIVE TIME: 10 minutes
TOTAL TIME: 20 minutes
MAKES: 12 side-dish servings

4	pounds sweet potatoes (5 medium), peeled and cut into 1½-inch chunks
4	tablespoons butter or margarine
3	tablespoons soy sauce
1	green onion, thinly sliced

1. In 5- or 6-quart saucepot, place sweet potatoes and enough water to cover; heat to boiling over high heat. Reduce heat to medium-low; cover and cook for 10 to 12 minutes or until potatoes are tender. Drain well and set aside.

2. In same saucepot, melt butter over medium heat. Remove saucepot from heat; add soy sauce and potatoes. With potato masher, mash potatoes until almost smooth. Transfer to serving bowl and sprinkle with green onion.

Each serving: About 150 calories, 2g protein, 27g carbohydrate, 4g total fat (1g saturated), 3g fiber, 310mg sodium

OVEN FRIES

You won't miss the fat in these hand-cut "fries." They bake beautifully in a jelly-roll pan with a spritz of nonstick cooking spray and a sprinkle of salt and pepper.

ACTIVE TIME: 10 minutes   **TOTAL TIME**: 30 minutes
MAKES: 4 side-dish servings

Nonstick cooking spray
3   medium baking potatoes, unpeeled (8 ounces each)
½   teaspoon salt
¼   teaspoon coarsely ground black pepper

1. Preheat oven to 500°F. Spray two 15½" by 10½" jelly-roll pans or two large baking sheets with nonstick cooking spray.

2. Scrub potatoes well, but do not peel. Cut each potato lengthwise in half. With each potato half cut-side down, cut lengthwise into ¼-inch-thick slices. Place potatoes in medium bowl and toss with salt and pepper.

3. Divide potato slices between pans and spray potatoes with nonstick cooking spray. Roast potatoes until tender and lightly browned, about 20 minutes, rotating pans between upper and lower racks halfway through roasting time.

Each serving: About 130 calories, 4g protein, 28g carbohydrate, 1g total fat (0g saturated), 3g fiber, 280mg sodium

ROSEMARY AND GARLIC OVEN FRIES

Prepare Oven Fries as above, but in step 3 add ½ **teaspoon dried rosemary**, crumbled, and **2 garlic cloves**, crushed with press.

10 DESSERTS

If you're worried that eating low-fat means you have to pass on sweet treats, take heart! We've collected recipes for cakes, cookies, puddings, and fruity and frozen desserts that will satisfy your hankerings. Most have fewer than 200 calories per serving (many come in at less than that) and all are low in fat, so you can dig in, guilt-free.

We open with fruit desserts: From pears steeped in wine sauce to Broiled Brown-Sugar Bananas, we make use of an entire fruit basket of options. We even include a mixed fruit salad smothered with a delectable vanilla bean syrup.

Then it's on to the baked goods: Enjoy Grilled Angel Food Cake with Strawberries and a slimmed-down version of carrot cake (the light cream-cheese frosting, made with reduced-fat cream cheese and low-fat milk, is so satisfying, you'll never know the difference). Or fill your cookie jar with our reduced-fat oatmeal raisin cookies, butterscotch blondies, or Healthy Makeover Brownies, where nonfat cocoa delivers delicious chocolatey goodness. If you're trying to get more grains into your diet, whip up a batch of Whole Wheat Sugar Cookies; you can use white whole wheat flour for a more traditional look and texture.

Last, but certainly not least, we offer creamy puddings and icy treats, like our dinner-party worthy panna cotta drizzled with a pretty blackberry sauce or a number of sophisticated sorbets and granitas.

CHIANTI-ROASTED PEARS

This is a super-easy dessert for company. Bosc pears become tender and caramelized on the outside when baked with a butter-and-sugar coating and basted with red wine.

ACTIVE TIME: 15 minutes
TOTAL TIME: 1 hour plus cooling
MAKES: 6 servings

1	large navel orange (12 to 14 ounces)
6	Bosc pears (8 ounces each)
$^1\!/_2$	cup hearty red wine, such as Chianti
$^1\!/_4$	cup water
$^1\!/_4$	cup granulated sugar
1	tablespoon butter or margarine, melted

1. Preheat oven to 450°F. With vegetable peeler, remove peel from orange in 2" by $^1\!/_2$" strips. Reserve orange for another use.

2. With melon baller or small knife, remove cores and seeds from pears by cutting through blossom end (bottom) of unpeeled pears. (Do not remove stems from pears.)

3. In shallow $1^1\!/_2$- to 2-quart glass or ceramic baking dish, combine orange peel, wine, and water. Place sugar in medium bowl. Hold pears, one at a time, over bowl of sugar with one hand (keep other hand dry). With dry hand, use pastry brush to brush pears with melted butter, then sprinkle pears with sugar until coated. Stand pears in baking dish. Sprinkle any remaining sugar into baking dish around pears.

4. Bake pears for 35 to 40 minutes or until tender when pierced with tip of small knife, basting occasionally with syrup in baking dish.

5. Cool pears slightly, for about 30 minutes, to serve warm. Or cool completely, then cover and refrigerate for up to 1 day. Reheat to serve warm, if you like.

Each serving: About 135 calories, 1g protein, 29g carbohydrate, 3g total fat (1g saturated), 4g fiber, 20mg sodium

Let's Talk Pears

Sweet, juicy, crisp, and aromatic—pears are versatile enough to play starring roles in desserts and supporting roles in stuffings, salads, and sides. Available year-round, pears are picked unripe, then ripen during shipping and storage. Select well-shaped, fairly firm fruit; the color depends on the variety. Avoid shriveled, discolored, cut, or bruised fruit.

For cooking, Bosc, Bartlett, or Anjou are good choices. The elegant shape of the Bosc pear makes it especially appealing for poaching. Knowing when a particular pear is ripe depends on the variety. Bartletts go from green to soft yellow; greenish brown Boscs turn the color of milk chocolate; and Anjous yield to pressure. Let firm pears ripen at room temperature in a brown paper bag for a few days (it may even take a week), then refrigerate and use within three to five days. Never refrigerate pears in an airtight plastic bag; the centers will turn dark brown. To prevent peeled or cut-up pears from browning, sprinkle with lemon juice.

LEMON-BLUEBERRY TIRAMISU

Impress your friends and family with this surprisingly low-fat tiramisu.

ACTIVE TIME: 20 minutes   **TOTAL TIME**: 25 minutes plus overnight chilling
MAKES: 9 servings

1 to 2	lemons
3³⁄₄	cups blueberries
³⁄₄	cup granulated sugar
4	tablespoons water
1	container (17.6 ounces) nonfat Greek yogurt
1	package (3 ounces) ladyfingers

Mint sprig, for garnish

1. From lemon(s), grate 1½ teaspoons peel and squeeze ¼ cup juice.

2. In medium saucepan, combine 1½ cups blueberries, ¼ cup sugar, and 1 tablespoon water. Heat over medium heat for 5 minutes or until blueberries soften and juices thicken, stirring occasionally. Transfer to medium bowl and stir in 1½ cups blueberries. Set aside.

3. Prepare lemon syrup: In microwave-safe small bowl, combine ¼ cup sugar and remaining 3 tablespoons water. Cook in microwave on high for 1 minute. Stir in 3 tablespoons lemon juice and 1 teaspoon lemon peel.

4. In medium bowl, stir together yogurt and remaining ¼ cup sugar, 1 tablespoon lemon juice, and ½ teaspoon lemon peel.

TIP

We tested this recipe with both soft and hard (Italian-style) ladyfingers (sometimes called savoiardi) and had good results with both.

5. In 8-inch square baking dish, arrange half of ladyfingers. Brush with half of lemon syrup. Spoon blueberry mixture over ladyfingers. Arrange remaining ladyfingers over blueberries. Brush with remaining lemon syrup. Spread yogurt mixture on top. Cover and refrigerate overnight. To serve, top tiramisu with ³/₄ cup blueberries and garnish with mint sprig.

Each serving: About 165 calories, 7g protein, 34g carbohydrate, 1g total fat (0g saturated), 2g fiber, 90mg sodium

THREE-FRUIT SALAD WITH VANILLA-BEAN SYRUP

If you don't have a vanilla bean, stir ½ teaspoon vanilla extract into the chilled syrup.

ACTIVE TIME: 30 minutes   **TOTAL TIME**: 40 minutes plus chilling

MAKES: 12 servings

2	large lemons
1	vanilla bean
³/₄	cup water
³/₄	cup granulated sugar
3	ripe mangoes, peeled and cut into 1-inch pieces
2	pints strawberries, hulled and cut in half, or into quarters if large
1	medium honeydew melon, peeled and cut into 1-inch pieces

1. From 1 lemon, with vegetable peeler, remove strips of yellow outer peel; from lemons, squeeze ¼ cup juice. Cut vanilla bean lengthwise in half. With small knife, scrape seeds from vanilla bean; reserve seeds and pod.

2. In 1-quart saucepan, combine lemon peel, vanilla seeds and pod, water, and sugar; heat to boiling over high heat. Reduce heat to medium; cook until syrup has thickened, about 5 minutes. Pour syrup mixture through sieve into bowl; stir in lemon juice. Cover and refrigerate syrup until chilled, about 2 hours.

3. Place mangoes, strawberries, and melon in large bowl; add syrup and toss.

Each serving: About 140 calories, 1g protein, 35g carbohydrate, 0g total fat, 3g fiber, 13mg sodium

BROILED BROWN-SUGAR BANANAS

This sweet, satisfying dessert has just four basic ingredients.

ACTIVE TIME: 5 minutes **TOTAL TIME**: 10 minutes
MAKES: 4 servings

4	ripe medium bananas, unpeeled
2	tablespoons brown sugar
1	tablespoon lower-fat margarine
1/8	teaspoon ground cinnamon

1. Preheat broiler.

2. Cut each unpeeled banana lengthwise almost in half, being careful not to cut all the way through and leaving 1 inch uncut at banana end.

3. In cup, with fork, blend together brown sugar, margarine, and cinnamon. Place bananas, cut-side up, on rack in broiling pan. Spoon brown-sugar mixture over split bananas.

4. Place pan in broiler at closest position to source of heat; broil until bananas are browned, about 5 minutes.

5. Serve bananas in skins and use spoon to scoop out fruit.

Each serving: About 150 calories, 1g protein, 34g carbohydrate, 2g total fat (1g saturated), 3g fiber, 20mg sodium

GRILLED ANGEL FOOD CAKE WITH STRAWBERRIES

Store-bought angel food cake goes gourmet when it's grilled and topped with sweetened balsamic-soaked strawberries.

TOTAL TIME: 15 minutes plus standing

MAKES: 6 servings

1½   pounds strawberries, hulled and cut in half, or into quarters if large
2   tablespoons balsamic vinegar
1   tablespoon granulated sugar
1   store-bought angel food cake (9 ounces)
Whipped cream, for serving (optional)

1. In medium bowl, toss strawberries with vinegar and sugar. Let stand at room temperature until sugar dissolves, at least 30 minutes, stirring occasionally.

2. Meanwhile, prepare outdoor grill for direct grilling over medium heat. Cut cake into 6 wedges.

3. Place cake on hot grill rack and grill for 3 to 4 minutes or until lightly toasted on both sides, turning over once. Spoon strawberries with their juice onto six dessert plates. Place grilled cake on plates with strawberries; serve with whipped cream, if you like.

Each serving (without whipped cream): About 155 calories, 3g protein, 35g carbohydrate, 1g total fat (0g saturated), 3g fiber, 320mg sodium

TIP

These days, fresh berries are found in stores year-round, but they can be expensive when not in-season, so it pays to freeze them. Do this when the berries are at their peak to preserve nutrients. Here's how: Rinse the berries in a colander, and if necessary, hull them. Freeze in zip-tight plastic bags and you'll have fresh berries year-round.

Eat Your Berries

They're not only delicious—they're berry, berry nutritious!

BLUEBERRIES contain powerful antioxidant compounds that may improve memory and coordination.

RASPBERRIES are loaded with 4 grams of fiber per half cup, and they boast high levels of antioxidants (although not the stratospheric levels found in blueberries).

STRAWBERRIES are rich in ellagic acid, a cancer fighter. One half cup provides 57% of your daily requirement for vitamin C.

BLACKBERRIES are rich in a compound that helps fight cancer and inflammation and may also reduce the risk of heart disease. They're also a good source of fiber, with 4 grams per half cup.

ELDERBERRIES, BLACK CURRANTS, AND CHOKEBERRIES are still scarce in the marketplace, but that may change as consumers learn about their high antioxidant content—they may have 50% higher antioxidant levels than the more common berries!

STUFFED FRESH FIGS

If you're lucky enough to have a fig tree, or to find ripe figs at your market, try this recipe.

TOTAL TIME: 25 minutes
MAKES: 6 servings

19	small ripe figs (1¼ pounds total)
¼	cup pure honey
½	cup part-skim ricotta cheese
¼	cup natural almonds, toasted and chopped

1. On plate, with fork, mash ripest fig with honey; set aside.

2. With sharp knife, trim stems from remaining figs, then cut a deep X in top of each, making sure not to cut through to bottom. Gently spread each fig open to make "petals."

3. In small bowl, combine ricotta and almonds. With back of spoon, press fig and honey mixture through sieve into 1-cup measure.

4. To serve, spoon ricotta mixture into figs. Arrange figs on platter and drizzle with fig honey.

Each serving: About 170 calories, 4g protein, 32g carbohydrate, 4g total fat (1g saturated), 4g fiber, 25mg sodium

Let's Talk Honey

There are hundreds of different honeys from different regions of the world, most of them named for the flower from which they originate. The color and flavor of each honey is derived from the flowers' nectar, which bees use to make honey. In general, the darker the honey, the stronger the flavor. Clover and orange blossom honey are both popular in the United States for their light, delicate fragrance and flavor.

HONEYED HOT FRUIT SALAD

A few turns on the grill transform fresh fruit into a sumptuously sweet finale.

ACTIVE TIME: 15 minutes   **TOTAL TIME**: 25 minutes
MAKES: 6 servings

½	cup honey
1	tablespoon fresh lemon juice
¼	cup loosely packed fresh mint leaves, thinly sliced
1	medium pineapple, cut lengthwise into 6 wedges, with leaves attached
2	large bananas, peeled and cut diagonally into thirds
3	medium plums, cut in half and pitted
2	medium nectarines or peaches, cut into quarters and pitted

1. Prepare outdoor grill for direct grilling over medium heat.

2. In cup, stir honey, lemon juice, and 1 tablespoon sliced mint.

3. With tongs, place fruit pieces on hot grill rack and grill, turning fruit occasionally and brushing it with honey mixture during last 3 minutes of cooking, until browned and tender, 10 to 15 minutes.

4. To serve, arrange grilled fruit on large platter; drizzle with any remaining honey mixture. Sprinkle with remaining mint.

Each serving: About 215 calories, 2g protein, 55g carbohydrate, 1g total fat (0g saturated), 5g fiber, 5mg sodium

FROZEN CHOCOLATE KAHLUA MOUSSE

When company's coming unexpectedly, or if you need a special dessert at the last minute, this delicate, rich-tasting confection rises to the occasion—and it's fat-free, too.

TOTAL TIME: 10 minutes plus freezing
MAKES: 6 servings

1	envelope unflavored gelatin
1	cup cold water
½	cup nonfat ricotta cheese
½	cup cold skim milk
6	tablespoons granulated sugar
½	cup Kahlua liqueur
3	tablespoons unsweetened cocoa powder

Pinch salt

1. In 1-quart saucepan, evenly sprinkle gelatin over cold water; let stand for 2 minutes to soften gelatin slightly. Cook over medium heat, stirring frequently, until gelatin has completely dissolved (do not boil).

2. In blender, combine gelatin mixture, ricotta, milk, sugar, liqueur, and cocoa. Blend until smooth, about 1 minute. Pour into dessert glasses and freeze for at least 2 hours.

Each serving: About 100 calories, 5g protein, 16g carbohydrate, 0g total fat, 1g fiber, 80mg sodium

TIP

The darker the chocolate, the better it is for you. Bittersweet chocolate is rich in flavonoids that have been found to reduce blood pressure and LDL ("bad") cholesterol.

HEALTHY MAKEOVER CARROT CAKE

A dessert with a vegetable in its name can't be that bad for you, right? Wrong! Here's a greatly slimmed-down version you can enjoy without guilt. For an even healthier treat, skip the icing altogether.

ACTIVE TIME: 20 minutes   **TOTAL TIME**: 1 hour 5 minutes plus cooling
MAKES: 20 servings

CARROT CAKE

Nonstick cooking spray with flour

2¼	cups all-purpose flour
2	teaspoons baking soda
2	teaspoons ground cinnamon
1	teaspoon ground ginger
1	teaspoon baking powder
1	teaspoon salt
2	large eggs
2	large egg whites
1	cup granulated sugar
¾	cup packed dark brown sugar
1	can (8 to 8¼ ounces) crushed pineapple in juice
⅓	cup canola oil
1	tablespoon vanilla extract
1	bag (10 ounces) shredded carrots
½	cup dark seedless raisins

CREAM-CHEESE ICING

2	ounces reduced-fat cream cheese
¾	cup confectioners' sugar
½	teaspoon low-fat (1%) milk
¼	teaspoon vanilla extract

1. Preheat oven to 350°F. Spray nonstick 12-cup Bundt-style pan with cooking spray with flour.

2. Prepare carrot cake: Combine flour, baking soda, cinnamon, ginger, baking powder, and salt.

3. In large bowl, with mixer on medium speed, beat eggs and egg whites until blended. Beat in granulated and dark brown sugars; beat for 2 minutes. On low speed, beat in pineapple with juice, oil, and vanilla. Add flour mixture; beat for 1 minute. Stir in carrots and raisins.

4. Pour batter into pan. Bake for 45 to 50 minutes or until toothpick inserted in center comes out clean. Cool in pan for 10 minutes. Invert cake onto rack; cool completely.

5. Prepare cream-cheese icing: In bowl, stir cream cheese and $^1/_4$ cup confectioners' sugar until smooth. Add milk, vanilla, and remaining confectioners' sugar; stir to a drizzling consistency. Drizzle icing over cake.

Each serving: About 210 calories, 3g protein, 40g carbohydrate, 5g total fat (1g saturated), 1g fiber, 295mg sodium

LEMON-MAPLE ICEBOX CAKE

This icebox cake combines layers of whole-grain graham crackers with lemon-maple filling for a quick and easy treat. The best part—the creamy filling is made with nonfat Greek yogurt, so you can enjoy this dessert guilt-free!

TOTAL TIME: 10 minutes plus chilling
MAKES: 6 servings

2¼	cups plain nonfat Greek yogurt
1	tablespoon maple syrup
½	teaspoon grated lemon peel, plus more for garnish
½	teaspoon vanilla extract
⅛	teaspoon no-calorie sweetener
6	full sheets low-fat whole-grain graham crackers, broken into halves

1. Line 8½" by 4½" loaf pan with plastic wrap, leaving overhang on the two long sides.

2. In a bowl, stir together yogurt, syrup, ½ teaspoon lemon peel, vanilla, and sweetener.

3. Line bottom of loaf pan with 3 graham cracker halves. Spread one-third of yogurt mixture over crackers. Repeat, layering twice. Top with remaining 3 graham cracker halves.

4. Using plastic overhang, wrap cake and refrigerate for at least 2 hours or up to 4 hours. Unwrap cake and, using overhanging plastic, pull cake out of pan. With serrated knife, gently cut cake into 6 slices. Garnish with lemon peel and serve.

Each serving: About 115 calories, 9g protein, 18g carbohydrate, 1g total fat (0g saturated), 1g fiber, 127mg sodium

WHOLE-GRAIN GINGERSNAPS

These treats aren't just pretty—they provide a healthy dose of whole wheat goodness.

ACTIVE TIME: 25 minutes plus chilling   **TOTAL TIME**: 35 to 45 minutes
MAKES: 42 cookies

1	cup all-purpose flour
1	cup whole wheat flour
1	teaspoon ground ginger
1	teaspoon baking soda
½	teaspoon ground cinnamon
½	teaspoon salt
½	cup granulated sugar
6	tablespoons trans-fat-free vegetable oil spread (60% to 70% oil)
1	large egg
½	cup dark molasses

Nonpareils or round while sprinkles, for decorating (optional)

1. On sheet of waxed paper, combine flours, ginger, baking soda, cinnamon, and salt.

2. In large bowl, with mixer on low speed, beat sugar and vegetable oil spread until blended. Increase speed to high; beat until light and creamy, occasionally scraping bowl with rubber spatula. Beat in egg and molasses. On low speed, beat in flour mixture just until blended. Cover bowl with plastic wrap and refrigerate until easier to handle (dough will be slightly sticky), 1 hour.

3. Preheat oven to 350°F. With lightly greased hands, shape cookie dough by heaping measuring teaspoons into 1-inch balls. If desired, dip top of each ball in nonpareils. Place balls, 2½ inches apart, on ungreased large cookie sheet. Bake until tops are slightly cracked, 9 to 11 minutes (cookies will be very soft). Cool on cookie sheet on wire rack for 1 minute. With wide metal spatula, transfer cookies to rack to cool completely. Repeat with remaining dough and nonpareils, if using.

4. Store cookies in cookie jar for up to 3 days.

Each cookie: About 55 calories, 1g protein, 9g carbohydrate, 2g total fat (0g saturated), 1g fiber, 75mg sodium

HONEY COOKIES

These slightly salty cookies are perfect for those who prefer their treats not too sweet.

ACTIVE TIME: 40 minutes plus chilling   **TOTAL TIME**: 1 hour to 1 hour 20 minutes
MAKES: 36 cookies

1	cup (2 sticks) butter or margarine, softened
1/4	cup honey (see Tip)
2	teaspoons vanilla extract
2	cups all-purpose flour
2	cups walnuts, chopped
1/2	teaspoon salt

1. Preheat oven to 325°F. In large bowl, with mixer on high speed, beat butter until creamy. Add honey and vanilla; beat until well blended. On low speed, beat in flour, walnuts, and salt until a dough forms. Cover bowl with plastic wrap and refrigerate for 1 hour.

2. With lightly floured hands, shape dough by heaping measuring teaspoons into 1/2-inch balls. Place balls, 2 inches apart, on ungreased large cookie sheet. Press floured four-tine fork across top of each ball. Bake until golden, 18 to 22 minutes. With wide metal spatula, transfer cookies to wire rack to cool completely. Repeat with remaining dough.

3. Store cookies in cookie jar for up to 1 week.

Each cookie: About 105 calories, 1g protein, 7g carbohydrate, 8g total fat (1g saturated), 1g fiber, 85mg sodium

TIP

In general, the darker the color of a honey, the stronger the flavor. Choose a light delicate variety, such as orange blossom honey, for these cookies.

Lighten Up Your Favorite Desserts!

You don't have to kiss your favorite recipes good-bye because they call for high-fat ingredients. Just make these easy swaps.

- Replace the semisweet chocolate chips in treasured cookie classics with half the amount of mini semisweet chips (they'll scatter through more of the dough than big chips, but still add that authentic richness). Or try using the full amount of low-fat baking chips; they taste best when the cookies are eaten warm from the oven.

- Omit up to half the butter, margarine, or oil in cakes, muffins, or quick breads and substitute with applesauce, prune puree, or a fruit-based fat replacement (such as Lighter Bake). These switches are especially successful in coffee cakes and bar cookies.

- Substitute plain nonfat or low-fat yogurt or reduced-fat sour cream for regular sour cream. The flavor comes very close to the original in muffins and cakes.

- Eliminate the bottom crust in fruit pies to significantly reduce calories and fat. Spoon the filling into a pie plate, add the top crust, and serve cobbler-style. (You don't even need to grease the plate—the saucy fruit will spoon right out.)

- Cut back on the amount of nuts in a recipe to a few tablespoons, finely chop, and sprinkle on top of cookies, brownies, cakes, and breads before baking—they'll get a nice toasty flavor in the oven, and you'll see and taste them first.

- Slip light cream cheese (Neufchâtel) into cheesecakes rather than its full-fat counterpart—you'll save about 6 grams of fat and 60 calories per slice.

- Use $1/4$ cup no-cholesterol egg substitute in place of each whole egg in quick breads, muffins, and cakes. Or substitute 2 whites for each egg, up to 2 eggs (too many whites can make the texture a bit rubbery).

- Count on lower-fat dairy products. Instead of whole or 2% milk, use 1% or skim. Rather than heavy cream (unless it must be whipped), pour in light cream or half-and-half—either will perform perfectly in most frostings, glazes, and doughs. If a pie or cookie calls for canned evaporated or sweetened condensed milk, get the fat-free or low-fat version.

- For mock whipped cream, beat evaporated skim milk. Chill the milk, bowl, and beaters in your freezer for at least 15 minutes; beat in 1 tablespoon lemon juice to stabilize the mixture and sweeten the taste. Serve immediately, because it collapses quickly. We won't lie to you—it's no double for the real thing—but it is creamy-looking, white, and fluffy.

- Don't grease baking pans with butter or margarine—try new nonstick pan liners, kitchen parchment, or a spritz of nonstick cooking spray with flour.

OATMEAL-RAISIN COOKIES

If you thought the words "delicious" and "low-fat" could never be used to describe the same cookie, think again. This one's chewy and sweet, with only 2 grams of fat per cookie.

ACTIVE TIME: 15 minutes   **TOTAL TIME**: 35 minutes

MAKES: About 48 cookies

2	cups all-purpose flour
1	teaspoon baking soda
$1/2$	teaspoon salt
$1/2$	cup (1 stick) light corn-oil spread (56 to 60% fat)
$3/4$	cup packed dark brown sugar
$1/2$	cup granulated sugar
2	large egg whites
1	large egg
2	teaspoons vanilla extract
1	cup quick-cooking oats, uncooked
$1/2$	cup dark seedless raisins

1. Preheat oven to 375°F. Grease two large cookie sheets. In medium bowl, combine flour, baking soda, and salt.

2. In large bowl, with mixer on low speed, beat corn-oil spread and brown and granulated sugars until well combined. Increase speed to high; beat until mixture is light and fluffy. Add egg whites, whole egg, and vanilla; beat until blended. With wooden spoon, stir in flour mixture, oats, and raisins until combined.

3. Drop dough by level tablespoons, 2 inches apart, on prepared cookie sheets. Bake until golden, 10 to 12 minutes, rotating cookie sheets between upper and lower racks halfway through baking. With wide spatula, transfer cookies to wire racks to cool completely.

4. Repeat with remaining dough.

Each cookie: About 65 calories, 1g protein, 12g carbohydrate, 2g total fat (0g saturated), 0g fiber, 72mg sodium

MOLASSES COOKIES

A classic, old-time favorite that everyone will enjoy.

ACTIVE TIME: 40 minutes plus freezing
TOTAL TIME: 1 hour 5 minutes to 1 hour 15 minutes
MAKES: 72 cookies

³/₄	cup (1½ sticks) butter or margarine
¼	cup light (mild) molasses
1¼	cups granulated sugar
1	large egg
2	cups all-purpose flour
2	teaspoons baking soda
1	teaspoon ground cinnamon
½	teaspoon ground ginger
½	teaspoon salt
¼	teaspoon ground cloves

1. Preheat oven to 375°F.

2. In 3-quart saucepan, melt butter over low heat. Remove saucepan from heat and, with wire whisk, beat in molasses and 1 cup sugar until blended. Whisk in egg. With wooden spoon, stir in flour, baking soda, cinnamon, ginger, salt, and cloves until mixed. Transfer dough to medium bowl and freeze until firm enough to handle, about 15 minutes.

3. Spread remaining ¼ cup sugar on sheet of waxed paper. With hands, shape dough into 1-inch balls; roll balls in sugar to coat. Place balls, 2½ inches apart, on large ungreased cookie sheet. Bake until cookies spread and darken, 10 to 12 minutes. Cool on cookie sheet on wire rack for 1 minute. With wide metal spatula, transfer cookies to rack to cool completely. Repeat with remaining dough and sugar.

4. Store cookies in cookie jar for up to 1 week.

Each cookie: About 45 calories, 1g protein, 7g carbohydrate, 2g total fat (0g saturated), 0g fiber, 75mg sodium

WHOLE WHEAT SUGAR COOKIES

We snuck some whole wheat flour into these sugar cookies with tasty results.

ACTIVE TIME: 1 hour   **TOTAL TIME**: 2 hours plus chilling
MAKES: About 72 cookies

1	cup all-purpose flour
1	cup white whole wheat flour
1/2	teaspoon baking powder
1/4	teaspoon salt
1	cup granulated sugar
1/2	cup (1 stick) trans-fat-free vegetable-oil spread (60 to 70% oil)
1	large egg
2	teaspoons vanilla extract

1. On sheet of waxed paper, combine all-purpose and whole wheat flours, baking powder, and salt.

2. In large bowl, with mixer on low speed, beat sugar and vegetable-oil spread until blended. Increase speed to high; beat until light and creamy, about 3 minutes, occasionally scraping down bowl with rubber spatula. Reduce speed to low; beat in egg and vanilla, then beat in flour mixture just until blended.

3. Divide dough in half; flatten each half into a disk. Wrap each disk with plastic wrap and refrigerate until dough is firm enough to roll, about 2 hours.

4. Preheat oven to 375°F.

5. On lightly floured surface, with floured rolling pin, roll one piece of dough to $^1/_8$-inch thickness. With 2-inch cookie cutters, cut out as many cookies as possible; wrap and refrigerate trimmings. With lightly floured spatula, place cookies 1 inch apart on ungreased cookie sheet.

6. Bake cookies until lightly browned, 10 to 12 minutes. With thin metal spatula, transfer cookies to wire rack to cool. Repeat with remaining dough and trimmings.

Each cookie: About 35 calories, 1g protein, 5g carbohydrate, 1g total fat (0g saturated), 0g fiber, 20mg sodium

Whole Wheat Flour that's White

Struggling to eat the recommended three servings of whole grains a day because you don't like the flavor and texture of whole wheat? Try baking with white whole wheat flour. Milled from a variety of white wheat, it's as healthy as traditional whole wheat—with the same levels of fiber, nutrients, and minerals—but it lacks the heartier taste and grainy heft.
It's ideal for all whole-grain recipes and can be substituted for up to half of the all-purpose flour in many baked goods without substantially changing the taste.

WHEAT-FREE ALMOND BUTTER COOKIES

The almond butter, flaxseeds, and sliced almonds in these treats are all loaded with omega-3 fatty acids. Plus, they're gluten- and dairy-free, so everyone can enjoy them.

ACTIVE TIME: 10 minutes **TOTAL TIME**: 22 to 34 minutes

MAKES: About 36 cookies

1	tablespoon ground flaxseeds or flaxseed meal (see Tip)
3	tablespoons water
1	cup smooth almond butter
1	cup packed brown sugar
1	teaspoon baking soda
½	teaspoon vanilla extract

Pinch salt

½	teaspoon pumpkin pie spice

Sliced almonds, for topping (optional)

1. Preheat oven to 350°F. Line two cookie sheets with parchment paper.

2. In small bowl, mix flaxseeds with water. Let stand for 5 minutes.

3. In mixer bowl, combine almond butter, brown sugar, baking soda, vanilla, salt, pumpkin pie spice, and soaked flaxseeds; mix on low speed until thoroughly combined. Using tablespoon measure, form dough into balls and place 1½ inches apart on prepared baking sheets. If desired, top balls with almonds.

4. Bake until slightly golden, 11 to 12 minutes, rotating cookie sheets between upper and lower racks halfway through baking. Set sheets on wire racks to cool. Repeat with remaining dough.

5. Store cookies in airtight container for up to 3 days, or freeze for up to 3 months.

Each serving: About 70 calories, 1g protein, 8g carbohydrate, 4g total fat (0g saturated), 13g fiber, 72mg sodium

TIP
Flaxseeds can be found in the natural food section of most supermarkets.

WHOLE-GRAIN FIG BARS

Made with whole wheat flour and dried figs (a fiber-packed miracle food in its own right), these soft, chewy goodies are good for you, too! For an additional whole-grain boost, sprinkle the batter with 2 tablespoons honey-crunch wheat germ before baking.

ACTIVE TIME: 15 minutes **TOTAL TIME**: 35 minutes
MAKES: 24 bars

4	ounces dried Calimyrna figs ($^3/_4$ cup)
$^1/_2$	cup all-purpose flour
$^1/_2$	cup whole wheat flour
$^1/_3$	cup packed dark brown sugar
1	teaspoon ground cinnamon
$^1/_2$	teaspoon ground ginger
$^1/_2$	teaspoon baking powder
$^1/_4$	teaspoon salt
$^1/_3$	cup light (mild) molasses
2	tablespoons butter, melted
1	teaspoon vanilla extract
1	large egg white

1. Preheat oven to 350°F. Grease 8-inch square metal baking pan. Line pan with foil; grease foil.

2. With kitchen shears, cut stems from figs; cut figs into small pieces. In large bowl with spoon, stir figs, all-purpose and whole wheat flours, brown sugar, cinnamon, ginger, baking powder, and salt until mixed. Stir in molasses, melted butter, vanilla, and egg white just until blended and evenly moistened. With metal spatula, spread butter in pan (batter will be sticky).

3. Bake until toothpick inserted in center comes out clean, 20 to 25 minutes. Cool completely in pan on wire rack. When cool, transfer with foil to cutting board. Cut into 3 strips, then cut each strip crosswise into 4 pieces. Cut each rectangle diagonally in half to make 24 triangles. Store cookies between layers of waxed paper in a tightly-covered container for up to 3 days or freeze for up to 3 months.

Each bar: About 65 calories, 1g protein, 13g carbohydrate, 1g total fat (0g saturated), 2g fiber, 45mg sodium

PIGNOLI COOKIES

Thanks to the food processor—and prepared almond paste—making these classic Italian cookies with a pine-nut topping is a breeze. Use a pastry bag to form the rounds and keep your fingers from getting sticky.

ACTIVE TIME: 25 minutes   **TOTAL TIME**: 35 to 45 minutes

MAKES: About 24 cookies

1	tube or can (7 to 8 ounces) almond paste
3/4	cup confectioners' sugar
1	large egg white
4	teaspoons honey
1/2	cup pine nuts (3 ounces)

1. Preheat oven to 350°F. Line two large cookie sheets with parchment paper.

2. Crumble almond paste into food processor with knife blade attached. Add sugar and process until paste has texture of fine meal; transfer to large bowl. Add egg white and honey. With mixer on low speed, beat until dough is blended. Increase speed to medium-high and beat until very smooth, about 5 minutes.

3. Spoon batter into pastry bag fitted with 1/2-inch round tip. Pipe 1 1/4-inch rounds, 2 inches apart, onto prepared cookie sheets. Brush cookies lightly with water and cover completely with pine nuts, pressing gently to make nuts stick.

4. Bake until golden brown, 10 to 12 minutes, rotating cookie sheets between upper and lower racks halfway through baking. Slide parchment onto wire racks and let cookies cool before peeling off paper. Repeat with remaining dough and pine nuts.

5. Store pignoli in an airtight container for up to 5 days, or freeze for up to 3 months.

Each cookie: About 75 calories, 2g protein, 9g carbohydrate, 4g total fat (0g saturated), 0g fiber, 5mg sodium

Let's Talk Almond Paste

This firm but pliable confection is made of blanched ground almonds and confectioners' sugar mixed with glucose, corn syrup, or egg whites. It's used in many Italian cookies, from macaroons to pignolis to amarettis, which feature a bitter-almond paste. Available in 6- to 8-ounce cans or tubes, almond paste is similar to marzipan, which is sweeter and softer. If your almond paste is too hard to work with, microwave on high for a few seconds to soften. Once opened, it should be wrapped tightly and refrigerated.

HEALTHY MAKEOVER BROWNIES

The rich texture and chocolaty goodness of these bake-sale favorites speak of decadence, but compare each square's 95 calories and 3 grams of fat to a regular brownie's doubly high calories and nearly quadrupled fat and you'll feel virtuous (and satisfied).

ACTIVE TIME: 15 minutes   **TOTAL TIME**: 35 minutes plus cooling

MAKES: 16 brownies

1	teaspoon instant coffee powder or granules	¼	teaspoon salt
2	teaspoons vanilla extract	1	cup granulated sugar
½	cup all-purpose flour	4	tablespoons trans-fat-free vegetable-oil spread (60 to 70% oil)
½	cup unsweetened cocoa powder		
¼	teaspoon baking powder	3	large egg whites

1. Preheat oven to 350°F. Line 8-inch square metal baking pan with foil; grease foil. In cup, dissolve coffee powder in vanilla extract.

2. On waxed paper, combine flour, cocoa, baking powder, and salt.

3. In medium bowl, whisk sugar, vegetable-oil spread, egg whites, and coffee mixture until well mixed, then blend in flour mixture. Spread in prepared pan.

4. Bake for 22 to 24 minutes or until toothpick inserted in brownies 2 inches from edge comes out almost clean. Cool completely in pan on wire rack for about 2 hours.

5. When cool, lift foil, with brownie, out of pan; peel foil away from sides. Cut brownies into 4 strips, then cut each strip crosswise into 4 squares (see Tip).

Each brownie: About 95 calories, 2g protein, 17g carbohydrate, 3g total fat (1g saturated), 1g fiber, 75mg sodium

TIP

If the brownies are difficult to cut, dip your knife in hot water; wipe dry, then cut. Repeat dipping and drying as necessary.

LOW-FAT BUTTERSCOTCH BLONDIES

These chewy treats are one of our test kitchen's favorites—and each has only 3 grams of fat!

ACTIVE TIME: 15 minutes   **TOTAL TIME**: 50 minutes

MAKES: 16 blondies

1	cup all-purpose flour
1/2	teaspoon baking powder
1/4	teaspoon salt
3	tablespoons butter or margarine
3/4	cup packed dark brown sugar
2	large egg whites
1/3	cup dark corn syrup
2	teaspoons vanilla extract
2	tablespoons finely chopped pecans

1. Preheat oven to 350°F. Grease 8-inch square baking pan. In bowl, combine flour, baking powder, and salt.

2. In large bowl, with mixer on medium speed, beat butter and sugar until well blended, about 2 minutes. Reduce speed to low; beat in egg whites, corn syrup, and vanilla until smooth. Beat in flour mixture just until combined. Spread batter in prepared pan. Sprinkle with pecans.

3. Bake until toothpick inserted in center comes out clean and edges are lightly browned, 35 to 40 minutes. Cool completely in pan on wire rack.

4. When cool, cut into 4 strips, then cut each strip crosswise into 4 pieces.

Each blondie: About 115 calories, 1g protein, 21g carbohydrate, 3g total fat (1g saturated), 0g fiber, 94mg sodium

CHOCOLATE PUDDING

This is retro food at its best—who doesn't love chocolate pudding? This clever version has only 2 grams of fat per serving and tastes divine warm or chilled.

ACTIVE TIME: 5 minutes
TOTAL TIME: 10 minutes plus chilling
MAKES: 4 servings

⅓	cup granulated sugar
¼	cup cornstarch
3	tablespoons unsweetened cocoa powder

Pinch salt

2	cups skim milk
1	square semisweet chocolate (1 ounce), finely chopped
1	teaspoon vanilla extract

1. In 2-quart saucepan, with wire whisk, mix sugar, cornstarch, cocoa, and salt until combined. Whisk in milk until blended. Heat mixture to boiling over medium heat, stirring constantly. Add chocolate; cook for 1 minute, stirring, until chocolate has melted and pudding thickens slightly. Remove from heat; stir in vanilla.

2. Spoon pudding into custard cups. Serve warm or place plastic wrap directly on surface of pudding and refrigerate to serve cold later.

Each serving: About 180 calories, 5g protein, 37g carbohydrate, 2g total fat (0g saturated), 1g fiber, 105mg sodium

HEALTHY MAKEOVER PUMPKIN BREAD

Treat family and friends to our slimmed-down quick bread. Gone is the traditional version's saturated fat, thanks to egg whites and a blend of low-fat yogurt and canola oil.

ACTIVE TIME: 20 minutes   **TOTAL TIME**: 1 hour 10 minutes
MAKES: 16 slices per loaf

1	cup packed light brown sugar
2	large egg whites
1	cup solid pack pumpkin (not pumpkin pie mix)
1/4	cup canola oil
1/3	cup plain low-fat yogurt
1	teaspoon vanilla extract
1	cup all-purpose flour
3/4	cup whole wheat flour
1 1/2	teaspoons baking powder
1	teaspoon ground cinnamon
1/2	teaspoon ground nutmeg
1/2	teaspoon baking soda
1/2	teaspoon salt

1. Preheat oven to 350°F. Spray 8 1/2" by 4 1/2" metal loaf pan with nonstick cooking spray with flour.

2. In large bowl, with wire whisk, combine brown sugar and egg whites. Add pumpkin, oil, yogurt, and vanilla; stir to combine.

3. In medium bowl, combine all-purpose flour, whole wheat flour, baking powder, cinnamon, nutmeg, baking soda, and salt. Add flour mixture to pumpkin mixture; stir until just combined. Do not overmix.

4. Pour batter into prepared pan. Bake for 45 to 50 minutes or until toothpick inserted in center of loaf comes out clean. Cool in pan for 10 minutes. Invert pumpkin bread onto wire rack; cool completely before slicing.

Each slice: About 140 calories, 2g protein, 25g carbohydrate, 4g total fat (0g saturated), 1g fiber, 165mg sodium

LEMON MERINGUE DROPS

These melt-in-your-mouth meringues are both crunchy and cloud-light, not to mention low in calories and fat-free.

ACTIVE TIME: 45 minutes   **TOTAL TIME**: 2 hours 15 minutes plus standing
MAKES: About 60 cookies

3	large egg whites
1/4	teaspoon cream of tartar
1/8	teaspoon salt
1/2	cup granulated sugar
2	teaspoons freshly grated lemon peel

1. Preheat oven to 200°F. Line two large cookie sheets with parchment paper.

2. In medium bowl with mixer on high speed, beat egg whites, cream of tartar, and salt until soft peaks form. With mixer running, sprinkle in sugar, 2 tablespoons at a time, beating until sugar dissolves and meringue stands in stiff, glossy peaks when beaters are lifted. Gently fold in lemon peel.

3. Spoon meringue into decorating bag fitted with 1/2-inch star tip. Pipe meringue into 1 1/2-inch stars, about 1 inch apart, on prepared cookie sheets.

4. Bake meringues until crisp but not brown, about 1 1/2 hours, rotating cookie sheets between upper and lower racks halfway through baking. Turn oven off; leave meringues in oven until dry, about 1 hour.

5. Remove meringues from oven and cool completely. Remove from parchment with wide metal spatula. Store meringues in airtight container for up to 1 month, or freeze for up to 3 months.

Each cookie: About 5 calories, 0g protein, 2g carbohydrate, 0g total fat, 0g fiber, 10mg sodium

BUTTERMILK PANNA COTTA WITH BLACKBERRY SAUCE

This smooth and creamy dessert features antioxidant-rich blackberries. (See photograph on page 420.)

ACTIVE TIME: 15 minutes **TOTAL TIME**: 25 minutes plus chilling
MAKES: 8 servings

1	envelope unflavored gelatin
1/4	cup plus 2 tablespoons water
2 3/4	cups buttermilk
1/2	cup plus 4 teaspoons granulated sugar
10	ounces frozen blackberries, thawed
1	teaspoon fresh lemon juice

1. In cup, evenly sprinkle gelatin over 1/4 cup water. Let stand for 2 minutes to allow gelatin to absorb liquid and soften.

2. In 3-quart saucepan, heat 1/2 cup buttermilk and 1/2 cup sugar over medium heat for 2 to 3 minutes or until sugar dissolves, stirring occasionally. Reduce heat to low; whisk in gelatin. Cook for 1 to 2 minutes or until gelatin dissolves, stirring. Remove saucepan from heat; stir in remaining 2 1/4 cups buttermilk.

3. Pour buttermilk mixture into eight 4-ounce ramekins or 6-ounce custard cups. Place ramekins in jelly-roll pan for easier handling. Cover pan with plastic wrap and refrigerate panna cotta for at least 4 hours or overnight, until well chilled and set.

4. Reserve 1/3 cup blackberries for garnish. In blender, puree remaining blackberries with lemon juice, remaining 2 tablespoons water, and 4 teaspoons sugar. Pour puree through sieve set over small bowl, stirring to press out fruit sauce; discard seeds. Cover and refrigerate sauce if not serving right away.

5. To unmold panna cotta, run tip of small knife around edge of ramekins. With hand, sharply tap side of each ramekin to break seal; invert onto eight dessert plates. Spoon sauce around each panna cotta. Garnish with reserved berries.

Each serving: About 115 calories, 4g protein, 24g carbohydrate, 1g total fat (1g saturated), 1g fiber, 90mg sodium

LOW-FAT CRÈME CARAMEL

Low-fat milk and a moderate number of eggs make this caramel custard guilt-free.

ACTIVE TIME: 15 minutes   **TOTAL TIME**: 55 minutes plus cooling and chilling
MAKES: 8 servings

³/₄	cup granulated sugar
1	large egg
2	large egg whites
2	cups low-fat (1%) milk
¹/₂	teaspoon vanilla extract

1. Preheat oven to 350°F. In heavy 1-quart saucepan, heat ¹/₂ cup sugar over medium heat, swirling pan occasionally, until sugar has melted and is amber in color. Immediately pour into eight 4- to 5-ounce ramekins.

2. In large bowl, with wire whisk, beat remaining ¹/₄ cup sugar, whole egg, and egg whites until well blended. Beat in milk and vanilla; pour into ramekins. Skim off foam.

3. Place ramekins in medium roasting pan; cover loosely with foil. Place pan on rack in oven. Carefully pour enough very hot water into pan to come halfway up sides of ramekins. Bake until knife inserted 1 inch from center comes out clean, 40 to 45 minutes. Transfer ramekins to wire rack to cool. Refrigerate until well chilled, 3 hours or up to overnight.

4. To serve, run tip of small knife around edge of custards. Invert ramekins onto dessert plates, shaking cups gently until custards slip out, allowing caramel syrup to drip onto custards.

Each serving: About 110 calories, 4g protein, 22g carbohydrate, 1g total fat (1g saturated), 0g fiber, 52mg sodium

PEACHY FROZEN YOGURT

Served as a fruity dessert or snack, this creamy frozen treat delivers a double dose of peach flavor and only 1 gram of fat per serving.

TOTAL TIME: 5 minutes

MAKES: 2½ cups or 4 servings

1	bag (10 to 12 ounces) frozen sliced peaches
2	containers (6 ounces each) low-fat peach yogurt
1	tablespoon granulated sugar

In food processor with knife blade attached, process frozen peaches until finely shaved. Add yogurt and sugar. Process just until smooth. Serve immediately. If not serving right away, pour into 9-inch square baking pan; cover and freeze for 1 hour for best texture.

Each serving: About 130 calories, 4g protein, 28g carbohydrate, 1g total fat (1g saturated), 2g fiber, 50mg sodium

PLUM YOGURT POPS

Forget store-bought popsicles. This super-fruity refresher will be a cool hit with kids of all ages. Make a day in advance to allow enough time for freezing.

TOTAL TIME: 15 minutes plus freezing
MAKES: 16 pops

1	pound ripe red or purple plums (4 medium), coarsely chopped
½	cup granulated sugar
1	tablespoon fresh lemon juice
2	cups vanilla low-fat yogurt

1. In blender, on medium speed, puree plums, sugar, and lemon juice. Pour plum puree into medium-mesh sieve set over medium bowl. With spoon, press puree against sieve to push through pulp and juice. Discard solids in sieve.

2. With wire whisk, mix yogurt and plum mixture until well combined.

3. Spoon yogurt mixture into sixteen 3-ounce paper cups; freeze for 4 hours or until partially frozen. Insert wooden ice cream-bar sticks and freeze until completely frozen. (Or, spoon yogurt mixture into sixteen 2-ounce popsicle molds; seal and insert sticks as manufacturer directs. Freeze overnight.)

Each pop: About 60 calories, 1g protein, 13g carbohydrate, 1g total fat (0g saturated), 0g fiber, 20mg sodium

SGROPPINO SORBET WITH PROSECCO AND MINT

Sgroppino is a classic after-dinner beverage from the Veneto region in northern Italy. It's usually made by whipping up lemon sorbet and Prosecco; a splash of vodka is sometimes added. Here, we've left the sorbet intact as a light and refreshing float—a luscious and low-cal end to dinner.

TOTAL TIME: 5 minutes
MAKES: 6 servings

1	pint lemon sorbet
2	cups Prosecco (Italian sparkling wine)

Fresh mint sprigs, for garnish

Evenly scoop sorbet into six wine goblets or dessert bowls. Pour $\frac{1}{3}$ cup Prosecco into each glass; garnish with mint. Serve immediately.

Each serving: About 135 calories, 0g protein, 22g carbohydrate, 0g total fat, 0g fiber, 10mg sodium

COFFEE GRANITA

Similar to sorbet but coarser, this coffee-flavored ice is a Neapolitan tradition. Substitute decaffeinated coffee, if you prefer.

TOTAL TIME: 5 minutes plus freezing
MAKES: 4 servings

²/₃   cup granulated sugar
2   cups hot coffee

1. Dissolve sugar in hot coffee. Pour mixture into 9-inch square metal pan. Cover; freeze for 2 hours. Stir to break up chunks. Freeze for 3 hours longer.

2. To serve, with fork, scrape granita into coffee cups or bowls.

Each serving: About 130 calories, 0g protein, 34g carbohydrate, 0g total fat, 0g fiber, 3mg sodium

Granita Know-How

The heat-beating Italian ice known as granita doesn't require any special equipment—just a metal baking pan. Cover and freeze the granita mixture until partially frozen, about 2 hours. Stir with a fork to break up the chunks. Cover again and return the pan to the freezer until the mixture is completely frozen, at least 3 hours or up to overnight. To serve the granita, let it stand at room temperature until slightly softened, about 15 minutes. Use a metal spoon or fork to scrape across surface, transferring the flavorful ice shards to chilled dessert dishes, wine goblets, or coffee cups without packing them.

BOLD BERRY GRANITA

Frosty, fruity, and fat-free, this mix of pureed raspberries and strawberries is the ultimate summer dessert.

TOTAL TIME: 20 minutes plus freezing
MAKES: 10 servings

½	cup granulated sugar
1	cup water
2	lemons
1	pound strawberries, hulled
1½	cups raspberries

1. In saucepan, heat sugar and water to boiling, stirring until sugar dissolves. Reduce heat to low and simmer, uncovered, for 5 minutes. Set aside to cool slightly.

2. Meanwhile, from lemons, grate 2 teaspoons peel and squeeze ¼ cup juice. In food processor with knife blade attached, blend berries until pureed. With back of spoon, press puree through sieve into bowl; discard seeds.

3. Stir sugar syrup, lemon juice, and lemon peel into berry puree. Pour into 9-inch square metal baking pan.

4. Cover and freeze mixture for 2 hours or until frozen around edges. With fork, scrape ice at edges into center. Cover and freeze until solid, at least 3 hours or overnight.

5. To serve, let granita stand at room temperature for 15 minutes. With fork, scrape across surface to form ice shards and spoon into chilled bowls.

Each serving: About 60 calories, 1g protein, 15g carbohydrate, 0g total fat, 2g fiber, 0mg sodium

METRIC EQUIVALENT CHARTS

The recipes that appear in this cookbook use the standard United States method for measuring liquid and dry or solid ingredients (teaspoons, tablespoons, and cups). The information on this chart is provided to help cooks outside the United States successfully use these recipes. All equivalents are approximate.

METRIC EQUIVALENTS FOR DIFFERENT TYPES OF INGREDIENTS

A standard cup measure of a dry or solid ingredient will vary in weight depending on the type of ingredient. A standard cup of liquid is the same volume for any type of liquid. Use the following chart when converting standard cup measures to grams (weight) or milliliters (volume).

Standard Cup	Fine Powder (e.g., flour)	Grain (e.g., rice)	Granular (e.g., sugar)	Liquid Solids (e.g., butter)	Liquid (e.g., milk)
1	140 g	150 g	190 g	200 g	240 ml
¾	105 g	113 g	143 g	150 g	180 ml
⅔	93 g	100 g	125 g	133 g	160 ml
½	70 g	75 g	95 g	100 g	120 ml
⅓	47 g	50 g	63 g	67 g	80 ml
¼	35 g	38 g	48 g	50 g	60 ml
⅛	18 g	19 g	24 g	25 g	30 ml

USEFUL EQUIVALENTS FOR LIQUID INGREDIENTS BY VOLUME

¼ tsp=					1 ml
½ tsp=					2 ml
1 tsp	=				5 ml
3 tsp	=	1 tbls =		½ fl oz =	15 ml
		2 tbls =	⅛ cup =	1 fl oz =	30 ml
		4 tbls =	¼ cup =	2 fl oz =	60 ml
		5⅓ tbls =	⅓ cup =	3 fl oz =	80 ml
		8 tbls =	½ cup =	4 fl oz =	120 ml
		10⅔ tbls =	⅔ cup =	5 fl oz =	160 ml
		12 tbls =	¾ cup =	6 fl oz =	180 ml
		16 tbls =	1 cup =	8 fl oz =	240 ml
		1 pt =	2 cups =	16 fl oz =	480 ml
		1 qt =	4 cups =	32 fl oz =	960 ml
				33 fl oz =	1000 ml = 1 L

USEFUL EQUIVALENTS FOR COOKING/OVEN TEMPERATURES

	Fahrenheit	Celsius	Gas Mark
Freeze Water	32°F	0° C	
Room Temperature	68°F	20° C	
Boil Water	212°F	100° C	
Bake	325°F	160° C	3
	350°F	180° C	4
	375°F	190° C	5
	400°F	200° C	6
	425°F	220° C	7
	450°F	230° C	8
Broil			Grill

USEFUL EQUIVALENTS FOR DRY INGREDIENTS BY WEIGHT

(To convert ounces to grams, multiply the number of ounces by 30.)

1 oz	=	⅟₁₆ lb	=	30g
4 oz	=	¼ lb	=	120g
8 oz	=	½ lb	=	240g
12 oz	=	¾ lb	=	360g
16 oz	=	1 lb	=	480g

USEFUL EQUIVALENTS LENGTH

(To convert inches to centimeters, multiply the number of inches by 2.5.)

1 in	=		2.5cm
6 in	= ½ ft =		15cm
12 in	= 1 ft =		30cm
36 in	= 3 ft = 1 yd	=	90cm
40 in	=		100cm = 1 m

PHOTOGRAPHY CREDITS

COVER: Mike Garten (front); clockwise from top left: Christopher Testani, Mike Garten, Con Poulos (x2), Mike Garten, Con Poulos (back)

© Antonio Achilleos: 311, 326

© Yossy Arefi: 261

© James Baigrie: 26, 31, 48, 78, 91, 129, 178, 235, 368, 389, 390, 425, 465

© Monica Buck: 119, 134

Depositphotos: © Czuber 357, © Andrii Gorulko 117, © Asimojet 337, © Kung Mangkorn 23, © Anna Mavritta 27, © Serreitor 219, © Sedneva 371, © Sommaill 147, © Spaxiax 353, © Timmary 445

© Tara Donne: 96, 148, 287, 301 (bottom), 435

Mike Garten: 3, 8, 29, 52, 57, 73, 75, 82, 92, 158, 167, 186, 204, 208, 220, 233, 246, 258, 268, 270, 276, 294, 315, 338, 340, 355, 375, 382, 411

Getty images: © Ansonsaw 401 (middle), © Cultura RM Exclusive/Brett Stevens 102, © Steve Brown Photography 15, 195, © Creative Crop 403 (top), Tara Donne 419, © Nicholas Eveleigh 402, © Philippe Desnerck 55, © Gusto Images/Science Photo Library 163, © Floortje 169, © Haoliang 396, © ICP 252, © Dave King 25, © Dorling Kindersley 196, 416, © Rob Lawson 301 (top), 365, © Joff Lee 401 (top), © Souders Studios 429, © Love Life 275, © Lisa Romerein 460, © Georgia Glynn Smith 463, © Brett Stevens 417, © Maximilian Stock Ltd. 373, 400, © Nash Photos 403 (bottom), © Myles New 453, © Ian O'Leary 299, © Judd Pilossof 456, © Kellie Walsh 401 (bottom), © Westend61 106, 351

© Brian Hagiwara: 67, 240, 297, 322, 325

© Lisa Hubbard: 431

iStockphoto: © Bluestocking 14, © Kelly Cline 395, © Clubfoot 39, © Creativeye99 105, © Floortje 409, © Mark Gillow 99, © Oliver Hoffmann 63, © Adam Korzekwa 21, © Mashuk 86, © Maxg71 267, © Morningarage 313, © Joanna Pecha 20, © Small Frog 414, © Vitalina Rybakova 16, 271

© Frances Janisch: 293, 346

© Yunhee Kim: 35, 40

© Rita Maas: 398

© Kate Mathis: 43, 85, 109, 111, 120, 123, 125, 145, 175, 176, 185, 203, 333, 345, 362, 378, 420, 455

© Ngoc Minh Ngo: 288

© Con Poulos: 12, 126, 133, 152, 155, 213, 257, 284, 319, 342, 436

© David Prince: 280

© Alan Richardson: 71, 151, 180, 239, 372

Emily Kate Roemer: 251, 272, 305, 317, 321, 361, 384

© Kate Sears: 188, 223, 227, 228, 237, 263, 377, 422, 462

Shutterstock: © Bienchen-s 107, 201, © Norman Chan 183

StockFood: © Chay 423, © Fotosearch RM 207, © Gräfe & Unzer Verlag / Jörn Rynio 461, © Keller & Keller Photography 279, 441, © Karl Newedel 449, © Magdalena Paluchowska 451, © Anthony Tieuli 143

© Ann Stratton: 387, 393

Studio D: Chris Eckert 7

© Christopher Testani: 6, 140, 214, 305

© Mark Thomas: 359

© Anna Williams: 88, 139, 164

INDEX

Note: Page numbers in *italics* indicate photos on pages separate from recipes.

A

Almonds. *See* Nuts and seeds
Angel food cake, grilled with strawberries, 428
Apple Cider-Braised Greens, 386–387
Apples
  Apple-Brie Pizza with Caramelized Onions, 201
  Apple-Oat Muffins, 48
  Chicken and Apple Meatloaves, 282–283
  Chicken Apple Burgers, 182
  Fruity Green Smoothie, 25
  Pork, Cabbage, and Apple Sauté, 328
  Spiced Apple Pancake, 45
Apricots
  about: freezing for smoothies, 21
  Granola-Yogurt Parfait, 31
  Lower-Fat Granola, 30
Aromatic Brown Rice, 402–403
Artichokes, couscous-stuffed, 370–371
Asian Brown Rice, 403
Asian Chicken Salad, 69
Asian-Style Flounder Baked in Parchment, 232
Asian Tuna Burgers, 172
Asparagus
  about: low-fat ways to dress, 395; nutritional benefits, 329; steaming and enjoying, 329
  Garden Greens and Pumpernickel Panzanella, 52, 97
  Grilled Asparagus and Shiitake Tacos, 186–187
  Orange Pork and Asparagus Stir-Fry, 329
  Ricotta, Yellow Pepper, and Asparagus Pizza, 198
  Shrimp and Asparagus Stir-Fry, 210
Avocados
  about: healthy fat and eating, 10
  Avocado Salsa, 178–179
  Black Bean and Avocado Salad, 63
  Roasted Shrimp and Poblano Salad, 82–83
  Tex-Mex Chicken Soup, 126–127

B

Bacon, 124–125, 380
Baked Snapper with Peppers and Mushrooms, 228–229
Balsamic Roasted Pork with Berry Salad, 332–333
Bananas
  about: buying, 20; freezing for smoothies, 21; nutritional benefits, 20; ripeness of, 20
  Banana Berry Blast Smoothie, 18
  Berry Satisfying Smoothie, 16
  Broiled Brown-Sugar Bananas, 427
  Chocolate-Banana Smoothie, 20
  Fruity Green Smoothie, 25
  Honeyed Hot Fruit Salad, 432
  Java Banana Smoothie, 22
  Low-Fat Banana Bread, 50
  Spiced Banana-Chocolate Muffins, 12, 47
Barbecue Chicken Burgers, 181
Barley
  about, 60
  Barley, Corn, and Tomato Salad, 60
  Barley Minestrone with Pesto, 118–119
  Beef and Barley with Mushrooms, 306–307
  Seven-Minute Multigrain Cereal, 26
Basic Chicken Burgers, 180
Basic Couscous, 400
Basil
  Basil and Balsamic Beets, 414
  Basil-Orange Chicken with Couscous, 252–253
  Grilled Whole Wheat Veggie Pizza, 202–203
  Light Pesto, 118–119
  Shrimp and Pineapple Salad with Basil, 90–91
  Summer Tuna Salad with Sweet Potato and Basil, 73
  Thai Chicken-Basil Soup, 130
  Thai Noodles with Beef and Basil, 310–311
  Whole Wheat Penne Genovese, 376–377
BBQ Brisket Tacos, 190
BBQ Ranch Chicken Wraps, 167
"BBQ" Salmon and Brussels Bake, 220–221
BBQ Sauce, 281
BBQ Tofu Sandwiches, 364
Beans and other legumes. *See also* Edamame; Peas
  about: dry (soaking, cooking, storing), 117; miso from soybeans, 241; nutritional and health benefits, 122

Bean and Corn-Stuffed Sweet Potatoes, 362–363
Black Bean and Avocado Salad, 63
Black Bean Burgers, 344–345
Black Bean Soup, 122–123
Brazilian Pork Chops, 331
Breakfast Tortilla Stack, 34–35
Bulgur Bean Burgers, 162–163
Chickpea Mango Salad, 88–89
Chutney-Glazed Shrimp with Lentils, 215
Cincinnati Chili, 152–153
Corn Fritters with Black Bean Salad, 342–343
Creamy Italian White-Bean Soup, 113
Falafel Sandwiches, 160
Greek Salad Pitas, 170–171
Grilled Chicken Taco Salad, 68
Healthy Club Sandwiches, 161
Huevos Rancheros, 37
Indian Cauliflower Stew, 368
Italian Tuna and White Bean Salad, 76
Kale and Bean Salad, 340
Macaroni, Cabbage, and Bean Soup, 114
Moroccan Sweet-Potato Stew, 346–347
Pasta e Fagioli with Sausage, 116
Six-Bean Salad with Tomato Vinaigrette, 95
South-of-the-Border Vegetable Hash, 36
Summer Tuna Salad with Sweet Potato and Basil, 73
Super Bowl Chili, 150–151
Swordfish with Summer Salad, 204, 244
Tex-Mex Turkey Cobb Salad, 64
Three-Bean Vegetable Chili, 146
Turkey and White Bean Chili, 148–149
Tuscan Tuna Salad Sandwiches, 169
Tuscan Veggie Stew, 140–141
Valentine's Day Red Chili, 144–145
Veggie Wraps with Goat Cheese, 166
Warm French Lentil Salad, 84–85
White-Bean and Tomatillo Chili, 341
Whole Wheat Penne Genovese, 376–377
Beef
  about: browning and braising, 143; cutting thin, 307; grilling (cuts to use), 299; selecting, 299

BBQ Brisket Tacos, 190
Beef and Barley with
    Mushrooms, 306–307
Beef Eye Round au Jus, 302
Caramelized Brisket with Glazed
    Shiitakes, 334
Cincinnati Chili, 152–153
Classic Beef Stew, 142
Korean Steak in Lettuce Cups,
    70–71
Lean Beef Stroganoff, 312–313
Meatloaf Burgers with Sautéed
    Carrots, 193
Osso Buco with Gremolata,
    336–337
Pastrami-Spiced Flank Steak
    Sandwiches, 296–297
Penne Rigate with Picadillo
    Sauce, 314
Roast Beef Waldorf Sandwiches,
    192
Sautéed Beef and Pepper Skillet
    with Fries, 294, 303
Slow-Braised Beef Ragu, 308–309
Steak and Oven Fries, 300–301
Steak and Pepper Fajitas, 298
Steak Sandwiches with Grilled
    Onions, 194–195
Super Bowl Chili, 150–151
Thai Noodles with Beef and
    Basil, 310–311
Ultimate Rub for, 190
Veal and Mushroom Stew, 157
Beets
    about: nutritional benefits, 96;
        subduing earthy flavor, 96
    Basil and Balsamic Beets, 414
    Not Your Grandma's Borscht, 112
    Shredded Beets with Celery and
        Dates, 96
    Valentine's Day Red Chili,
        144–145
Berries
    about: blackberries, 429; black
        currants, 429; blueberries,
        18, 429; chokeberries, 429;
        elderberries, 429; freezing, 21,
        428; nutritional benefits, 14, 19,
        429; raspberries, 429; selecting,
        18, 21; strawberries, 14, 19, 429
    Balsamic Roasted Pork with
        Berry Salad, 332–333
    Banana Berry Blast Smoothie, 18
    Berry Satisfying Smoothie, 16
    Bold Berry Granita, 464–465
    Brown Rice and Cranberry
        Stuffing, 405
    Buttermilk Panna Cotta with
        Blackberry Sauce, 420, 458
    Coulis, 32

Grilled Angel Food Cake with
    Strawberries, 428
Jump-Start Smoothie, 19
Lemon-Blueberry Tiramisu,
    424–425
Mango Strawberry Smoothie, 14
Strawberry Chia Smoothie, 17
Strawberry Granola Yogurt
    Parfait, 32
Three-Fruit Salad with Vanilla
    Bean Syrup, 426
Whole-Grain Blueberry Muffins, 49
Whole-Grain Pancakes, 40–41
Black beans. See Beans and other
    legumes
Blackberries and blueberries. See
    Berries
Blondies, low-fat butterscotch, 452
Bold Berry Granita, 464–465
Borscht, 112
Brazilian Pork Chops, 331
Breads. See also Pancakes and
    waffles; Pizza; Sandwiches and
    wraps
    about: low-fat tips, 440
    Apple-Oat Muffins, 48
    Garden Greens and
        Pumpernickel Panzanella, 52,
        97
    Grilled Chicken Bruschetta,
        256–257
    Healthy Makeover Pumpkin
        Bread, 454–455
    Panzanella Salad with Grilled
        Chicken, 65
    Savory Pear and Cornbread
        Stuffing, 412
    Skinny Carrot Muffins, 51
    Spiced Banana-Chocolate
        Muffins, 12, 47
    Whole-Grain Blueberry Muffins, 49
Breakfasts and brunches, 13–51.
    See also Pancakes and waffles;
    Smoothies
    about: overview of recipes, 13
    Apple-Oat Muffins, 48
    Breakfast Tortilla Stack, 34–35
    California Frittata, 38–39
    Granola-Yogurt Parfait, 31
    Healthy Makeover French Toast,
        42–43
    Huevos Rancheros, 37
    Lower-Fat Granola, 30
    Low-Fat Banana Bread, 50
    Paprika Parmesan Granola Bars,
        28–29
    Seven-Minute Multigrain Cereal, 26
    Skinny Carrot Muffins, 51
    South-of-the-Border Vegetable
        Hash, 36

Spiced Banana-Chocolate
    Muffins, 12, 47
Spinach Soufflé, 33
Strawberry Granola Yogurt
    Parfait, 32
Whole-Grain Blueberry Muffins, 49
Broccoli
    about: low-fat ways to dress, 394;
        nutritional and health benefits,
        200
    Broccoli-Mushroom Pizza, 200
    Broccoli Pesto Spaghetti, 365
    Slow-Cooker Sesame-Garlic
        Chicken, 272–273
    Soba Noodles Primavera with
        Miso, 381
    Tangerine Chicken Stir-Fry,
        262–263
    Veggie Lo Mein, 382–383
Broiled Brown-Sugar Bananas,
    427
Broth, chicken, 137
Broth, vegetable, 136
Brownies, healthy makeover,
    450–451
Browning and braising meats, 143
Brown rice. See Rice and wild rice
Brussels sprouts
    Bacon and Brussels Sprout
        Penne, 380
    "BBQ" Salmon and Brussels Bake,
        220–221
Bulgur
    about: benefits and uses, 163
    Bulgur and Cashew Stuffed
        Eggplant, 360–361
    Bulgur and Grape Salad with
        Dried Figs and Almonds, 80
    Bulgur Bean Burgers, 162–163
    Cabbage and Bulgur Casserole,
        358–359
    Seven-Minute Multigrain Cereal, 26
Buttermilk-Chive Dressing, 59
Buttermilk Panna Cotta with
    Blackberry Sauce, 420, 458
Butterscotch blondies, low-fat, 452

C
Cabbage
    Barley Minestrone with Pesto,
        118–119
    Cabbage and Bulgur Casserole,
        358–359
    Crunchy Carrot Coleslaw, 99
    Grilled Plum and Pork Salad,
        74–75
    Macaroni, Cabbage, and Bean
        Soup, 114
    Not Your Grandma's Borscht, 112
    Nutty Chicken Noodles, 258–259

Pork, Cabbage, and Apple Sauté, 328
Caesar pasta salad, kale, 56–57
Caesar salad, grilled, 72
Cakes. See Desserts
California Frittata, 38–39
Cantaloupe. See Melons
Caper Vinaigrette, 384, 413
Caramelized Brisket with Glazed Shiitakes, 334
Caramelized Chile Shrimp, 212–213
Caramel, low-fat crème, 459
Carrots
    Carrot and Dill Soup, 106–107
    Crunchy Carrot Coleslaw, 99
    Ginger-Spiced Carrot Soup, 108–109
    Healthy Makeover Carrot Cake, 324–325
    Meatloaf Burgers with Sautéed Carrots, 193
    Mixed Vegetable Minestrone, 120–121
    Skinny Carrot Muffins, 51
    Soba Noodles Primavera with Miso, 381
    Soba Noodles with Shrimp, Snow Peas, and Carrots, 134–135
    Three-Bean Vegetable Chili, 146
    Tuscan Veggie Stew, 140–141
    Veggie Lo Mein, 382–383
Cauliflower
    about: low-fat ways to dress, 395; using stems as snack, 410
    Cauliflower "Popcorn," 410–411
    Chili-Lime "Popcorn," 410
    Indian Cauliflower Stew, 368–369
    Skillet Vegetable Curry, 366
    Truffle "Popcorn," 410
Celery
    Fruity Green Smoothie, 25
    Shredded Beets with Celery and Dates, 96
Chard. See Swiss chard
Cheese
    about: low-fat tips, 440
    Chicken Quesadillas with Avocado Salsa, 178–179
    Cincinnati Chili, 152–153
    Cream-Cheese Frosting, 434–435
    Paprika Parmesan Granola Bars, 28–29
    pasta with. See Pasta
    pizza with. See Pizza
    Stuffed Fresh Figs, 430–431
Cherries
    Tart Cherry Sauce, 292
    Wheat Berry Salad with Dried Cherries, 87
Chianti-Roasted Pears, 422–423

Chicken
    about: breast meat, 253, 275; minimizing fat intake, 275; overview of recipes, 247
    Asian Chicken Salad, 69
    Barbecue Chicken Burgers, 181
    Basic Chicken Burgers, 180
    Basil-Orange Chicken with Couscous, 252–253
    BBQ Ranch Chicken Wraps, 167
    Chicken Adobo over Gingery Rice, 260–261
    Chicken and Apple Meatloaves, 282–283
    Chicken and Escarole Soup, 115
    Chicken Apple Burgers, 182
    Chicken Bolognese, 254
    Chicken Breasts with Two Quick Sauces, 248
    Chicken Caesar Pitas, 174–175
    Chicken Cakes with "Roasted" Tomato Salsa, 173
    Chicken Chilaquiles, 250–251
    Chicken Noodle Stir-Fry, 265
    Chicken Quesadillas with Avocado Salsa, 178–179
    Chicken Soup, Bouillabaisse-Style, 128–129
    Chicken Thighs Provençal, 266–-267
    Crispy Chicken Tenders with BBQ Sauce, 280–281
    Curried Chicken Salad with Cantaloupe Slaw, 66–67
    Gingery Chicken in Lettuce Cups, 177
    Gourmet Ramen, 132–133
    Grilled Chicken Bruschetta, 256–257
    Grilled Chicken Taco Salad, 68
    Healthy Makeover Fried Chicken, 278–279
    Herb Chicken Burgers, 181
    Homemade Chicken Broth, 137
    Honey-Mustard Chicken and Potatoes, 274–275
    Lemon-Oregano Chicken, 264
    Mango Chicken Lettuce Wraps, 176
    Maple-Glazed Sausages and Figs, 335
    Moroccan Olive and Orange Chicken, 276–277
    Nutty Chicken Noodles, 258–259
    Pancetta Chicken, 246, 249
    Panzanella Salad with Grilled Chicken, 65
    Ratatouille Pasta, 270
    Red-Cooked Chicken, Slow-Cooker Style, 255

Slow-Cooker Sesame-Garlic Chicken, 272–273
    Southwestern Chicken Stew, 154–155
    Spicy Turkey Sausage Jambalaya, 291
    Sweet and Sticky Chicken with Snow Peas, 268–269
    Tangerine Chicken Stir-Fry, 262–263
    Teriyaki Chicken Burgers, 181
    Tex-Mex Chicken Soup, 126–127
    Thai Chicken-Basil Soup, 130
Chickpeas (garbanzo beans)
    about: nutritional and health benefits, 122
    Chickpea Mango Salad, 88–89
    Falafel Sandwiches, 160
    Greek Salad Pitas, 170–171
    Healthy Club Sandwiches, 161
    Indian Cauliflower Stew, 368
    Moroccan Sweet-Potato Stew, 346–347
    Six-Bean Salad with Tomato Vinaigrette, 95
    Swordfish with Summer Salad, 204, 244
    Veggie Wraps with Goat Cheese, 166
Chili-Lime "Popcorn," 410
Chilis
    Cincinnati Chili, 152–153
    Super Bowl Chili, 150–151
    Three-Bean Vegetable Chili, 146
    Turkey and White Bean Chili, 148–149
    Valentine's Day Red Chili, 144–145
    White-Bean and Tomatillo Chili, 341
Chilled Buttermilk and Corn Soup, 105
Chilled Tuscan-Style Tomato Soup, 102, 104
Chinese Ginger Sauce, 248
Chocolate
    about: low-fat tips, 440; types and nutritional benefits, 433
    Chocolate-Banana Smoothie, 20
    Chocolate Pudding, 453
    Frozen Chocolate Kahlua Mousse, 433
    Healthy Makeover Brownies, 450–451
    Spiced Banana-Chocolate Muffins, 12, 47
Chutney-Glazed Shrimp with Lentils, 215
Cincinnati Chili, 152–153

Citrus
about: boosting flavors with, 55;
grated peel and juice uses, 55
Banana Berry Blast Smoothie, 18
Basil-Orange Chicken with
Couscous, 252–253
Chili-Lime "Popcorn," 410
Honey-Lime Vinaigrette, 58
Jump-Start Smoothie, 19
Lemon-Blueberry Tiramisu,
424–425
Lemon-Maple Icebox Cake,
436–437
Lemon Meringue Drops, 456–457
Lemon-Oregano Chicken, 264
Lemon-Parsley Brown Rice, 403
Lemony Crab Linguine, 233
Lime Couscous, 401
Moroccan Olive and Orange
Chicken, 276–277
Orange-Cilantro Brown Rice, 403
Orange-Ginger Vinaigrette, 58
Orange Pork and Asparagus Stir-
Fry, 329
Pasta Salad with Lemon and
Peas, 54
Roasted-Lemon Orzo, 316–317
Tangerine Chicken Stir-Fry,
262–263
Tomato-Orange Vinaigrette, 58
Clam sauce, red, 245
Classic Beef Stew, 142
Cobb salad, Tex-Mex turkey, 64
Cod, dishes with, 124–125, 138–139,
226–227, 230
Coffee
about: ice cubes of, 23
Coffee Granita, 463
Java Banana Smoothie, 22
Perfect Cold-Brewed Coffee, 23
Collard greens, 386–387, 394
Cookies. See Desserts
Corn
Barley, Corn, and Tomato Salad, 60
BBQ Ranch Chicken Wraps, 167
Bean and Corn-Stuffed Sweet
Potatoes, 362–363
Chilled Buttermilk and Corn
Soup, 105
Corn Fritters with Black Bean
Salad, 342–343
Huevos Rancheros, 37
Millet with Corn and Green
Chiles, 406
Minted Corn and Brown Rice
Salad, 81
Polenta with Garlicky Greens,
350–351
Savory Pear and Cornbread
Stuffing, 412

Tex-Mex Chicken Soup, 126–127
Coulis, 32
Couscous
about, 371
Basic Couscous, 400
Basil-Orange Chicken with
Couscous, 252–253
Couscous-Stuffed Artichokes,
370–371
Lamb and Root Vegetable Tagine,
156
Lime Couscous, 401
Moroccan Couscous, 401
Moroccan Sweet-Potato Stew,
346–347
Pan-Seared Scallops with Lemon
Couscous, 218
Spiced Couscous with
Vegetables, 348
Sun-Dried Tomato and Green
Onion Couscous, 401
Crab dishes, 216, 233
Cracked Wheat with Greens, 397
Cream-Cheese Frosting, 434–435
Cream, reducing fat intake, 441
Creamy Italian White-Bean Soup, 113
Creamy Kale Smoothie, 24
Creamy Ranch Dressing, 59
Creamy Vegan Linguine with Wild
Mushrooms, 338, 349
Crispy Chicken Tenders with BBQ
Sauce, 280–281
Crispy Roasted Potatoes with Caper
Vinaigrette, 384, 413
Crunchy Carrot Coleslaw, 99
Curried Chicken Salad with
Cantaloupe Slaw, 66–67
Curry, skillet vegetable, 366

D
Dairy, fat and, 10, 440, 441
Deep-Dish Supreme Pizza, 158, 199
Desserts, 421–465. See also Sauces,
sweet
about: almond paste for, 449;
lightening up fat content,
440–441; mock whipped cream,
441; overview of recipes, 421;
whole wheat flour for, 445
Bold Berry Granita, 464–465
Broiled Brown-Sugar Bananas,
427
Buttermilk Panna Cotta with
Blackberry Sauce, 420, 458
Chianti-Roasted Pears, 422–423
Chocolate Pudding, 453
Coffee Granita, 463
Cream-Cheese Frosting, 434–435
Frozen Chocolate Kahlua
Mousse, 433

Grilled Angel Food Cake with
Strawberries, 428
Healthy Makeover Brownies,
450–451
Healthy Makeover Carrot Cake,
434–435
Healthy Makeover Pumpkin
Bread, 454–455
Honey Cookies, 439
Honeyed Hot Fruit Salad, 432
Lemon-Blueberry Tiramisu,
424–425
Lemon-Maple Icebox Cake,
436–437
Lemon Meringue Drops, 456–457
Low-Fat Butterscotch Blondies,
452
Low-Fat Crème Caramel, 459
Molasses Cookies, 443
Oatmeal-Raisin Cookies, 442
Peachy Frozen Yogurt, 460
Pignoli Cookies, 448
Plum Yogurt Pops, 461
Sgroppino Sorbet with Prosecco
and Mint, 462
Stuffed Fresh Figs, 430–431
Three-Fruit Salad with Vanilla
Bean Syrup, 426
Wheat-Free Almond Butter
Cookies, 446
Whole-Grain Fig Bars, 447
Whole-Grain Gingersnaps, 438
Whole Wheat Sugar Cookies,
444–445
Dill, in Carrot and Dill Soup, 106–107
Duck breasts, crispy with tart cherry
sauce, 292–293

E
Edamame
about: nutritional benefits, 147;
snacks and other uses, 147
Asian Chicken Salad, 69
Gingery Chicken in Lettuce Cups,
177
Mixed Vegetable Minestrone,
120–121
Six-Bean Salad with Tomato
Vinaigrette, 95
Sweet Potato Cakes with Kale
and Bean Salad, 340
Three-Bean Vegetable Chili, 146
Veggie Lo Mein, 382–383
Eggplant
about: low-fat ways to dress,
395; mellowing flavor of, 361;
nutritional and health benefits,
361
Bulgur and Cashew Stuffed
Eggplant, 360–361

Grilled Eggplant Caponata Salad, 78–79

Ratatouille Pasta, 270

Eggs. *See also* Pancakes and waffles

about: low-fat substitute for, 440

Breakfast Tortilla Stack, 34–35

California Frittata, 38–39

Healthy Makeover French Toast, 42–43

Huevos Rancheros, 37

Spinach Soufflé, 33

Escarole, in Chicken and Escarole Soup, 115

F

Fajitas, steak and pepper, 298

Fajitas, turkey, 184–185

Falafel Sandwiches, 160

Farfalle Livornese with Tuna, 236–237

Farro

about, 94

Farro Risotto with Butternut Squash, 352–353

Warm Farro Salad with Roasted Vegetables, 94

Fast Fried Rice, 367

Fat

bottom line, 11

dairy, healthiness of, 10

Dietary Guidelines (2015) and, 9

dressing veggies to minimize, 394–395

"healthy," calorie intake and, 10–11

lightening up desserts, 440–441

"moderate" fat diet, 11

new thinking about, 9–11

oil types and, 9–10

plant-based vs. animal-based, 9–10

trans-fats, 11

unsaturated vs. saturated, 9–10

Fattoush, 86

Fiber, benefits and sources, 27

Figs

Bulgur and Grape Salad with Dried Figs and Almonds, 80

Maple-Glazed Sausages and Figs, 335

Stuffed Fresh Figs, 430–431

Whole-Grain Fig Bars, 447

Fish and shellfish, 205–245

about: Asian fish sauce, 130; cleaning, preparing mussels, 206; overview of recipes, 205; prepping scallops, 219

Almond-Crusted Creole Salmon, 224

Asian-Style Flounder Baked in Parchment, 232

Asian Tuna Burgers, 172

Baked Snapper with Peppers and Mushrooms, 228–229

"BBQ" Salmon and Brussels Bake, 220–221

Caramelized Chile Shrimp, 212–213

Chutney-Glazed Shrimp with Lentils, 215

Crab Boil, 216

Farfalle Livornese with Tuna, 236–237

Greek-Style Tilapia, 222–223

Hearty Fish Chowder, 124–125

Island-Spiced Fish Sticks, 226–227

Italian Tuna and White Bean Salad, 76

Lemony Crab Linguine, 233

Linguine with Red Clam Sauce, 245

Mediterranean Seafood Stew, 138–139

Miso-Glazed Salmon, 240–241

Moules à la Marinière, 206

Mussels with Tomatoes and White Wine, 206–207

Mustard-Dill Salmon with Herbed Potatoes, 242

Pan-Roasted Cod on Cabbage and Apples, 230

Pan-Seared Scallops with Lemon Couscous, 218

Roasted Halibut with Fennel and Potatoes, 231

Roasted Shrimp and Poblano Salad, 82–83

Salt-Baked Fish, 238

Saucy Creole Shrimp, 214

Seafood Fra Diavolo, 243

Seared Scallops with Olive and Tomato Compote, 217

Shrimp and Asparagus Stir-Fry, 210

Shrimp and Pineapple Salad with Basil, 90–91

Shrimp and Zucchini Scampi, 208–209

Snapper Livornese, 225

Soba Noodles with Shrimp, Snow Peas, and Carrots, 134–135

Spring Vegetable Risotto with Shrimp, 211

Steamed Scrod Fillets, 239

Summer Tuna Salad with Sweet Potato and Basil, 73

Swordfish with Summer Salad, 204, 244

Tuna au Poivre with Lemon-Caper Lentils, 234–235

Tuscan Tuna Salad Sandwiches, 169

Flounder, dishes with, 225, 228–229, 232

Flour, whole wheat, 445

Flowers, in soup, 110–111

Freezing fruit, 21, 428

French toast, healthy, 42–43

Fried chicken, healthy makeover, 278–279

Frozen Chocolate Kahlua Mousse, 433

Fruit. *See also specific fruit*

about: colorful, benefits of, 62; freezing, 21, 429

Fruity Green Smoothie, 25

Honeyed Hot Fruit Salad, 432

Three-Fruit Salad with Vanilla Bean Syrup, 426

G

Garbanzo beans. *See* Chickpeas

Garden Greens and Pumpernickel Panzanella, 52, 97

Garden Turkey Sandwiches, 183

Ginger

Chicken Adobo over Gingery Rice, 260–261

Chinese Ginger Sauce, 248

Ginger-Spiced Carrot Soup, 108–109

Gingery Chicken in Lettuce Cups, 177

Orange-Ginger Vinaigrette, 58

Whole-Grain Gingersnaps, 438

Gourmet Ramen, 132–133

Grains. *See also* Breads; Bulgur; Corn; Granola; Oats; Pasta; Rice and wild rice

about: farro, 94; millet, 406; nutritional benefits, 94, 357, 406; wheat berries, 357

Cracked Wheat with Greens, 397

Farro Risotto with Butternut Squash, 352–353

Millet with Corn and Green Chiles, 406

Polenta with Garlicky Greens, 350–351

Seven-Minute Multigrain Cereal, 26

Warm Farro Salad with Roasted Vegetables, 94

Wheat-Berry Pilaf with Green Beans, 356–357

Granita, berry, 464–465

Granita, coffee, 463

Granola

Granola-Yogurt Parfait, 31

Lower-Fat Granola, 30
Paprika Parmesan Granola Bars, 28–29
Strawberry Granola Yogurt Parfait, 32
Grapes and raisins
  Bulgur and Grape Salad with Dried Figs and Almonds, 80
  Granola-Yogurt Parfait, 31
  Lower-Fat Granola, 30
  Oatmeal-Raisin Cookies, 442
  Pork Tenderloin with Roasted Grapes, 322–323
  Sautéed Swiss Chard with Golden Raisins and Capers, 388
Greek Salad Pitas, 170–171
Greek-Style Tilapia, 222–223
Green beans
  about: low-fat ways to dress, 394
  Chicken Adobo over Gingery Rice with, 260–261
  Farfalle Livornese with Tuna, 236–237
  Green Beans with Caramelized Onions, 392–393
  Mixed Vegetable Minestrone, 120–121
  Sesame Green Beans, 396
  Six-Bean Salad with Tomato Vinaigrette, 95
  Veggie Wraps with Goat Cheese, 166
  Wheat-Berry Pilaf with Green Beans, 356–357
Greens. See Collard greens; Salads; Spinach; Swiss chard
Gremolata, 337
Grilled Angel Food Cake with Strawberries, 428
Grilled Asparagus and Shiitake Tacos, 186–187
Grilled Caesar Salad, 72
Grilled Chicken Bruschetta, 256–257
Grilled Chicken Taco Salad, 68
Grilled Eggplant Caponata Salad, 78–79
Grilled Plum and Pork Salad, 74–75
Grilled Whole Wheat Veggie Pizza, 202–203

H
Halibut, roasted with potatoes, 231
Hash, vegetable, 36
Healthy Club Sandwiches, 161
Healthy Makeover Brownies, 450–451
Healthy Makeover Carrot Cake, 434–435
Healthy Makeover French Toast, 42–43

Healthy Makeover Fried Chicken, 278–279
Healthy Makeover Pumpkin Bread, 454–455
Hearty Fish Chowder, 124–125
Herb Chicken Burgers, 181
Hoisin Pork Tenderloin with Grilled Pineapple, 326–327
Homemade Chicken Broth, 137
Homemade Vegetable Broth, 136
Honey Cookies, 439
Honeydew melon. See Melons
Honeyed Hot Fruit Salad, 432
Honey-Lime Vinaigrette, 58
Honey-Mustard Chicken and Potatoes, 274–275
Honey, types of, 430, 439
Hot and Spicy Pork Noodles, 321
Huevos Rancheros, 37

I
Ice cubes, coffee, 23
Indian Cauliflower Stew, 368–369
Island-Spiced Fish Sticks, 226–227
Italian Tuna and White Bean Salad, 76

J
Jambalaya, spicy turkey sausage, 291
Java Banana Smoothie, 22
Jump-Start Smoothie, 19

K
Kahlua mousse, frozen chocolate, 433
Kale
  Creamy Kale Smoothie, 24
  Kale Caesar Pasta Salad, 56–57
  Kale "Chips," 389
  Sweet Potato Cakes with Kale and Bean Salad, 340
  Tuscan Veggie Stew, 140–141
Kiwifruit, in Strawberry Chia Smoothie, 17
Korean Steak in Lettuce Cups, 70–71

L
Lamb
  about: browning and braising, 143; grilling (cuts to use), 299; selecting, 299
  Lamb and Root Vegetable Tagine, 156
Lemon(s) and Lime(s). See Citrus
Lentils
  Chutney-Glazed Shrimp with Lentils, 215
  Tuna au Poivre with Lemon-Caper Lentils, 234–235
  Warm French Lentil Salad, 84–85
Lettuce wraps and cups, 176, 177
Light Mashed Potatoes, 416

Light Pesto, 118–119
Lower-Fat Granola, 30
Low-Fat Banana Bread, 50
Low-Fat Butterscotch Blondies, 452
Low-Fat Crème Caramel, 459

M
Macaroni, Cabbage, and Bean Soup, 114
Mango
  Chickpea Mango Salad, 88–89
  Fruity Green Smoothie, 25
  Mango Chicken Lettuce Wraps, 176
  Mango Strawberry Smoothie, 14
  Three-Fruit Salad with Vanilla Bean Syrup, 426
Maple-Glazed Sausages and Figs, 335
Maple-Roasted Squash, 415
Marsala, about, 157
Mashed Sweet Potatoes, 417
Meatloaf Burgers with Sautéed Carrots, 193
Meatloaves, chicken and apple, 282–283
Meats. See also specific meats
  browning and braising, 143
  grilled, best cuts by meat, 299
  lean red, overview of recipes, 295
  selecting, 299
Mediterranean Seafood Stew, 138–139
Melons
  Cantaloupe Slaw, 66–67
  Melon Salsa, 315
  Prosciutto Turkey Cutlets with Melon, 286–287
  Three-Fruit Salad with Vanilla Bean Syrup, 426
Meringues, lemon, 456–457
Mesclun with Pears and Pumpkin Seeds, 100
Metric equivalent charts, 466
Millet with Corn and Green Chiles, 406
Minestrone, 118–119, 120–121
Mint
  Minted Corn and Brown Rice Salad, 81
  Minted Yogurt Sauce, 189
  Sgroppino Sorbet with Prosecco and Mint, 462
  Tomato and Mint Tabbouleh, 98
Miso
  about, 241
  Miso-Glazed Salmon, 240–241
  Soba Noodles Primavera with Miso, 381

Mixed Pea Pod Stir-Fry, 398–399
Mixed Vegetable Minestrone, 120–121
Molasses Cookies, 443
Moroccan Couscous, 401
Moroccan Olive and Orange Chicken, 276–277
Moroccan Sweet-Potato Stew, 346–347
Mousse, frozen chocolate Kahlua, 433
Mushrooms
    Baked Snapper with Peppers and Mushrooms, 228–229
    Beef and Barley with Mushrooms, 306–307
    Broccoli-Mushroom Pizza, 200
    Brown Rice and Vegetable Pilaf, 404
    Caramelized Brisket with Glazed Shiitakes, 334
    Creamy Vegan Linguine with Wild Mushrooms, 338, 349
    Deep-Dish Supreme Pizza, 158, 199
    Grilled Asparagus and Shiitake Tacos, 186–187
    Grilled Whole Wheat Veggie Pizza, 202–203
    Lean Beef Stroganoff, 312–313
    Orecchiette with Morels and Peas, 374–375
    PLT Sandwiches, 164–165
    Veal and Mushroom Stew, 157
    Veggie Wraps with Goat Cheese, 166
    Wild Rice and Mushroom Stuffing, 408–409
    Wild Rice and Orzo Pilaf, 407
Mussels, 138–139, 206–207, 243
Mustard-Dill Salmon with Herbed Potatoes, 242
Mustard greens, 386–387

N
Nectarines. See Peaches and nectarines
Not Your Grandma's Borscht, 112
Nuts and seeds
    about: almond paste, 449; appetite impact of nuts, 50; buying, 17, 50, 446; chia seeds, 15, 17; flaxseeds, 15, 446; healthy smoothie additions, 15; low-fat tips, 440; nut benefits, 50; nut butters, 15; nutritional benefits, 15; peanut sauce alternative, 259; toasting nuts, 101; toasting sesame seeds, 70

Almond-Crusted Creole Salmon, 224
Apple-Oat Muffins, 48
Bulgur and Cashew Stuffed Eggplant, 360–361
Bulgur and Grape Salad with Dried Figs and Almonds, 80
Granola-Yogurt Parfait, 31
Lower-Fat Granola, 30
Low-Fat Banana Bread, 50
Mesclun with Pears and Pumpkin Seeds, 100
Nutty Chicken Noodles, 258–259
Paprika Parmesan Granola Bars, 28–29
Pignoli Cookies, 448
Strawberry Chia Smoothie, 17
Stuffed Fresh Figs, 430–431
Warm Quinoa Salad with Toasted Almonds, 101
Wheat-Free Almond Butter Cookies, 446

O
Oats
    about: benefits of, 15; in smoothies, 15
    Apple-Oat Muffins, 48
    Berry Satisfying Smoothie, 16
    Granola-Yogurt Parfait, 31
    Lower-Fat Granola, 30
    Oatmeal-Raisin Cookies, 442
    Paprika Parmesan Granola Bars, 28–29
    Seven-Minute Multigrain Cereal, 26
    Spiced Banana-Chocolate Muffins, 12, 47
    Whole-Grain Blueberry Muffins, 49
Oils, types of, 9–10
Olives
    Grilled Eggplant Caponata Salad, 78–79
    Olive and Tomato Compote, 217
    Risotto Puttanesca, 354–355
    Spinach and Feta Pizza, 197
Onions
    about: nutritional benefits, 191
    Apple-Brie Pizza with Caramelized Onions, 201
    Green Beans with Caramelized Onions, 392–393
    Grilled Whole Wheat Veggie Pizza, 202–203
    Steak Sandwiches with Grilled Onions, 194–195
    Sun-Dried Tomato and Green Onion Couscous, 401
    Tarragon Peas and Pearl Onions, 390–391

Orange(s). See Citrus
Orecchiette with Morels and Peas, 374–375
Osso Buco with Gremolata, 336–337
Oven Fries, 418–419

P
Pancakes and waffles
    Healthy Makeover French Toast, 42–43
    Pumpkin Pancakes, 44
    Spiced Apple Pancake, 45
    Ultimate Classic Waffle, 46
    Whole-Grain Pancakes, 40–41
Pancetta Chicken, 246, 249
Panna cotta, buttermilk with blackberry sauce, 420, 458
Pan-Roasted Cod on Cabbage and Apples, 230
Pan-Seared Scallops with Lemon Couscous, 218
Panzanella Salad with Grilled Chicken, 65
Paprika Parmesan Granola Bars, 28–29
Parsnips, 136, 156
Pasta
    about: adding vegetables to, 271; Asian noodle types (bean thread, Chinese wheat, rice, soba, udon), 131; cooking, 271; fiber content, 373; flavoring tips, 271; healthy options, 271, 373; overview of mains recipes, 339; rice noodles, 77, 131; speedy sauce for, 271; whole wheat and multigrain, 373
    Bacon and Brussels Sprout Penne, 380
    Broccoli Pesto Spaghetti, 365
    Chicken and Escarole Soup, 115
    Chicken Bolognese, 254
    Chicken Noodle Stir-Fry, 265
    Cincinnati Chili, 152–153
    Creamy Vegan Linguine with Wild Mushrooms, 338, 349
    Farfalle Livornese with Tuna, 236–237
    Gourmet Ramen, 132–133
    Greek-Style Tilapia, 222–223
    Hot and Spicy Pork Noodles, 321
    Kale Caesar Pasta Salad, 56–57
    Lasagna Toss with Spinach and Ricotta, 372–373
    Lean Beef Stroganoff, 312–313
    Lemony Crab Linguine, 233
    Linguine with Red Clam Sauce, 245
    Macaroni, Cabbage, and Bean Soup, 114

Mixed Vegetable Minestrone, 120–121
Nutty Chicken Noodles, 258–259
Orecchiette with Morels and Peas, 374–375
Parmesan and Sausage Bolognese, 304–305
Pasta e Fagioli with Sausage, 116
Pasta Salad with Lemon and Peas, 54
Penne Rigate with Picadillo Sauce, 314
Pork Tenderloin with Roasted-Lemon Orzo, 316–317
Ratatouille Pasta, 270
Rice Noodles with Many Herbs, 77
Shrimp and Zucchini Scampi, 208–209
Soba Noodles Primavera with Miso, 381
Soba Noodles with Shrimp, Snow Peas, and Carrots, 134–135
Southwestern Chicken Stew, 154–155
"Spaghetti" and Meatballs alternative, 290
Spaghetti with Roasted Sweet Potato, 378–379
Thai Chicken-Basil Soup, 130
Thai Noodles with Beef and Basil, 310–311
Veggie Lo Mein, 382–383
Vietnamese Noodle Salad, 92–93
Wild Rice and Orzo Pilaf, 407
Pastrami-Spiced Flank Steak Sandwiches, 296–297
Peaches and nectarines
about: freezing for smoothies, 21
Honeyed Hot Fruit Salad, 432
Peaches and Greens, 62
Peachy Frozen Yogurt, 460
Whole-Grain Pancakes, 40–41
Pears
about, 423; avoiding browning of, 289, 423; refrigerating, 423; ripening, 423; varieties and uses, 423
Chianti-Roasted Pears, 422–423
Fruity Green Smoothie, 25
Mesclun with Pears and Pumpkin Seeds, 100
Savory Pear and Cornbread Stuffing, 412
Turkey Cutlets with Pears and Tarragon, 288–289
Peas
Ginger-Spiced Carrot Soup, 108–109
Mixed Pea Pod Stir-Fry, 398–399

Orecchiette with Morels and Peas, 374–375
Pasta Salad with Lemon and Peas, 54
Snap Pea Salad, 61
Soba Noodles with Shrimp, Snow Peas, and Carrots, 134–135
Spring Pea Soup, 110–111
Spring Vegetable Risotto with Shrimp, 211
Sweet and Sticky Chicken with Snow Peas, 268–269
Tarragon Peas and Pearl Onions, 390–391
Penne. See Pasta
Peppers
about: nutritional benefits, 267
Baked Snapper with Peppers and Mushrooms, 228–229
Chicken Thighs Provençal, 266–267
Deep-Dish Supreme Pizza, 158, 199
Millet with Corn and Green Chiles, 406
Ricotta, Yellow Pepper, and Asparagus Pizza, 198
Roasted Shrimp and Poblano Salad, 82–83
Sautéed Beef and Pepper Skillet with Fries, 294, 303
Steak and Pepper Fajitas, 298
Turkey Fajitas, 184–185
Pesto, 118–119, 365
Pignoli Cookies, 448
Pineapple
Banana Berry Blast Smoothie, 18
Creamy Kale Smoothie, 24
Hoisin Pork Tenderloin with Grilled Pineapple, 326–327
Honeyed Hot Fruit Salad, 432
Shrimp and Pineapple Salad with Basil, 90–91
Pitas. See Sandwiches and wraps
Pizza, 196–203
about: buying whole wheat dough for, 202
Apple-Brie Pizza with Caramelized Onions, 201
Broccoli-Mushroom Pizza, 200
Deep-Dish Supreme Pizza, 158, 199
Grilled Whole Wheat Veggie Pizza, 202–203
Quick Homemade Pizza Dough, 196
Ricotta, Yellow Pepper, and Asparagus Pizza, 198
Spinach and Feta Pizza, 197
PLT Sandwiches, 164–165

Plums
about: freezing for smoothies, 21
Grilled Plum and Pork Salad, 74–75
Honeyed Hot Fruit Salad, 432
Plum Glaze, 324
Plum Yogurt Pops, 461
Polenta with Garlicky Greens, 350–351
Pork
about: browning and braising, 143; grilling (cuts to use), 299; selecting, 299
Bacon and Brussels Sprout Penne, 380
Balsamic Roasted Pork with Berry Salad, 332–333
Brazilian Pork Chops, 331
Grilled Plum and Pork Salad, 74–75
Hoisin Pork Tenderloin with Grilled Pineapple, 326–327
Hot and Spicy Pork Noodles, 321
Orange Pork and Asparagus Stir-Fry, 329
Pancetta Chicken, 246, 249
Parmesan and Sausage Bolognese, 304–305
Pasta e Fagioli with Sausage, 116
Pork, Cabbage, and Apple Sauté, 328
Pork Steak with Plum Glaze, 324–325
Pork Tenderloin with Melon Salsa, 315
Pork Tenderloin with Roasted Grapes, 322–323
Pork Tenderloin with Roasted-Lemon Orzo, 316–317
Prosciutto Turkey Cutlets with Melon, 286–287
Sesame Pork Stir-Fry, 330
Soy-Honey Pork with Sweet Potatoes, 318–319
Sweet and Savory Pork, 320
Vietnamese Noodle Salad, 92–93
Potatoes
about: low-fat ways to dress, 395
California Frittata, 38–39
Crispy Roasted Potatoes with Caper Vinaigrette, 384, 413
Honey-Mustard Chicken and Potatoes, 274–275
Light Mashed Potatoes, 416
Mustard-Dill Salmon with Herbed Potatoes, 242
Oven Fries, 418–419
Roasted Halibut with Fennel and Potatoes, 231
Rosemary and Garlic Oven Fries, 418

Sautéed Beef and Pepper Skillet
with Fries, 294, 303
South-of-the-Border Vegetable
Hash, 36
Steak and Oven Fries, 300–301
Turkey Shepherd's Pie, 284
Poultry, 247–293. *See also* Chicken;
Turkey
about: breast meat, 253, 275;
minimizing fat intake, 275;
overview of recipes, 247
Crispy Duck Breasts with Tart
Cherry Sauce, 292–293
Prosciutto Turkey Cutlets with
Melon, 286–287
Provençal Sauce, 248
Pudding, chocolate, 453
Pumpkin
Healthy Makeover Pumpkin
Bread, 454–455
Mesclun with Pears and
Pumpkin Seeds, 100
Pumpkin Pancakes, 44

Q
Quesadillas, chicken, 178–179
Quick Homemade Pizza Dough, 196
Quinoa
Granola-Yogurt Parfait, 31
Lower-Fat Granola, 30
Warm Quinoa Salad with
Toasted Almonds, 101

R
Ragu, slow-braised beef, 308–309
Raisins. *See* Grapes and raisins
Ramen, gourmet, 132–133
Ranch dressing, creamy, 59
Raspberries. *See* Berries
Ratatouille Pasta, 270
Red-Cooked Chicken, Slow-Cooker
Style, 255
Rice and wild rice
about: brown rice, 369; noodles,
77; nutritional benefits, 369;
types of, 369
Aromatic Brown Rice, 402–403
Asian Brown Rice, 403
Brown Rice and Cranberry
Stuffing, 405
Brown Rice and Vegetable Pilaf,
404
Brown-Rice Risotto with
Butternut Squash, 353
Chicken Adobo over Gingery
Rice, 260–261
Fast Fried Rice, 367
Indian Cauliflower Stew, 368–369
Minted Corn and Brown Rice
Salad, 81

Orange-Cilantro Brown Rice, 403
Paprika Parmesan Granola Bars,
28–29
Rice Noodles with Many Herbs, 77
Risotto Puttanesca, 354–355
Sesame Pork Stir-Fry, 330
Slow-Cooker Sesame-Garlic
Chicken, 272–273
Spicy Turkey Sausage Jambalaya,
291
Spring Vegetable Risotto with
Shrimp, 211
Tangerine Chicken Stir-Fry,
262–263
Vietnamese Noodle Salad, 92–93
Wheat-Berry Pilaf with Green
Beans, 356–357
Wild Rice and Mushroom
Stuffing, 408–409
Wild Rice and Orzo Pilaf, 407
Ricotta, Yellow Pepper, and
Asparagus Pizza, 198
Risotto. *See* Farro; Rice and wild rice
Roast Beef Waldorf Sandwiches, 192
Roasted Halibut with Fennel and
Potatoes, 231
Roasted-Lemon Orzo, 316–317
Roasted Shrimp and Poblano Salad,
82–83
Rosemary and Garlic Oven Fries, 418
Rosemary Roast Turkey Breast, 285
Rub, ultimate, 190

S
Salads, 53–101
about: colorful fruits and
vegetables for, 62; overview of
recipes, 53; pears in, 423
Asian Chicken Salad, 69
Balsamic Roasted Pork with
Berry Salad, 332–333
Barley, Corn, and Tomato Salad, 60
Black Bean and Avocado Salad, 63
Bulgur and Grape Salad with
Dried Figs and Almonds, 80
Chickpea Mango Salad, 88–89
Corn Fritters with Black Bean
Salad, 342–343
Crunchy Carrot Coleslaw, 99
Curried Chicken Salad with
Cantaloupe Slaw, 66–67
Fattoush, 86
Garden Greens and
Pumpernickel Panzanella, 52,
97
Greek Salad Pitas, 170–171
Grilled Caesar Salad, 72
Grilled Chicken Taco Salad, 68
Grilled Eggplant Caponata Salad,
78–79

Grilled Plum and Pork Salad,
74–75
Honeyed Hot Fruit Salad, 432
Italian Tuna and White Bean
Salad, 76
Kale and Bean Salad, 340
Kale Caesar Pasta Salad, 56–57
Korean Steak in Lettuce Cups,
70–71
Mesclun with Pears and
Pumpkin Seeds, 100
Minted Corn and Brown Rice
Salad, 81
Panzanella Salad with Grilled
Chicken, 65
Pasta Salad with Lemon and
Peas, 54
Peaches and Greens, 62
Rice Noodles with Many Herbs,
77
Roasted Shrimp and Poblano
Salad, 82–83
Shredded Beets with Celery and
Dates, 96
Shrimp and Pineapple Salad
with Basil, 90–91
Six-Bean Salad with Tomato
Vinaigrette, 95
Skinny Salad Dressings, 58–59.
See also Sauces and dressings
Snap Pea Salad, 61
Summer Tuna Salad with Sweet
Potato and Basil, 73
Swordfish with Summer Salad,
204, 244
Tex-Mex Turkey Cobb Salad, 64
Three-Fruit Salad with Vanilla
Bean Syrup, 426
Tomato and Mint Tabbouleh, 98
Vietnamese Noodle Salad, 92–93
Warm Farro Salad with Roasted
Vegetables, 94
Warm French Lentil Salad, 84–85
Warm Quinoa Salad with
Toasted Almonds, 101
Wheat Berry Salad with Dried
Cherries, 87
Salmon, dishes with, 220–221, 224,
240–241, 242
Salt-Baked Fish, 238
Sandwiches and wraps, 159–195. *See
also* Pizza
about: overview of recipes, 159
Asian Tuna Burgers, 172
Barbecue Chicken Burgers, 181
Basic Chicken Burgers, 180
BBQ Brisket Tacos, 190
BBQ Ranch Chicken Wraps, 167
BBQ Tofu Sandwiches, 364
Black Bean Burgers, 344–345

Bulgur Bean Burgers, 162–163
Chicken Apple Burgers, 182
Chicken Caesar Pitas, 174–175
Chicken Cakes with "Roasted"
 Tomato Salsa, 173
Chicken Quesadillas with
 Avocado Salsa, 178–179
Falafel Sandwiches, 160
Garden Turkey Sandwiches, 183
Gingery Chicken in Lettuce Cups,
 177
Greek Salad Pitas, 170–171
Grilled Asparagus and Shiitake
 Tacos, 186–187
Healthy Club Sandwiches, 161
Herb Chicken Burgers, 181
Mango Chicken Lettuce Wraps,
 176
Meatloaf Burgers with Sautéed
 Carrots, 193
Pastrami-Spiced Flank Steak
 Sandwiches, 296–297
PLT Sandwiches, 164–165
Roast Beef Waldorf Sandwiches,
 192
Steak Sandwiches with Grilled
 Onions, 194–195
Teriyaki Chicken Burgers, 181
Turkey Burgers with Minted
 Yogurt Sauce, 188–189
Turkey Fajitas, 184–185
Turkey Meatball Pitas, 191
Tuscan Tuna Salad Sandwiches,
 169
Vegetarian Souvlaki, 168
Veggie Wraps with Goat Cheese,
 166
Saturated vs. unsaturated fat, 9–10
Sauces and dressings
 about: Asian fish sauce, 130;
  low-fat ways to dress veggies,
  394–395; speedy pasta sauce,
  271
 Avocado Salsa, 178–179
 BBQ Sauce, 281
 Broccoli Pesto, 365
 Buttermilk-Chive Dressing, 59
 Caper Vinaigrette, 384, 413
 Chinese Ginger Sauce, 248
 Creamy Ranch Dressing, 59
 Honey-Lime Vinaigrette, 58
 Light Pesto, 118–119
 Melon Salsa, 315
 Minted Yogurt Sauce, 189
 Olive and Tomato Compote, 217
 Orange-Ginger Vinaigrette, 58
 Picadillo Sauce, 314
 Plum Glaze, 324
 Provençal Sauce, 248
 Red Clam Sauce, 245

"Roasted" Tomato Salsa, 173
Skinny Salad Dressings, 58–59
Slow-Braised Beef Ragu, 308–309
Tart Cherry Sauce, 292
Tomato-Orange Vinaigrette, 58
Tomato Vinaigrette, 95
Ultimate Rub, 190
Sauces, sweet
 about: mock whipped cream, 441
 Blackberry Sauce, 458
 Coulis, 32
 Cream-Cheese Frosting, 434–435
 Vanilla Bean Syrup, 426
Saucy Creole Shrimp, 214
Sausage
 Maple-Glazed Sausages and
  Figs, 335
 Parmesan and Sausage
  Bolognese, 304–305
 Pasta e Fagioli with Sausage, 116
 Spicy Turkey Sausage Jambalaya,
  291
Sautéed Beef and Pepper Skillet
 with Fries, 294, 303
Savory Pear and Cornbread Stuffing,
 412
Scallops, 217, 218–219
Sesame Green Beans, 396
Sesame Pork Stir-Fry, 330
Seven-Minute Multigrain Cereal, 26
Sgroppino Sorbet with Prosecco and
 Mint, 462
Shepherd's pie, turkey, 284
Shrimp. See Fish and shellfish
Side dishes, 385–418
 about: low-fat ways to dress
  veggies, 394–395; overview of
  recipes, 385; pears in, 423
 Apple Cider-Braised Greens,
  386–387
 Aromatic Brown Rice, 402–403
 Asian Brown Rice, 403
 Basic Couscous, 400
 Basil and Balsamic Beets, 414
 Brown Rice and Cranberry
  Stuffing, 405
 Brown Rice and Vegetable Pilaf,
  404
 Cauliflower "Popcorn," 410–411
 Chili-Lime "Popcorn," 410
 Cracked Wheat with Greens, 397
 Crispy Roasted Potatoes with
  Caper Vinaigrette, 384, 413
 Green Beans with Caramelized
  Onions, 392–393
 Kale "Chips," 389
 Lemon-Parsley Brown Rice, 403
 Light Mashed Potatoes, 416
 Lime Couscous, 401
 Maple-Roasted Squash, 415

Mashed Sweet Potatoes, 417
Millet with Corn and Green
 Chiles, 406
Mixed Pea Pod Stir-Fry, 398–399
Moroccan Couscous, 401
Orange-Cilantro Brown Rice, 403
Oven Fries, 418–419
Rosemary and Garlic Oven Fries,
 418
Sautéed Swiss Chard with
 Golden Raisins and Capers, 388
Savory Pear and Cornbread
 Stuffing, 412
Sesame Green Beans, 396
Sun-Dried Tomato and Green
 Onion Couscous, 401
Tarragon Peas and Pearl Onions,
 390–391
Truffle "Popcorn," 410
Wild Rice and Mushroom
 Stuffing, 408–409
Wild Rice and Orzo Pilaf, 407
Six-Bean Salad with Tomato
 Vinaigrette, 95
Skillet Vegetable Curry, 366
Skinny Carrot Muffins, 51
Slow-Braised Beef Ragu, 308–309
Slow-Cooker Sesame-Garlic
 Chicken, 272–273
Smoothies
 about: freezing fruit for, 21;
  healthy additions for, 15; nut
  butters and seeds for, 15; oats,
  oat bran for, 15
 Banana Berry Blast Smoothie, 18
 Berry Satisfying Smoothie, 16
 Chocolate-Banana Smoothie, 20
 Creamy Kale Smoothie, 24
 Fruity Green Smoothie, 25
 Java Banana Smoothie, 22
 Jump-Start Smoothie, 19
 Mango Strawberry Smoothie, 14
 Strawberry Chia Smoothie, 17
Snap Pea Salad, 61
Snapper, dishes with, 225, 228–229,
 238
Snow peas. See Peas
Soba Noodles Primavera with Miso,
 381
Soba Noodles with Shrimp, Snow
 Peas, and Carrots, 134–135
Sorbet, 462
Soups and stews, 103–157. See also
 Chilis
 about: Asian noodle types and,
  131; benefits of soup, 107;
  browning and braising meats
  for, 143; dry beans for, 117; edible
  flowers in, 110; overview of
  recipes, 103; reheating chili, 147

Barley Minestrone with Pesto, 118–119

Black Bean Soup, 122–123

Carrot and Dill Soup, 106–107

Chicken and Escarole Soup, 115

Chicken Soup, Bouillabaisse-Style, 128–129

Chilled Buttermilk and Corn Soup, 105

Chilled Tuscan-Style Tomato Soup, 102, 104

Classic Beef Stew, 142

Creamy Italian White-Bean Soup, 113

Ginger-Spiced Carrot Soup, 108–109

Gourmet Ramen, 132–133

Hearty Fish Chowder, 124–125

Homemade Chicken Broth, 137

Homemade Vegetable Broth, 136

Indian Cauliflower Stew, 368–369

Lamb and Root Vegetable Tagine, 156

Macaroni, Cabbage, and Bean Soup, 114

Mediterranean Seafood Stew, 138–139

Mixed Vegetable Minestrone, 120–121

Moroccan Sweet-Potato Stew, 346–347

Not Your Grandma's Borscht, 112

Pasta e Fagioli with Sausage, 116

Soba Noodles with Shrimp, Snow Peas, and Carrots, 134–135

Southwestern Chicken Stew, 154–155

Spring Pea Soup, 110–111

Tex-Mex Chicken Soup, 126–127

Thai Chicken-Basil Soup, 130

Tuscan Veggie Stew, 140–141

Veal and Mushroom Stew, 157

South-of-the-Border Vegetable Hash, 36

Southwestern Chicken Stew, 154–155

Souvlaki, vegetarian, 168

Soy-Honey Pork with Sweet Potatoes, 318–319

Spaghetti. See Pasta

"Spaghetti" and Meatballs, 290

Spiced Apple Pancake, 45

Spiced Banana-Chocolate Muffins, 12, 47

Spiced Couscous with Vegetables, 348

Spices, whole, 296

Spicy Turkey Sausage Jambalaya, 291

Spinach

about: low-fat ways to dress, 394; nutritional benefits,

183; tempering taste of, 183; thawing frozen, 197

Fruity Green Smoothie, 25

Garden Turkey Sandwiches, 183

Lasagna Toss with Spinach and Ricotta, 372–373

Spinach and Feta Pizza, 197

Spinach Soufflé, 33

Veggie Lo Mein, 382–383

Spring Pea Soup, 110–111

Spring Vegetable Risotto with Shrimp, 211

Sprouts (alfalfa), in Healthy Club Sandwiches, 161

Sprouts (bean), in Thai Noodles with Beef and Basil, 310–311

Squash

about: low-fat ways to dress, 394

Brown-Rice Risotto with Butternut Squash, 353

Deep-Dish Supreme Pizza, 158, 199

Farro Risotto with Butternut Squash, 352–353

Grilled Whole Wheat Veggie Pizza, 202–203

Maple-Roasted Squash, 415

Shrimp and Zucchini Scampi, 208–209

"Spaghetti" and Meatballs, 290

Steak. See Beef; Pork

Steamed Scrod Fillets, 239

Stews. See Chilis; Soups and stews

Strawberries. See Berries

Stroganoff, lean beef, 312–313

Stuffed Fresh Figs, 430–431

Stuffing

about: pears in, 423

Brown Rice and Cranberry Stuffing, 405

Savory Pear and Cornbread Stuffing, 412

Wild Rice and Mushroom Stuffing, 408–409

Sugar cookies, whole wheat, 444–445

Summer Tuna Salad with Sweet Potato and Basil, 73

Super Bowl Chili, 150–151

Sweet and Savory Pork, 320

Sweet and Sticky Chicken with Snow Peas, 268–269

Sweet potatoes

Bean and Corn-Stuffed Sweet Potatoes, 362–363

Lamb and Root Vegetable Tagine, 156

Mashed Sweet Potatoes, 417

Moroccan Sweet-Potato Stew, 346–347

Soy-Honey Pork with Sweet Potatoes, 318–319

Spaghetti with Roasted Sweet Potato, 378–379

Summer Tuna Salad with Sweet Potato and Basil, 73

Sweet Potato Cakes with Kale and Bean Salad, 340

Swiss chard

about: low-fat ways to dress, 394

Apple Cider-Braised Greens, 386–387

Cracked Wheat with Greens, 397

Maple-Glazed Sausages and Figs, 335

Mixed Vegetable Minestrone, 120–121

Polenta with Garlicky Greens, 350–351

Roasted-Lemon Orzo, 316–317

Sautéed Swiss Chard with Golden Raisins and Capers, 388

Swordfish with Summer Salad, 204, 244

T

Tabbouleh, tomato and mint, 98

Tacos, 186–187, 190

Taco salad, grilled chicken, 68

Tangerine Chicken Stir-Fry, 262–263

Tarragon Peas and Pearl Onions, 390–391

Tart Cherry Sauce, 292

Teriyaki Chicken Burgers, 181

Tex-Mex Chicken Soup, 126–127

Tex-Mex Turkey Cobb Salad, 64

Thai Chicken-Basil Soup, 130

Thai Noodles with Beef and Basil, 310–311

Three-Bean Vegetable Chili, 146

Three-Fruit Salad with Vanilla Bean Syrup, 426

Tiramisu, lemon-blueberry, 424–425

Tofu

BBQ Tofu Sandwiches, 364

Fast Fried Rice, 367

Soba Noodles Primavera with Miso, 381

Tomatillos, in White-Bean and Tomatillo Chili, 341

Tomatoes

about: nutritional and health benefits, 39; speedy pasta sauce, 271

Chilled Tuscan-Style Tomato Soup, 102, 104

Mussels with Tomatoes and White Wine, 206–207

Olive and Tomato Compote, 217

other soups and stews with. *See*
  Chilis; Soups and stews
Picadillo Sauce, 314
"Roasted" Tomato Salsa, 173
salads with. *See* Salads
sandwiches with. *See*
  Sandwiches and wraps
Sun-Dried Tomato and Green
  Onion Couscous, 401
Tomato-Orange Vinaigrette, 58
Tomato Vinaigrette, 95
Tortillas
  BBQ Brisket Tacos, 190
  Breakfast Tortilla Stack, 34–35
  Chicken Chilaquiles, 250–251
  Chicken Quesadillas with
    Avocado Salsa, 178–179
  Grilled Asparagus and Shiitake
    Tacos, 186–187
  Grilled Chicken Taco Salad, 68
  Huevos Rancheros, 37
  Shrimp and Pineapple Salad
    with Basil, 90–91
  Steak and Pepper Fajitas, 298
  Turkey Fajitas, 184–185
  Veggie Wraps with Goat Cheese,
    166
Trans-fats, 11
Truffle "Popcorn," 410
Tuna. *See* Fish and shellfish
Turkey
  about: minimizing fat intake, 275
  Garden Turkey Sandwiches, 183
  Prosciutto Turkey Cutlets with
    Melon, 286–287
  Rosemary Roast Turkey Breast, 285
  "Spaghetti" and Meatballs, 290
  Spicy Turkey Sausage Jambalaya,
    291
  Tex-Mex Turkey Cobb Salad, 64
  Turkey and White Bean Chili,
    148–149
  Turkey Burgers with Minted
    Yogurt Sauce, 188–189
  Turkey Cutlets with Pears and
    Tarragon, 288–289
  Turkey Fajitas, 184–185
  Turkey Meatball Pitas, 191
  Turkey Shepherd's Pie, 284
Tuscan Tuna Salad Sandwiches, 169
Tuscan Veggie Stew, 140–141

U
Ultimate Classic Waffle, 46
Ultimate Rub, 190
Unsaturated vs. saturated fat, 9–10

V
Valentine's Day Red Chili, 144–145
Vanilla Bean Syrup, 426

Veal
  about: grilling (cuts to use), 299;
    selecting, 299
  Osso Buco with Gremolata,
    336–337
  Veal and Mushroom Stew, 157
Vegetable mains. *See also* Grains;
  specific grains
  about: overview of recipes, 339
  Bacon and Brussels Sprout
    Penne, 380
  BBQ Tofu Sandwiches, 364
  Black Bean Burgers, 344–345
  Broccoli Pesto Spaghetti, 365
  Corn Fritters with Black Bean
    Salad, 342–343
  Couscous-Stuffed Artichokes,
    370–371
  Creamy Vegan Linguine with
    Wild Mushrooms, 338, 349
  Fast Fried Rice, 367
  Indian Cauliflower Stew, 368–369
  Lasagna Toss with Spinach and
    Ricotta, 372–373
  Moroccan Sweet-Potato Stew,
    346–347
  Orecchiette with Morels and
    Peas, 374–375
  Polenta with Garlicky Greens,
    350–351
  Skillet Vegetable Curry, 366
  Soba Noodles Primavera with
    Miso, 381
  Spaghetti with Roasted Sweet
    Potato, 378–379
  Spiced Couscous with
    Vegetables, 348
  Sweet Potato Cakes with Kale
    and Bean Salad, 340
  Veggie Lo Mein, 382–383
  White-Bean and Tomatillo Chili,
    341
  Whole Wheat Penne Genovese,
    376–377
Vegetables. *See also specific vegetables*
  about: colorful, benefits of, 62;
    low-fat ways to dress, 394–395
  Brown Rice and Vegetable Pilaf,
    404
  California Frittata, 38–39
  sandwiches with. *See*
    Sandwiches and wraps
  soup with. *See* Chilis; Soups and
    stews
  South-of-the-Border Vegetable
    Hash, 36
  Spring Vegetable Risotto with
    Shrimp, 211
Vegetarian Souvlaki, 168
Vietnamese Noodle Salad, 92–93

W
Waffles, 46
Warm Farro Salad with Roasted
  Vegetables, 94
Warm French Lentil Salad, 84–85
Warm Quinoa Salad with Toasted
  Almonds, 101
Wheat-Berry Pilaf with Green Beans,
  356–357
Wheat Berry Salad with Dried
  Cherries, 87
Whipped cream mock, 441
White beans. *See* Beans and other
  legumes
Whole-Grain Blueberry Muffins, 49
Whole-Grain Fig Bars, 447
Whole-Grain Gingersnaps, 438
Whole-Grain Pancakes, 40–41
Whole wheat flour, 445
Whole Wheat Penne Genovese,
  376–377
Wild Rice and Mushroom Stuffing,
  408–409
Wild Rice and Orzo Pilaf, 407
Wine
  about: cooking with, 301;
    Marsala, 157
  Chianti-Roasted Pears, 422–423
  Mussels with Tomatoes and
    White Wine, 206–207
  Sgroppino Sorbet with Prosecco
    and Mint, 462
Wraps. *See* Sandwiches and wraps

Y
Yogurt
  about: benefits and uses, 31;
    Greek-style, 31; low-fat tips,
    440
  Berry Satisfying Smoothie, 16
  Granola-Yogurt Parfait, 31
  Jump-Start Smoothie, 19
  Lemon-Maple Icebox Cake,
    436–437
  Minted Yogurt Sauce, 189
  Peachy Frozen Yogurt, 460
  Plum Yogurt Pops, 461
  Strawberry Granola Yogurt
    Parfait, 32

Z
Zucchini. *See* Squash

THE GOOD HOUSEKEEPING TRIPLE-TEST PROMISE

At Good Housekeeping, we want to make sure that every recipe we print works in any oven, with any brand of ingredient, no matter what. That's why, in our test kitchens at the **Good Housekeeping Research Institute**, we go all out: We test each recipe at least three times—and, often, several more times after that.

When a recipe is first developed, one member of our team prepares the dish and we judge it on these criteria: it must be **delicious, family-friendly, healthy**, and **easy to make**.

1. The recipe is then tested several more times to fine-tune the flavor and ease of preparation, always by the same team member, using the same equipment.

2. Next, another team member follows the recipe as written, **varying the brands of ingredients** and **kinds of equipment**. Even the types of stoves we use are changed.

3. A third team member repeats the whole process **using yet another set of equipment** and **alternative ingredients**.

By the time the recipes appear on these pages, they are guaranteed to work in any kitchen, including yours. WE PROMISE.